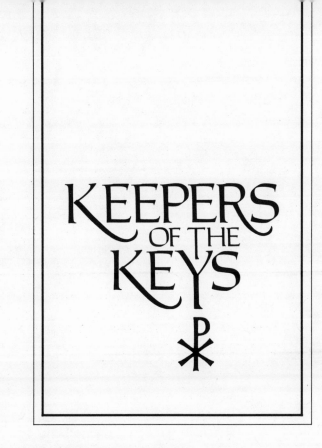

KEEPERS
OF THE
KEYS

WILTON WYNN

KEEPERS OF THE KEYS

JOHN XXIII
PAUL VI
and JOHN PAUL II
Three Who Changed the Church

Random House / New York

Library of Congress Cataloging-in-Publication Data

Wynn, Wilton, 1920-
  Keepers of the keys.

  Includes index.
  1. John XXIII, Pope, 1881–1963. 2. Paul VI, Pope,
1897–1978. 3. John Paul II, Pope, 1920-
4. Popes—Biography. 5. Papacy—History—20th century.
I. Title.
BX1389.W96 1988 282′.092′2 [B]   87-43230
ISBN 0-394-55762-X

Manufactured in the United States of America

2 3 4 5 6 7 8 9

First Edition

Typography and binding design by
Marsha Cohen/Parallelogram

CONTENTS

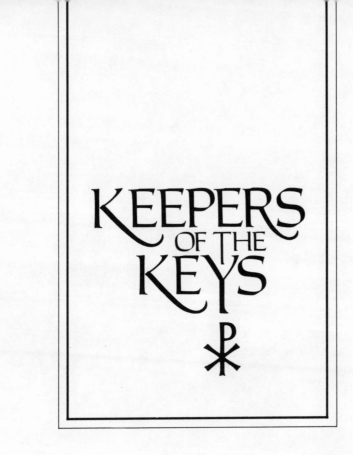

KEEPERS
OF THE
KEYS

INTRODUCTION: COVERING THE PAPACY

The telephone in my Liechtenstein hotel room rings to disturb an afternoon nap. "Come down here in a hurry!" shouts a colleague. "The pope wants to see you."

His idea of a joke irritates me as much as being awakened from my siesta, but I manage to play along: "What a day! Reagan rings me up at breakfast, and Gorbachev has been trying to reach me all day, and now the pope . . ."

Then I hang up. Popes don't ask to see journalists. The rule is that successors to Saint Peter, the "keepers of the keys," do not give press interviews or conduct news conferences and, for the most part, are inaccessible to the media. It is unthinkable that a pope would ask to talk with a working newsman. Somebody is trying to be funny.

But Rudi Frey, the photographer with whom I have been working, comes charging into the room to change my mind.

"Get moving!" he screams. "The pope is asking for you! It's *true!*"

In considerable bewilderment I crawl out of bed and scamper

3

down the hill to the little Gothic church where Pope John Paul II is meeting with teachers and students from Catholic schools. The Vatican's top security man, Camillo Cibin, positions me beside the church near the papal automobile.

When the pope emerges and sees me, he breaks into a smile and strides over with both arms outstretched. He seizes my hands in a double handshake and speaks with his characteristic warmth: "I understand that you are retiring." I nod, dumbstruck. "I congratulate you and bless your retirement and wish you a happy future. And please accept this gift."

The pontiff hands me a beautifully carved black rosary as a memento of my years as a Vatican correspondent, dating back to 1962.

During that time it was my privilege to cover three remarkable pontiffs, John XXIII, Paul VI, and John Paul II—a most challenging assignment. I had come to Rome after a decade of following wars, revolutions, and riots in the Middle East, and at first I expected the Vatican to be a soft and unexciting assignment, somewhat like covering the women's missionary society back home. Instead, I found following the papacy one of the most productive, stimulating, and exciting newsbeats any journalist could handle.

Telling the story of three popes has involved investigating international terrorism and major bank scandals, traveling to the ends of the earth, covering diplomatic crises when nations were on the verge of war. I remember the day in 1970 when I entered a dismal Manila jail, walked down corridors inexplicably lined with exhibits of human fetuses floating in jars of alcohol, and interviewed in his cell the Bolivian artist who had tried to kill Pope Paul. I had never expected to do murder stories when I began covering the Vatican.

Gathering information on the papacy has been at times a taxing and difficult task. To get beyond the routine communiqués handed out by the Vatican press office, a reporter must work relentlessly to build the confidence of persons close to the pope, gumshoe through the corridors of the Holy See to talk to those who *have* talked to the pope, and, in most cases, conceal his sources.

My coverage of the modern popes began on October 11, 1962, when I sat in the Hall of Benedictions looking down into the great High Renaissance nave of St. Peter's Basilica to watch Pope John XXIII march in, preceded by more than two thousand bishops he had summoned from around the world; it was a scene of age-old pageantry opening what would be the most forward-looking Church council in history. I reported on the remarkable series of moves the aging pope made toward Protestants, non-Christians, and, above all, the Soviet Union. And eventually I reported on a daily basis the details of his long terminal illness, a time when his great humanity shone through more brightly than ever.

After covering the funeral of "Good Pope John," I stood in St. Peter's Piazza on the day Giovanni Battista Montini was elected as Pope Paul VI and watched him deliver from the balcony his first papal blessing, "Urbi et Orbi" ("To the City and to the World"). I covered the main events of his long reign and did the reporting for three *Time* magazine cover stories on him.

Pope Paul offered journalists a new opportunity for "pope-watching" when he introduced the era of papal international travel with his historic flight to Jerusalem on January 6, 1964. Being on the aircraft with him for days at a time gave the press a far closer look at the pontiff than we had ever had before. For my purposes, the most productive of his trips was a ten-day, 28,000-mile voyage to the Far East that took us all the way to the Samoan Islands. Paul himself would come back to the press section to shake hands and exchange pleasantries, and I learned much about him and his activities from long talks on the plane with the men around him, such as Archbishop (now Cardinal) Agostino Casaroli, then the Vatican's "foreign minister," and Bishop Paul Marcinkus, best known today as president of the Vatican Bank but in those days chief organizer of papal trips and an intimate of the pope.

John Paul II has traveled far more than did Paul—more, in

fact, than all his predecessors put together. Scarcely three months after he was elected, we were on John Paul's plane heading for Mexico. In the hope that he would come back and chat with us, I positioned myself toward the head of the press section to be able to speak to him as soon as he appeared. When he stepped into our section, I was not sure whether I could ask him a question of substance or whether he intended only to exchange greetings, as had Paul. Nonetheless I bluntly asked him if he intended to visit the United States, and to my surprise I got a straight answer immediately.

"I think it will be necessary," he answered in his fluent but heavily accented English. "Only the date has not yet been fixed."

It was the first indication that John Paul intended to visit the United States (the trip took place that autumn), and his reply made headlines. We journalists were proud to have at last an impeccable, quotable source on a Vatican story—the pope himself. My question broke the ice, and shortly we were quizzing the pontiff on complicated questions like liberation theology—and again getting direct answers.

That Mexico trip convinced me that the way to get to know this pope was through his travels, and I made up my mind to make every trip with him, if possible. I was then chief of the Rome bureau of *Time* magazine and in position to assign myself to papal travel, somewhat selfishly taking away this choice story from other correspondents on my staff.

Pope Paul had made only nine trips in fifteen years; John Paul does four a year. Until a health crisis (and the relentless march of age) forced me to give it up, I was on the papal plane each time it took off, logging more than 150,000 miles on eighteen international flights with the pontiff, traveling over the North Pole and across the equator, to the great rain forests of the Congo and the vast Amazon Basin, to the White House in Washington and the Imperial Palace of Japan.

John, Paul, and John Paul have propagated the same basic message, but they have performed in such refreshingly individual styles that in all my years of covering the papacy I've never had a sense of "déjà vu." In physical appearance, temperament, and way of working they presented sharp contrasts.

There was the dumpy, homely, wide-mouthed John, a foxy Italian who was born a peasant, eternally optimistic, a lovable extrovert who savored to the full the good things of this life while anticipating the joys of the life to come; who enjoyed a convivial glass of wine with friends even against the doctor's orders and once telephoned the Vatican grocery himself to obtain just the right foods to suit his gourmet tastes; who was a traditional Catholic in his own thinking and yet basically so tolerant that he unleashed a revolution inside the Church.

Next came the introverted, intellectual Milanese, Paul, slightly built and frail, with sunken eyes, hooded lids, and hooked nose, a deeply spiritual mystic whose approach to piety involved inflicting physical pain on his own flesh; who projected an image of pessimism and suffering, bearing his burdens with infinite patience; who was so indecisive that his detractors often called him Amleto (Hamlet), yet withal strong enough to reign fifteen years and keep John's revolution on the track while struggling to keep it from getting out of hand.

Finally, after the brief reign of John Paul I, there arrived the handsome, athletic, white-haired and ruddy-faced John Paul II, a Pole who had worked in factories and mines, acted on the stage, and written plays and poetry before becoming a priest; an outdoor man who used to enjoy mountain climbing and canoeing and who even as pope likes to swim and occasionally slips out of the Vatican for a bit of skiing in the high mountains (the only pope in history who ever skied); a leader whose unfailing sense of humor, infectious charm, and external warmth cloak an iron will and rigorous sense of discipline, who befriends non-Catholics and non-Christians to an unprecedented degree but never gives an inch on orthodox Church teaching, who does his best to reimpose discipline in the Church in the wake of John's revolution.

In June 1969 I heard Pope Paul VI give an eloquent analysis

of what might be called the "diversity in continuity" of the papacy. I had flown with the pope to Geneva—often called the Protestant Rome, where local elders once banned Catholic "masses, images, idols and other papal abuses"—to hear him speak before the Protestant-dominated World Council of Churches. The seemingly frail Paul had the courage to begin his speech with the phrase "Our name is Peter . . ."

The message was clear. As the 259th successor to Saint Peter,* Paul VI was custodian of the Rock of Faith, the unchanging body of doctrine, which cannot be watered down as the price of Christian unity. To those Protestants it sounded like the beginning of an unfriendly speech. But the tension eased when the pope went on to say, "The name which we have taken, that of Paul, fully indicates the orientation which we have wished to give our apostolic ministry." Like the New Testament Paul, he meant to be a man of dialogue with other cultures and religions and to travel to many lands. But he also was saying that the name under which each pope chooses to reign stands for papal individuality, for diversity, for the vast innovations that each pope can introduce through the impact of his style and temperament, his personal and individual response to changing circumstances. The three popes I have covered chose their papal names for very special reasons, which pointed to the innovations each would bring to the office.

It is the purpose of this book to compare these three popes as a way of explaining how individual personalities can make a difference in an office that has remained in many ways unchanging for nearly two thousand years. I will describe the impact each has made in his own way on the Church and the world (and each

---

*There is some confusion regarding the number of popes, partly because the Vatican occasionally revises its own list to eliminate those of doubtful historicity or legitimacy. For example, the Vatican recently has dropped from its list a presbyter named Stephen who was elected March 23, 752, but died three days later, before he could be consecrated as pontiff. Church historians have noted that, according to the canon law of the time, he never in fact became pope. Another cause of confusion is the fact that in the eleventh century Benedict IX was elected—and reigned—three different times. In the latest Vatican list published in the *Annuario Pontificio*, Paul VI is number 260, or the 259th successor to Saint Peter, who, of course, is listed as number one.

has made a powerful impact), giving something of each pope's background and the sometimes fortuitous developments that led him to the throne of Peter; the men they have relied on as intimate advisors and collaborators; their decision-making processes and ways of governing; how they communicate in private and in public; how they handle problems as diverse as international diplomacy, finances, and modern moral issues; and how each has responded to the winds of change that have blown through the Church in this era.

Except for a bit of radio broadcasting in the early years, my reporting on popes was done for *Time* magazine. It is my belief that *Time* has given more attention to the Vatican over the past decades than any other secular publication in the United States, an interest originally kindled by the magazine's founder and long-time editor-in-chief, Henry Luce, who believed that religion was as vital a field of news as politics or economics.

The *Time* system of group journalism is a process in which it often is difficult to determine where one correspondent's reporting ends and another's begins, or whether what appears in print is the product of the New York–based writer or the man in the field. And so, throughout this book, my own reporting has often been supplemented by that of correspondents who have come and gone through the Rome bureau in the many years of my own experience there. I should mention in particular—in chronological order—Robert Kaiser, Jordan Bonfante, Roland Flamini, and Roberto Suro. Each has made a great contribution to *Time*'s coverage of the Holy See.

My warm gratitude goes to those scores of Vatican sources whose names in my dispatches to *Time* so often were accompanied by the warning "N.F.A." (Not For Attribution) but who have given so unselfishly of their time to help me break through to Vatican mysteries. I have warm memories of Popes John and Paul, but I would like to extend a special word of appreciation to their successor, John Paul II, for his kindness and helpfulness, both indirect and direct.

1

THE PATH TO
THE PAPACY

The Papal Tombola—Choosing a Pope

"The change from one pope to another altered all conditions in Rome, as in a 'tombola,' or lottery wheel."

So wrote German historian Ferdinand Gregorovius in the middle of the nineteenth century, but the election of a pope is still as unpredictable as a game of chance. The choice of a pontiff takes place in absolute secrecy, according to a system that has evolved over the centuries with the aim of insulating electors from political pressure or lobbying. This unpredictability is summed up in the Roman saying "He who goes in a pope comes out a cardinal"—whoever goes into the election as the favorite will not be the winner.

The uncertainties in such elections are reflected in the way that Angelo Giuseppe Roncalli, Giovanni Battista Montini, and Karol Wojtyla became Popes John XXIII, Paul VI, and John Paul II. Their experience shows that the path to the papacy rarely runs in a straight line. There are frequent detours, temporary obstacles, and wrong turns, with many an incident or accident of history making—or breaking—a potential *papabile* (papal candidate). Two of the three—Roncalli and Wojtyla—were surprise choices. The third, Montini, appeared destined for the papacy from early in his career and yet because of a special chain of circumstances almost missed it.

When Christ handed to Peter the keys of the kingdom (and therefore, Catholics believe, made him the first pope), he said nothing about how Peter's successors should be chosen. From the beginning it was assumed that the choice should be inspired by the Holy Spirit, and for nearly two millennia the Church has groped for a formula that would guarantee maximum opportunity for the Spirit to prevail. It seems to have been much easier in the early centuries, when the Church was a scattered community living under the shadow of persecution. In the year 236 a farmer named Fabian wandered into Rome and stopped to watch the clergy and people select their pope. A dove landed on Fabian's head, and the assembly instantly acclaimed him pope, assuming that the dove was a sign from the Holy Spirit. Unfortunately for simplicity, that method of selection could not be repeated, and other systems had to be tried.

Popes of today are elected by the cardinals in a procedure known as the conclave (in Latin, "with key" or "locked"). When a pope dies, the cardinals are summoned to Rome from all over the world, locked up in the Vatican Palace, and kept there, completely out of contact with the world, until they elect a new head of the Church. The conclave system dates back to the reign of Pope Gregory X, whose own election in 1271 followed two years, nine months, and two days of quarreling, resolved only after local citizens tore the roof off the palace to expose the cardinals to the elements and put them on bread and water till they reached agreement. To discourage such behavior in subsequent elections, Gregory drew up new rules, establishing the conclave system and adding some stern regulations to encourage the cardinals to reach an early decision. If they failed to elect a pope within three days, their ration of food would be reduced to one dish daily, and if after five more days they had not made up their minds, they would get only wine, bread, and water till they chose a pontiff. During the entire conclave, their salaries and incomes would be withheld.

The rule of no pay and short rations no longer is in effect; even so, a conclave is an exhausting experience. Cardinal Giuseppe Siri of Genoa, a veteran of four papal elections, says "in a sense one is buried alive."

The site of conclaves today—the Vatican Palace—is a rambling structure of dull gray walls and dusty tiled roofs which has been rebuilt, expanded, and modified many times since popes first took up residence there in the fifth century. The palace contains both residence and administrative offices for the pope, and it definitely was not built to house cardinals when they gather to elect a pontiff. Temporary cells have to be set up, converted from offices, closets, corridors, and assigned by lot; most of them lack private baths or toilets. The furnishings are spartan—an iron bed, a commode, a plastic clip-on bedside lamp, a writing table, two chairs, a kneeler, a small mirror and a crucifix on the wall. Meals are taken in the ornate Borgia Apartment, which is a magnificent sight to behold but rather crowded when one hundred twenty cardinals are crammed into it at long tables. (The number of cardinals varies from one conclave to another, depending on how many have been appointed by the most recent pope.) One bit of recently added Italian comfort is a stand-up espresso bar inside the conclave area, where cardinals can have coffee or "other liquid refreshment" between ballots. Heating is so poor that in the 1958 conclave, which took place in chilly late October, fifty-one hot water bottles were taken into the palace each night to warm the feet of the cardinals, whose average age was seventy-four. (That was the time a consignment of spoiled cured ham made nearly a third of the cardinals sick.)

Once locked inside the palace, the "princes of the church" are totally cut off from any contact with the outside world. Food and essential messages are brought in through turntables in one door. To guarantee the secrecy of the conclave, no one is allowed to bring in a tape recorder, camera, or any other kind of recording machine. Before the balloting begins, the premises are "swept" by electronic devices to make sure the place is not bugged. Until the last conclave, the windows were even painted over so that no one could signal to outsiders.

Voting takes place in the beautiful Sistine Chapel, where the cardinals sit at twelve long tables beneath the frescoes of "The Creation of the World" and "The Last Judgment" of Michelangelo. Inside the chapel is a silvery-gray iron stove, its pipe elbowing upward and outward, in which, after each vote is taken, the ballots and tally sheets are burned. In front of the altar sit three cardinals, called *scrutatores,* who supervise the balloting and count the votes.

Each cardinal is given a four-by-five-inch ballot inscribed "Eligo Summum Pontificem," on which he will write the name of his choice, disguising his handwriting. Absolute silence is imposed during the voting. In order of seniority, each cardinal takes his ballot between two fingers of his right hand, pauses to say a brief prayer, and drops the ballot into a chalice in front of the altar. When the voting is complete, the *scrutatores* begin the count; the first of them takes the ballot from the chalice, looks at it, and hands it to the next, who then passes it to the final *scrutator* to read aloud.

For election, a two-thirds-plus-one majority is necessary. Two ballots are taken in the morning, two in the afternoon, until a pope is elected. After each voting session, the *scrutatores* string the ballots and tally sheets on a cord, stuff them into the stove, and burn them, together with a chemical cartridge selected to produce either black or white smoke: white to announce to the world that a pope has been elected, black to report that the balloting has been inconclusive. (At one of the 1978 conclaves, the cardinals almost suffocated when the first ballots were burned before someone noticed that the stovepipe was broken, and the chapel filled with smoke.)

When a candidate gets the necessary majority, there usually is a round of unceremonial applause and cheering. Before the winner officially becomes pope, however, the senior cardinal-deacon must approach him solemnly to ask: "Acceptasne electionem de te canonice factam in Summum Pontifice?" ("Do you accept your election as Supreme Pontiff according to the Canons?")

If the reply is affirmative, the cardinal-deacon's next question is "Quo nomine vis vocari?" ("By what name do you wish to be known?")

The new pope then reveals the name he has chosen and gives some explanation for the choice. This practice goes back to 1009, when a man named Peter was elected pope and immediately changed his name to Sergius IV. It would have been presumptuous to use his own name, the same as that of the first pope. In addition, the new pope had good reasons for not using the name by which he had been generally known. The Vatican's staid *Annuario Pontificio* observes in a footnote that Peter "had the nickname of 'Os Porci' or 'Bucca Porca' [Pig-Mouth], which could have provided the motive for changing his name." Whatever his motives, Peter the Pig-Mouth set a precedent that by now has been written into the rules of the conclave.

The white smoke alerts the public that a pope has been chosen, but the announcement of his identity is delayed by further formalities inside the Sistine Chapel. First, the newly elected pope is conducted into a dressing room, where he removes his crimson cardinal's robes and dons papal attire—a white cassock and red elbow-length cape. To ensure that the costume fits the new pontiff at least approximately, the Vatican tailor always makes three sizes, large, medium, and small. Red slippers are prescribed, but at the last conclave the newly elected John Paul II rejected them in favor of ordinary black street shoes. The new pope's first official act is to reconfirm the *camerlengo,* or appoint a new one; the *camerlengo* is the cardinal who presides over the Vatican between the death of a pope and the election of his successor, and the post cannot be left vacant even for an hour.

The pontiff returns to the chapel and sits on a throne. The *camerlengo* slips the pontifical ring onto his finger, after which the pope hands it to the master of ceremonies, who will have the new pope's name inscribed in it. Now one by one the cardinals approach to embrace him and kiss his hand. He leads the cardinals in a Te Deum and gives them his benediction, the first blessing of his pontifical reign. The senior cardinal-deacon precedes the pope onto the central loggia of St. Peter's Basilica to announce to the crowd: "Annuntio vobis gaudium magnum. Habemus papam!" ("I announce to you joyful news. We have a pope!")

This is followed by the name of the new pope and the name under which he has chosen to reign. The pope himself then appears, receives the applause of the crowd, makes an impromptu speech, and gives his apostolic blessing "to the City and to the World."

The conclave system differs totally from that practiced in the early centuries of the Church, when the successor to Peter was chosen by the clergy and the people of Rome. That may sound democratic to Western ears, but in fact "the people" usually were powerful families or factions who didn't hesitate to wage war with each other to put their man on the papal throne. A bloody battle over the papacy in the year 366 left 137 corpses in the streets of Rome. Ruling popes have been strangled, poisoned, driven into exile by ambitious rivals. In the tenth century there lived an infamous woman named Marozia who was called the murderess of popes because of her demonstrated ability to eliminate an incumbent head of the Church. For many years after the return of the papal capital to Rome from Avignon there were two sitting pontiffs, one a pope, the other an anti-pope (the designation depending on which side you happened to support). In 1409 a general council of the Church gathered in Pisa to resolve a dispute between two reigning popes. As a compromise, the council chose a third candidate. Since neither of the other two accepted the compromise candidate, the Church had no less than three popes at once. It was clear that the Church had to establish a system that would insulate the election against such squabbles.

The election also had to be protected against massive interference by secular powers—emperors, kings, princes—because after the collapse of the Roman Empire the papacy became a secular as well as an ecclesiastical prize well worth fighting for. From A.D. 754 until 1870 popes ruled like secular monarchs over a kingdom, the Papal States, that originally stretched from Ravenna in the north to Benevento in the south. Called in Italy the pope-kings, these rulers maintained their own powerful armies (and some popes, notably Julius II in the sixteenth century, personally led their troops in bloody campaigns aimed blatantly at territorial conquest).

The worldly power of the papacy ended in 1870 when the army of modern Italy conquered Rome and brought the Papal States to an end. The pope is still a temporal sovereign, but his "kingdom" is the world's smallest independent country, the 108.7 acres of the State of Vatican City. His "army" consists of seventy Swiss Guards, who look like museum pieces in their brilliant red-yellow-and-blue uniforms and plumed helmets; remnants of a fighting force once ready to defend their pope to the last man, they now serve mainly as sentries at the gates of Vatican City.

Yet despite the loss of the pope's earthly power, the election of a pope is considered a major event around the world. While the cardinals are deliberating in the secrecy of the conclave the Rome press corps is drawing up lists of *papabili*, doing endless analyses of who is "liberal" and who "conservative," trying to distinguish blocs or factions of cardinals as if the event were a political convention. Dedicated Catholics speculate on whether the new pope will relax discipline on issues like priestly celibacy and ordination of women. Castro's ambassador to the Holy See watches to see if a pope will emerge who will support liberation theology in Latin America. The American ambassador to the Vatican files lengthy dispatches to Washington on the possibilities that the conclave will produce changes in Vatican policy toward the Communist world. The Soviets watch to see if a pontiff is elected who might be their ally in nuclear disarmament negotiations. Stalin could ask contemptuously, "How many divisions has the pope?" but his successors, like the rest of the world, await with the greatest of interest the latest turn of the papal tombola.

John XXIII's Roundabout Road to the Papacy

The election of aging Angelo Giuseppe Roncalli as Pope John XXIII in 1958 was so totally unexpected that some were tempted to say it was "just plain luck," while others saw in it the mysterious workings of Divine Providence. For one thing, if the rules of today had been in force at the 1958 conclave, Roncalli by that time would have been retired for two years and probably out of the running. Today bishops and Latin patriarchs retire at the age of seventy-five, and at the 1958 conclave Roncalli was only one month short of seventy-seven. He would no longer have been patriarch of Venice and thus would not have been active enough to be a viable candidate.

Secondly, Roncalli was lucky even to have been a cardinal at the time, and if he had not been a cardinal he would not have become pope. Born into a peasant family in a northern Italian village, he entered the priesthood early, put in a decade as secretary to the bishop of Bergamo, filled some rather insignificant Vatican posts, was sent to Bulgaria on a mission for the Vatican, and stayed there as apostolic delegate (papal representative to the bishops of the area but without diplomatic status). From Sofia he was moved to Istanbul as apostolic delegate to Turkey and Greece, not a tremendously important post considering the meager Catholic population in both countries.

Roncalli's performance in Turkey did not endear him to his superior back in Rome, Archbishop Domenico Tardini, who as undersecretary for external affairs was in effect "foreign minister" of the Holy See. Tardini thought him naïve in taking seriously Hitler's ambassador to Ankara, Franz Von Papen, who in the last years of World War II convinced the apostolic delegate that a powerful faction in Germany was ready to overthrow Hitler if the Allies would accept a negotiated peace. Tardini, in a note to the Vatican secretary of state, once wrote condescendingly "Roncalli is . . . a *pacioccone*" (an easygoing fellow), who obviously was not a person of much weight. Roncalli's finest performance while serving in Turkey was the assistance he gave to Jewish refugees fleeing from German-controlled territory, but even there his judgment, at least in hindsight, was somewhat erratic. In 1943, he sent a message to the Vatican saying that he thought it unwise to encourage Jewish emigration to Palestine because "more and more it becomes clear that the reconstruction of the kingdom of Judah and Israel is nothing more than a Utopia."

When Roncalli later was named papal nuncio (ambassador of the Holy See, with full diplomatic status) to Paris, Tardini noted that the appointment had been leaked prematurely to the French news agency, and he wrote in his own hand, "Who has spoken?" The implication was clear that he believed an indiscreet Roncalli was the source of the leak.

The blunt and outspoken Tardini made no secret of his unhappiness at the papal choice. Roncalli stopped off in Rome on his way to France and himself expressed surprise at getting such a high-level post. Tardini growled back: "We all were surprised. Your appointment came from the Holy Father, and only from him. I can assure you that I had nothing to do with it!"

The appointment as papal nuncio to Paris meant that Roncalli certainly would later become a cardinal and enter that select group eligible to be elected pope. Yet in truth he got the appointment by default, the result of a series of historical accidents that kept two other men from serving in the post.

It was late in 1944, when Charles de Gaulle was consolidating his power as chief of state of a recently liberated France. The unforgiving general adamantly refused to accept any ambassador who had been accredited to the Vichy regime, and he insisted that Pope Pius XII remove Archbishop Valerio Valeri, who had served as nuncio since 1936 in Paris and Vichy under a succession of regimes. Pius was furious at the de Gaulle demand, calling it an action "which shows little friendship to the Holy See" and "contrary to normal international practice" and "injurious, discourteous and painful." But in the end the pope had no choice; he recalled Valeri under protest and agreed to send someone else as nuncio.

At this point de Gaulle added another complication. He was

determined that on New Year's Day the doyen of the diplomatic corps address a special greeting to him, as president of a newly liberated France. In Catholic countries, including France, the papal nuncio normally is doyen. But if no nuncio was appointed in time, the senior diplomat and acting doyen would have been the Soviet ambassador. De Gaulle absolutely would not have a Russian delivering that New Year's message, and so he informed Pope Pius that his new nuncio must be in Paris by January first, without fail.

The pope understood the importance of getting his man to Paris on time, and he and his team at the Secretariat of State decided to nominate immediately Archbishop Giuseppe Fietta, then papal representative in Buenos Aires. Tardini made it clear to Fietta that the appointment was conditional on his reaching Paris by the first day of 1945 to deliver that address to de Gaulle. This posed a problem, because Fietta suffered from a heart ailment, and his doctor insisted that he could not fly; he would have to return to Europe by boat, and there was not enough time to make the sea journey. On December 4, the cable came in from Fietta to Tardini, explaining that reasons of health obliged him to refuse the Paris post.

Within hours the pope told the stunned Tardini that his third choice (after Valeri and Fietta) was that "easygoing fellow" in Istanbul, Angelo Giuseppe Roncalli. On the morning of December 5 Tardini sent a message to Roncalli: "The Holy Father wishes to transfer Your Most Reverend Excellency to Paris as nuncio . . ." Roncalli accepted without hesitation.

It was not easy to fathom the mind of Pius XII, or to explain his choice of Roncalli for Paris. He certainly did not act on the recommendation of his own team in the Secretariat of State. There was little in Roncalli's record in Istanbul to commend him for such a position. One theory is that the angry Pius was showing de Gaulle his displeasure by sending him a second-echelon diplomat as nuncio. (One perhaps apocryphal story quotes Pius as saying, "If they don't want an aristocrat [Valeri], then let them have a peasant!")

When Roncalli stopped in Rome on the way to Paris, the pope gave him scant attention, only a five-minute interview with the briefest of instructions. Yet with that appointment, Pius XII put Roncalli on the path to the papacy.

In those days there were only a few top-level Vatican diplomatic posts that inevitably led to a cardinal's hat at the end of the term. Specifically, they were Rome, Lisbon, Brussels, Madrid, Washington, and Paris. It is tempting to speculate that had Valeri been acceptable to de Gaulle, or if Fietta's doctor had permitted him to fly, Roncalli might have ground out his career in lesser posts.

Even when Roncalli was made a cardinal in 1953 and was named patriarch of Venice, he still was far from being a front-runner among the *papabili*. A third accident of history enhanced his chances. For reasons we will explore later, Pius XII had blocked the candidacy of the man whom many considered "born to be pope," Giovanni Battista Montini. During a long career in the Secretariat of State, Montini had been something of an alter ego to Pius and at one time was widely regarded as the heir apparent. There even was speculation on the name he would choose when eventually elected, and many predicted he would reign as Pius XIII. By the time Pius died, Montini was archbishop of Milan, the greatest diocese in Europe. He was eminently *papabile*— except that he was not a cardinal. Pius had refrained from making Montini a cardinal and thereby guaranteed that he would not be his successor. While it is theoretically possible for a non-cardinal to be elected pope, in fact it is unthinkable today. The last time it happened was in 1378. As one cynic has put it, "If the cardinals had to go outside the College to find a pope, they would be admitting that none of them was good enough for the job."

With Montini out of the running, there was no clear favorite to succeed Pius when the cardinals gathered in conclave in October of 1958. Had Montini been a cardinal Roncalli would not even have been considered.

Only fifty-one cardinals turned up for the election (two were absent, Aloysius Stepinac, who was in prison in Yugoslavia, and

Jozsef Mindszenty, who had found asylum in the American embassy in Budapest to escape imprisonment by the Communist regime). The conclave was a gathering of old men, their average age seventy-four. One irreverent Roman observer said, "There is one requirement for the pope to be elected by this conclave—he must be able to walk."

Though Montini's absence meant that Roncalli was among those who had a chance at election, he was by no means the favorite. His name was included on most of the long lists of *papabili* compiled by journalists, diplomats, and other observers of Vatican affairs, but few put him at or even near the top. An American journalist covering the conclave wrote at the time: "Roncalli . . . short and rotund . . . would be considered an intellectual lightweight compared to the stronger candidates. Jolly but intolerant (he was influential in shutting down a Christian Democratic newspaper which veered slightly to the left), Roncalli probably is too old at 77 to become pope, surely too old to make his mark if elected."

The field was so wide open at the time that one Rome newspaper prepared biographies of thirty-seven *papabili* to be sure to have the right one ready when the time came to put an "Extra" on the streets. Among the candidates most seriously spoken of, however, was the saintly, deeply intellectual Cardinal Gregory Peter Agagianian, patriarch of the Armenian Catholic Church, who had served for many years in top posts in the Roman Curia. Although those in the conclave theoretically are sworn to secrecy, many of them eventually do divulge certain details, and it later became known that at one point in the balloting the Armenian cardinal came within three votes of election.

In the end, the cardinals backed away from electing Agagianian for several reasons. Although sixty-three, he was considered a bit young by the standards of the time. After the nineteen-year reign of Pius, most of the cardinals were in the mood for a short-term pope, one so old that he could not hope to live long. And then, although Agagianian had spent much of his life in Rome, had once served as pastor of a Latin congregation in

Italy, and had held high office in the Roman Curia, he was not Italian. The Italian bloc of cardinals was not nearly ready to give up the monopoly on the papacy that they had held since 1523. Nor was there much of a spirit of adventure in that conclave. One conclavist afterwards reported, only half in jest, that "many of the cardinals refused to vote for a pope with a beard."

Agagianian had a fine gray beard, and the beard was a reminder of his alien origin. He was born in Tbilisi, in what is now Soviet Georgia, and as a boy attended the same seminary as Josef Stalin. Agagianian's sister still lived in the Soviet Union. No doubt conservative old cardinals shuddered at the thought that Moscow one day might hold a pope's sister hostage. No, the conservative gathering of cardinals in 1958 had not yet reached the point of experimenting with a pope from the Communist bloc.

In the midst of all the uncertainty prevailing on the eve of the conclave, there was one person who was sure of the outcome and that was Angelo Giuseppe Roncalli. It is hard to understand why, but Roncalli was confident that he would be elected. The day before the conclave began, Roncalli met a leading Christian Democratic politician, Giulio Andreotti, who later served several times as prime minister of Italy. He had earlier sought the help of Andreotti in settling the ownership of some Church property in Venice, and now he wanted to wind up the affair, "so as not to leave anything pending in Venice." He told Andreotti it would have been logical to elect Montini as pope, "but it is not possible to overcome the tradition of choosing a cardinal." He spoke of receiving a message of greetings from de Gaulle but said he had no intention of voting for a French cardinal. He dismissed the candidacy of Agagianian by arguing that "it is easier for an Italian or some other European" to deal with the Oriental world than for an Armenian. The stunned Andreotti reported: "I understood then that Roncalli felt sure that he would come out of the conclave the pope."

The foxy old Roncalli knew what the cardinals thought they were getting when they chose him. He later wrote: "When the cardinals designated me to the supreme responsibility of the government of the Church, at seventy-seven years of age, the belief was widespread that I would be a provisional pope of transition." As a Vatican journalist wrote at the time, "After the long reign of Pius, most cardinals would prefer a cooling-off period, time to revamp the Church's organizational structure, to get on with the quiet business of the Holy See. They will favor not a strong or willful man but a less talented cardinal—of proven reliability—who will ploddingly but surely put through unexciting but badly needed reforms." That was the job description the cardinals thought Roncalli fit, and so they elected him. (Eventually they got "badly needed reforms," but these were certainly not "unexciting.")

On the first day of balloting, there were two false alarms. In the morning, the smoke that billowed out of the pipe from the Sistine Chapel at first looked white as cotton. An emotional Vatican Radio announcer screamed, "Bianco, bianco, bianco, bello bianco!" ("White, white, white, beautiful white!"). But his enthusiasm waned quickly; the smoke turned gray and then black. The same thing happened in the afternoon. Eventually it took four days to elect Roncalli, as the cardinals groped to find the middle-of-the-road pope they thought they needed.

Roncalli sat serenely through the long days of balloting but never lost his confidence. When he finally was elected and asked by what name he would reign, he replied by pulling a well-prepared speech out of his pocket. He was ready.

In explaining his choice of the name John, he displayed a premonition that he would not have a long reign: "Twenty-two Johns of indisputable legitimacy have been pope, and almost all had brief pontificates."

After election, John went into the dressing room and nervously tried on one of the three papal cassocks available. It was far too small even to button. Under pressure to move on with the ceremonies, he hastily squeezed into a second cassock and barely managed to button it around his massive girth. He didn't want to waste time trying on the third outfit. Hardly able to breathe, his garments almost bursting, he went through the rest of that memorable day in considerable discomfort and embarrassment, especially painful for a person who always insisted on neatness in dress.

At seven o'clock the following morning the Vatican tailor, Bonaventura Gammarelli (whose family has dressed popes since 1800) got a phone call from Monsignor Enrico Dante, prefect of pontifical ceremonies, who gave him a dressing-down for not providing a cassock that at least approximated the Roncalli size. The puzzled Gammarelli replied that in fact he had prepared one cassock exactly to fit Roncalli, who he thought might well be elected, and he asked if the new pope had tried on all three costumes available. Told that Roncalli in his haste had tried only two of them, Gammarelli suggested that Pope John try the third cassock. John did so, and it fit like a glove.

Paul's Election after Roadblocks and Frustrations

The man who became known as Good Pope John acted quickly to remove the obstacles that Pius XII had placed in Giovanni Battista Montini's path to the papacy. Less than two months after his election, he made Montini a cardinal (the first cardinal he created), and in many ways John made it clear that the archbishop of Milan was his choice as a successor. At one point he said to friends, "I am here to prepare the place for Montini." When the Vatican Council opened in the autumn of 1962, Montini was the only cardinal John invited to stay with him as a guest in the Vatican Palace. He named Montini one of the moderators of the council and depended heavily on him to reconcile divergent points of view among the council fathers. He sent Montini on important missions and later, as he began to see his own death drawing near, the old pope urged some of the other cardinals to vote for Montini at the coming conclave. During his terminal illness, John reassured a visitor about the future: "Providence has most worthy priests all ready to take my place," he said serenely. "The first of them all is Montini."

For Montini, it was quite a different situation from his remarkable relationship with Pius XII. Early in Montini's career he had become a favorite of Cardinal Eugenio Pacelli, the future Pius XII, who first spotted the young man in 1930 when the cardinal was secretary of state. Pacelli remarked to a friend, "I like that intense young man," and he brought him along rapidly in a Vatican career. In 1937 Pacelli made the "intense young man" his *sostituto*, or undersecretary for ordinary affairs in the Secretariat of State. By 1952, when his mentor was pope, Montini became pro-secretary of state for ordinary affairs, with the pope himself holding the post of secretary of state. By now it had become clear to everyone that Montini was the man to see on papal business, and during Pius's long bouts of illness it was Montini who passed on papal orders to the Roman Curia. Few doubted that Montini would succeed Pius on the papal throne, just as the latter had succeeded his mentor, Pius XI. (In the 1939 conclave, Pacelli's election was taken for granted; he was chosen in one of the shortest conclaves in history, almost by acclamation.)

But it was not to be. Something strange happened in what had looked like a perfect understanding between pope and pupil. A friend of Montini once explained: "It was a sort of father-son relationship, and it created complexes in the son. He was never liberated by the father. I saw him weep once, out of frustration at something Pius was doing."

An obvious turning point came in 1953, when Pius called a consistory to create new cardinals—and Montini was not among them. During the consistory, the pope announced that Montini and Tardini (who worked in tandem just below the pope at the Secretariat of State) had both refused his offer to make them cardinals. On that occasion Pius explained to the assembled College of Cardinals, "It was our intention to add to the ranks of your Sacred College the two distinguished prelates who are in charge of the offices of the Secretariat of State and whose names headed the list of cardinals chosen by us and drawn up with our own hand. Nevertheless, the above-mentioned prelates, thus giving outstanding proof of virtue, begged us so insistently to be dispensed from this lofty dignity that we thought it best to accept their repeated requests and their wishes."

This "refusal" was never clearly explained. Certainly, neither man objected in principle to becoming a cardinal, since both later accepted red hats from John XXIII. But both were dedicated to their work in the Secretariat, and it seems that Pius offered them cardinalates without specifying what their new duties would be, which meant taking them away from work they loved and assigning them to unknown areas. Montini without doubt would have accepted if the Pope had nominated him secretary of state, a perfectly logical promotion which would have required that he be made a cardinal. Instead, Pius insisted on himself being secretary of state, thereby ruling out the job for Montini.

The next and final turning point came in November 1954, when Pius removed Montini from the Secretariat of State and made him archbishop of Milan. On the surface, this looked like a generous reward for all the years of hard work the pupil had put in for the pope. Milan is, as noted, a post of vast prestige, the largest diocese in Europe, the second largest in the world. But again Pius did not make Montini a cardinal, the first time in six hundred years that an archbishop of Milan was not a cardinal. In not making Montini a cardinal at that time, Pius finally guaranteed that his longtime pupil would not succeed him. When fifty-one cardinals gathered in the conclave of 1958 to choose a new pontiff, Archbishop Montini of Milan was not among them.

What had happened between pope and pupil? A very close friend of Pius XII has given an explanation: "Though Pius recognized that Montini was very intelligent and a clever person, the pope was disturbed that he was involved in many activities beyond his work at the Secretariat of State, especially in his connection with youth movements. Pius felt that Montini had overdone it, and a certain loss of confidence developed. But Pius was a very kind man, and so he 'promoted' Montini to the archdiocese of Milan."

The pope and his pupil in fact had been growing apart intellectually for many years and had developed very different political views. Pius was obsessed with a fear of Marxism. As former Jesuit Malachi Martin writes in his book *Three Popes and the Cardinal,* Pacelli's years in Germany as apostolic nuncio "had left indelible marks on him: a fear and foreboding of Soviet Bolshevism as direful as the fear and foreboding of Christians in the fifth century of Attila and the Huns." To Montini the great threat, more than Marxism, was Fascism. As early as July 1923, Montini in a letter to his parents called Mussolini's rise to power "a new triumph of the areligious—if not anti-religious—tendencies."

Back in the thirties, when right-wing dictatorships had taken root in Germany, Italy, and Spain and were threatening the democracies, Montini became an ardent member of a clique of French Catholic intellectuals centered on the philosopher Jacques Maritain, who had become an uncompromising opponent of the totalitarian state. Young Montini translated Maritain's books and used his thinking as the ideological basis for an Italian Catholic youth organization. He was instrumental in setting up a publishing house for promoting the works of Maritain and his followers. Movements sponsored by Montini formed the nucleus of the Catholic Left which flourished in Italy in the early years following World War II.

By 1950 there were signs that Montini was coming under a cloud because of these activities. In that year the Vatican's Holy Office complained about the "leftist" tendencies of Studium, the Montini-sponsored publishing house. At about the same time, the Jesuit journal *La Civiltà Cattolica* (whose articles must always be approved by the Vatican) launched an attack on Maritain. These attacks could not have been made without the knowledge and approval of Pius XII. It was clear that pope and pupil were not on the same track politically. Montini never got a red hat from his longtime mentor—and so did not become pope in 1958.

It was a fortunate development for Montini's candidacy that the cardinals in 1958 elected an old man whose reign would be short. Montini was sixty-one when John was elected. If someone of his own age had been chosen, Montini might well have been too old and infirm to be in the running at the following conclave. But John reigned less than five years, and when the 1963 conclave was summoned, Montini was only sixty-five, an age considered appropriate for a pope in those days.

The future Pope Paul VI had been deeply saddened when Pius sent him to Milan, away from the work he loved so much inside the Vatican. Leaving the father-figure Pius was a traumatic experience, which he described as "feeling like an orphan." But, good soldier that he was, he made the best of the situation and turned in a stellar performance running the sprawling archdiocese of Milan, the commercial and industrial capital of Italy. It was a cold and wet day when he drove into Milan to take possession of his archdiocese, but Montini insisted on getting out of the car to kiss the ground. At a meeting with industrial workers in the ugly, Communist-dominated suburb Sesto San Giovanni, Archbishop Montini said, "I pray that the day will come when the noise of your machines and the smoke from these chimneys may become incense, rising like a hymn of praise to the Lord."

The new archbishop spent so much time in factories, mines, and working-class quarters of the city that he became known as the workers' archbishop. Because he carried a mass kit in a brief-case on his visits to factories, business-minded Milanese nick-named him Jesus Christ's chairman of the board. He also became known as the builder of churches in Milan; during his term ninety-seven churches were either constructed or begun.

And so when Pope John died on June 3, 1963, Montini was the overwhelming choice to become the next pope. Cardinal Francis Koenig of Vienna told me that when he arrived in Rome for that conclave the secretary of state, Cardinal Amleto Cicognani, told him, "There is only one candidate—Montini." The Rome daily *Il Tempo* wrote that the only question was "Montini or not," adding, "If the answer is yes, it will be a short conclave. If it is no, it will take a long time for the cardinals to choose someone else."

Activity among the cardinals in the days immediately before they were locked up pointed to an easy Montini victory. German

Cardinal Joseph Frings called together a group of liberal colleagues at the hill town of Grottaferrata just outside Rome, and they committed themselves to support Montini. Agagianian, still considered *papabile* by some, insisted that he was not available and asked his colleagues not to vote for him. The darling of the conservatives was Cardinal Giuseppe Siri of Genoa, though at fifty-six he seemed too young to many. And he was too conservative to command a majority of the college. Cardinal Giacomo Lercaro of Bologna was *papabile* but too liberal to hope for a majority.

One of the few who refused to predict victory for Montini was Montini himself. Just before leaving Milan to attend the conclave, he was urged to wind up some diocesan business so as not to leave it hanging in case he was elected pope and had to stay in Rome. He answered quickly, "Next week, after the conclave, we will take up the matter."

At Milan's airport when he was leaving for the conclave, Montini's chauffeur-valet, Antonio Mopello, wished him a safe journey and good luck. Montini answered, "Oh, I will be back. I will be back!" He also had scheduled a trip to Norway a few days after the conclave.

Perhaps Montini was recalling the old rule "He who goes in a pope comes out a cardinal." This old Roman saying had been violated in the case of Pius XII, who went in the favorite and quickly came out as pope, but in the vast majority of modern conclaves it has proven correct.

On the first morning of balloting, it began to look as if Montini's caution was justified. A bloc of conservatives, led by some cardinals of the Roman Curia, launched a "stop Montini" maneuver. They were those who shared Pius's worries about Montini's alleged leftist tendencies. Some of them also resented the role he once had played as the favorite of Pius at the time when they could reach the pope only by going through Montini.

The first ballot showed Montini in the lead, but he was far short of the 54 votes needed for a two-thirds-plus-one majority. The conservatives focused on the candidacy of Cardinal Ildebrando Antoniutti, a former diplomat who was conservative but more moderate than Siri and thus conceivably able to attract some centrist votes. Another bloc of votes went to Lercaro, possibly as a way of siphoning support away from Montini, thereby keeping him from getting a majority and forcing the conclave to cast around for a compromise candidate.

At this point, conclave protocol was shattered. Cardinal Gustavo Testa, one of those whom Pope John had urged to support Montini, stood up and interrupted the voting with an outburst aimed at the conservatives supporting Antoniutti, calling on them to drop their maneuvers lest they "destroy the patrimony left us by Pope John!" Cardinal Siri rose to complain that Testa's outburst violated the rule of strict silence during the voting. For a moment it looked as if the session would break up in a shouting match, but order was quickly restored. Everyone returned to his place, and voting resumed in silence. Even so, Testa's message got through. A strong trend for Montini developed in the afternoon session, and at the end of the day he was only four votes short of victory. There was no doubt that on the next ballot, to be taken the following morning, Giovanni Battista Montini would be elected as the 259th successor to Saint Peter.

The great moment at last had come, after all the frustrations, the obstacles, the disappointments, the bitterness. Montini was to be placed at the pinnacle of the Church, as the Vicar of Christ on earth, the highest calling a priest can dream of. But when that moment came, it was almost more than the frail man could bear.

Montini's cell was situated immediately beside that of Cardinal Koenig. On the evening of the first day's voting the patriarch of Venice, Cardinal Giovanni Urbani, dropped in on Koenig with an expression of great concern on his face. "It would be a good thing if you would call on your neighbor," Urbani told Koenig. "He seems to be in a strange state of agitation and needs comfort."

Koenig went to Montini's cell and found him in a deep depression. The Austrian cardinal tried to cheer the poor man up with what he thought was a happy prediction: "It seems that tomorrow morning we will have a pope, and all the arrows are pointing to you."

To Montini it was not a happy prediction at all. His cheeks stained with tears, he looked up at Koenig and answered, "I hope it will not be true. I am in a terrible state of confusion. I feel as if I am in the dark."

Late that night, one of the cardinals saw Montini kneeling in prayer in the darkness of the Pauline chapel.

The following morning, as Koenig had predicted, white smoke billowed forth to announce to the world that a pope had been elected on the fifth ballot of the conclave. The new pope was Montini, who reportedly got 75 out of the 80 votes in the final tabulation. The senior cardinal-deacon, Alfredo Ottaviani, stood on the main loggia of St. Peter's to tell the crowd, "Habemus papam!" He didn't get through the name before they all knew it was the archbishop of Milan. When Ottaviani said, "Giovanni Battista—" the rest of the name was drowned out by the earthquake of applause and cheering that shook St. Peter's Square.

Standing on the loggia to bless the crowd, Paul VI appeared composed and serene, as if during that night of agony and prayer he somehow had found the strength to face the ordeal ahead. But the sadness still showed when he told the crowd, "With Christ I am nailed to the Cross. Perhaps the Lord has called me to this service so that I will suffer for the Church."

John Paul II, a Pope from the Communist World

Pope Paul "suffered" through a fifteen-year reign, and during that decade and a half a sweeping change came over the Church that destroyed the Italian monopoly on the papacy. Following the suggestions of the Vatican Council, Paul internationalized the government of the Church and in so doing reduced the Italians to a small minority in the College of Cardinals. By 1978, they no longer had the numerical strength to dictate the choice of a pope.

The change in the college completed a historical process that had begun earlier in the century. For more than half a millennium, the nationality of cardinals had been more or less determined by the place of residence of the pope. When the papal residence was moved to Avignon, in France, in 1308, the College of Cardinals became overwhelmingly French. In 1331, during the reign of Pope John XXII in Avignon, seventeen of the twenty cardinals were French. And French cardinals elected French popes. All seven popes who resided in Avignon were French. After the papacy was moved back to Rome in 1378, the great majority of cardinals were Italian, and Italy kept that majority until well into the twentieth century. From 1378 until 1978, only three popes were not Italian.

The last non-Italian pope, the Dutch Adrian VI (1522–1523), was considered a disaster by the easy-living Romans of the Renaissance. Pious, otherwordly, and austere, Adrian had been a grand inquisitor in Spain and reportedly had ordered thirty thousand Spanish heretics burned at the stake. He was shocked by the loose morality of Rome and once ordered that the walls of the Sistine Chapel be whitewashed to cover up the "pornography" painted there by Michelangelo. (He died before the order was carried out.) When he passed away after a twenty-month reign, no Roman mourned him. Some sadistic persons put laurels on the door of the papal physician who had failed to save Adrian's life, hailing the doctor as the liberator of his country.

After the experience with Adrian, what the Romans called the Dutch curse was placed on any non-Italian aspirant for the papacy. Until 1978 the predominantly Italian College of Cardinals routinely chose Italians as popes.

Things had begun to change, almost imperceptibly, as early as the election of Pius XII in 1939, when thirty-five of sixty-two cardinals were Italian. By 1958, the proportion had dropped to eighteen out of fifty-three, and in 1963 there were only twenty-nine Italian cardinals out of eighty-two. But the Italians remained the largest single group and, more important, they continued to hold almost all the offices in the Roman Curia, the government of the Church, and so still held enough power to dominate the selection of successors to Saint Peter.

The great leap forward came during the reign of Paul VI, who not only expanded the total number of cardinals but also diversified their nationalities to an unprecedented degree. Pope John had made a long step toward diversification in 1960, when he created the first black cardinal in Church history, Laurean Rugambwa of Tanganyika. Paul continued this trend, and by the time of his death the College of Cardinals included not only Europeans and Americans but also cardinals from Third World areas such as South Korea, black Africa, Pakistan, and India. When Paul died on August 6, 1978, there were only twenty-seven Italian cardinals out of one hundred twelve in the college. With them were twelve African cardinals, thirteen from Asia or Oceania, nineteen from Latin America and eleven North Americans. Altogether fifty nations were represented, and for the first time ever a majority were non-European. The Italians still were the largest single group, but they were far too few to impose their will.

Even with the decline of Italian strength, when the cardinals gathered to choose the successor to Paul in that hot conclave of August 1978, the consensus was that yet another Italian should be chosen. The problem was to find the kind of Italian the cardinals wanted. For the first time in many centuries, pastoral cardinals (those serving as bishops of dioceses in the field rather than in curial administrative or diplomatic jobs) held power in the college, and they made it clear that the Italian they chose must be a pastor, not another diplomat or Roman curial official. As a Roman priest said at the time, "It is one thing to interpret the faith and another to convey it to the people in the parishes. And that is something the bishops understand better than the curialists at their little desks in Rome."

This elimination of curial candidates gave Cardinal Giovanni Benelli of Florence the opportunity to act as "pope-maker." Only fifty-seven years old at the time, Benelli was generally considered too young to be elected himself, but he wielded much influence among the cardinals from outside Rome, and he used this power. For many years he had served, in effect, as Pope Paul's chief of staff (his title was undersecretary of state in those years), and in that role he had come to know most of the important archbishops around the globe. Cardinals from abroad not familiar with the Italian scene looked to Benelli for guidance.

Benelli's choice was the patriarch of Venice, Cardinal Albino Luciani, a lovable man with an infectious smile who had spent his entire career in pastoral work. He was not a strong man, and few Vatican observers considered him more than an outside possibility among the *papabili.* Nevertheless, he did have some admirable credentials. As patriarch of Venice, he had given a fine example of what Pope Paul had called "apostolic simplicity." He showed his contempt for worldly treasures by auctioning off two pectoral crosses on golden chains belonging to the patriarchate and a ring given him by Pope Paul, all for $16,000. To those who criticized him for this, he answered simply, "The real treasures of the Church are the poor, the disinherited, the little ones who must be helped."

Although not so liberal as to attract the hostility of conservatives, Luciani had shown a progressive inclination when he expressed kind words for the parents of a "test-tube baby" at a time when such experiments were being condemned by the Vatican. Another evidence of his liberal tendencies was the fact—revealed later by his secretary—that when he went into the conclave, Luciani had intended to vote for Brazilian cardinal Aloisi Lorscheider, who had gained widespread attention for his support of movements associated with liberation theology in Latin America.

Though Luciani did not "go in a pope," he was elected in amazingly quick time. Just before seven P.M. on the first day of the conclave the smoke belching out of the pipe looked gray, and swarms of people began pouring into St. Peter's Square. In the near-dusk, it was hard to see if the smoke was black or white, and a Vatican Radio announcer admitted, "There still is uncertainty about the color of that smoke."

Exuberant cardinals were to blame for the ambiguity. When

Luciani was elected, many of them were so elated that they threw their own tally sheets into the stove before the chemicals could be added, thereby producing grayish smoke. There was nothing doubtful about the outcome. In the morning balloting, votes had been widely dispersed, but in the first afternoon session the trend for Luciani had become clear. A bloc of diehard conservatives stuck with Siri as their candidate to the last, and this may have influenced others to vote for Luciani as a way of ensuring that the archconservative Siri would not be the winner.

The "smiling pope," who chose to reign under the name of John Paul I, lacked the strength to bear the burdens of the office, and he was the first to understand this. When votes for him began to pile up and he realized he was going to be elected, Luciani became terribly and visibly agitated. Dutch cardinal Jan Willebrands was sitting on one side of him and Portuguese cardinal Antonio Ribeiro on the other, and both realized that the man was in an emotional crisis. One told him, "Courage. If the Lord gives a burden he also gives the strength to carry it." The other said to him, "Don't be afraid. The whole world prays for a new pope."

Their kind words gave Luciani little comfort. He was afraid. When the result was announced, he appeared "red and flustered" in his seat underneath Pinturicchio's fresco of the Baptism of Christ. When the senior cardinal-deacon, Pericle Felici, approached him to ask if he accepted, his first words were "May God forgive you for what you have done to me."

When he sat on his throne before the altar receiving the first obeisance of the cardinals, the Belgian cardinal Leo Joseph Suenens approached to embrace him and said, "Holy Father, thank you for saying yes." To which Luciani replied, "Perhaps it would have been better if I had said no."

Poor Luciani, who had suffered from a tubercular condition in his younger days, obviously was neither physically nor emotionally strong enough to bear the overwhelming burdens of the papal office. Thirty-three days after his election he died in bed, apparently from a heart attack. And with his death, the unbroken string of Italian popes came to an end.

. . .

Once again cardinals had to be rounded up from all over the world for yet another conclave. Once again they were disposed to choose an Italian, so long as he was "pastoral," but by now they were nearing the end of the possibilities. The indestructible Siri remained the choice of archconservatives, though it was clear he never would be able to win.

As before, Benelli was a key figure in the conclave. The difference this time was that instead of simply acting as pope-maker he now opted to make a supreme bid for the papacy himself, notwithstanding his relative youth. His supporters quietly began canvassing for votes among the arriving cardinals. Just a week before the conclave began, a Benelli aide went to the Polish Church on Rome's Via delle Botteghe Oscure (the Street of the Dark Shops) to meet three Polish bishops—Archbishops Andrzej Deskur and Wladyslaw Rubin, both Vatican functionaries, and Cardinal Karol Wojtyla, archbishop of Krakow—reportedly to ask their support for Benelli, now archbishop of Florence. Their response is not known.

There also was some blatant campaigning for Siri. Members of the conservative but powerful religious order Opus Dei openly lobbied for him. A newspaper in Venice carried an unprecedented front-page endorsement of Siri's candidacy as "the heir of Luciani." His supporters pointed out that, with all Siri's conservatism, "the seminaries are full" in his Genoa diocese, while in most other areas there were shortages of vocations.

For the conclave that began on October 14, 1978, there were 111 cardinals present (112 were eligible to vote, but Cardinal Boleslaw Filipak of Poland was too ill to travel to Rome). None of the cardinals was accompanied by an assistant (called a conclavist) except the American cardinal John Wright, who was in a wheelchair and helped by his secretary, Father Donald Wuerhl. (The Pauline rules allowed for a conclavist if a cardinal was seriously ill.)

As in the August conclave, there was no obvious front-runner this time, no one "going in a pope." Cardinal Joseph Malula

of Zaire estimated that more than half the cardinals had not decided on their choice when the conclave began. There was even
more uncertainty than there had been in August.

On the first day of balloting, October 15, it was mainly a
contest between Siri and Benelli. Siri was strong during the
morning session, leading the field with 46 votes, but still far short
of the 75 needed to win. When the cardinals broke for lunch and
siesta, it still looked like an all-Italian election. But before the day
was out, it had become clear that no Italian would come out of
this conclave a pope. Some Romans called that day "the Italian
cardinals' last stand."

Benelli passed Siri in the afternoon voting, but he, too, failed
to approach the magic number 75. There was a scattering of votes
for other Italians and isolated ballots for non-Italians, such as
Cardinals Eduardo Pironio of Argentina and Basil Hume of Britain. As black puffs of smoke emerged after the fourth and last
ballot of that day, the cardinals understood that neither Siri's
supporters nor Benelli's would give way to the other side.
Benelli's followers considered him the rightful heir of the progressive Pope Paul, and they adamantly refused to accept a man as far
to the right as Siri. On the other hand, there were many supporters of Siri from the Roman Curia who detested Benelli—who not
only suspected his liberalism but also could not forgive him for
the way he often ran roughshod over them when he was Pope
Paul's "top sergeant."

Beyond Benelli and Siri no Italian cardinal had the stature to
command much of a following. When they gathered for dinner
in the Borgia Apartment that evening, there was more uncertainty among the cardinals than ever. If it was not to be an Italian,
who could it be? There were, of course, many outstanding non-
Italians, but no focus on any particular one. The National Opinion Research Center in Chicago had done a simulated conclave in
a computer, and results indicated a non-Italian could win. It listed
first among the non-Italians with a chance the black African cardinal Bernardin Gantin of Benin, who then headed the Pontifical
Commission for Justice and Peace. After Gantin, it listed in order

Pironio, Hume, and Willebrands. But cardinals in a conclave are not concerned with computer projections. Years later, Cardinal Koenig described to me the mood of that evening of uncertainty: "We dined together but there was very little discussion, no lobbying. In the fresh evening air of the courtyard of San Damaso, we took our walks silently. We felt a strange tension in our minds. There was no human explanation for the choice that we made the next day."

That "tension in the minds" was strong as the balloting began on the morning of the second day. When the *scrutatores* began reading the names on the ballots, the cardinals sensed something historically dramatic was about to happen. "Willebrands . . . Siri . . . Hume . . ." And then a name that had not been heard before in that conclave: "Wojtyla."

The moment that name was pronounced, the election was decided. It was as if the dove had landed on Karol Wojtyla's head. On the following ballot, a Wojtyla majority began to form, a majority that soon swelled into a flood tide for a cardinal who had scarcely been mentioned in public speculation. Cardinal Malula later reported that in the pre-conclave consultations, "I never once heard the name of Wojtyla mentioned." *Time* magazine was probably the only widely circulated publication that had even listed him among the *papabili,* and then only as a remote possibility. It seems that the only publication in the world that predicted the outcome was the Harvard *Crimson.* In 1976 Cardinal Wojtyla gave a lecture at Harvard and so impressed the students that the *Crimson* at the time captioned his photograph "The Future Pope."

Wojtyla himself had given no indication that he expected to be elected, but he was spiritually and emotionally prepared for that great event. He had packed lightly in coming to Rome from Kraków, as if he thought the conclave would be short. He had brought along a scarred, discolored overnight satchel of imitation leather, a few cheap shirts and changes of linen, an old shaving brush. Because he hates to waste even a single odd minute, Wojtyla always takes along some reading matter wherever he goes, and during those long periods of voting in the conclave he was calmly perusing a book of political theory by Karl Marx. When a fellow cardinal asked if he didn't feel it sacrilegious to read such an author in that sacred place, he answered with a good-natured smile, "My conscience is clear."

Wojtyla had not been so calm during the August conclave. Seven years later at dinner with him I learned a fact till then unknown and unpublished: Cardinal Wojtyla had gotten "a small but significant number of votes" in the August conclave that had elected John Paul I. The votes for Wojtyla apparently had come from the German-speaking bloc of cardinals led by the Austrian Koenig. It was the first time in his life that Wojtyla had faced the realistic possibility that he might become pope, and that looming possibility threw him into a panic. He recalled that as his name was read by the *scrutator* he was seized by "a severe agitation" approaching fear at the idea that he might have such a massive responsibility placed on his shoulders.

It was different when he returned for the October conclave. Although he did not, like Roncalli, predict his own election, he was at peace and fully prepared for whatever might happen. He told me that "by the beginning of the second day, it all had become clear. I could feel that the Holy Spirit was working among the cardinals, and I could sense the outcome."

In fact, the election of Wojtyla was not as surprising as it sounds, once it became clear that no Italian could be chosen. He had become very well known to most of the cardinals, if not to the world media. As a young bishop, he had attended the Vatican Council and had delivered eight speeches and one written report to that body, on subjects ranging from the sacraments to religious liberty. He had gotten even more exposure from his activity at the World Synod of Bishops, established by Pope Paul as a body of representative bishops from around the world which the pope would summon every two or three years to give him counsel on major questions. Wojtyla had attended all the synods from 1967 through 1977, and in 1971 he was elected a member of the permanent council of the synod, which brought him often to Rome. At the 1969 synod, he presided over the commission that produced the final document, and in the 1974 synod he delivered an important paper on evangelization. During the Lenten season of 1976, Pope Paul invited the cardinal from Kraków to be the preacher to the Lenten retreat for the pope and the curia.

The German cardinals knew Wojtyla well; he had visited their country only four months before. The Americans, led by the Polish-American cardinal John Krol, had gotten acquainted with him in the days when he attended the Eucharistic Congress in Philadelphia in 1976, and four of them had more than once been Wojtyla's guest in Poland. He thus was no stranger to the cardinals gathered in that conclave in October 1978.

The swing in the voting to Wojtyla was led by Cardinal Koening, who was quickly followed by other Europeans—French, German, Spanish, and Eastern Europeans. They were soon joined by the Americans, and in the afternoon the Italian cardinals—both curialists and pastorals—switched over to Wojtyla. On the final ballot of that day—the eighth of the conclave—it was Wojtyla by a landslide. Some sources say he got 94 of the 111 votes, far beyond the 75 needed for election.

How does it feel to be elected pope? I put this question to John Paul II, and he answered calmly, "I felt the choice resulted from the work of the Holy Spirit, and I know that if the Holy Spirit gives you a role to play, he also gives you the grace and strength to shoulder the burden."

The pope then sensed that he had to put it more clearly to the layman-journalist he was addressing. He paused to think a bit and then expressed the feeling in a manner he thought I might understand: "It was like you felt when you got married—making a lifetime commitment."

While inside the Sistine Chapel Karol Wojtyla was making his lifelong commitment to be John Paul II, all the streets leading to St. Peter's Square were jammed as at least a hundred thousand Romans who had seen the white smoke poured in to wait for the great announcement. The pontifical band marched in, followed by detachments of that last remnant of papal military strength, the

Swiss Guards, who in turn were followed by an honor guard of the Italian armed forces, all taking their places in formation in a reserved space in front of the basilica. The senior cardinal-deacon, Pericle Felici, walked slowly onto the loggia and for the second time in less than two months announced to the world that a new pope had been elected. Felici was a man of wry humor with a keen sense of the dramatic, and he obviously enjoyed immensely the moment of suspense as he dragged out the phrase "Annuntio vobis gaudium magnum. Habe-mus pa-pam!"

When Felici reached the point of revealing the new pope's first name—"Most Eminent and Most Reverend . . . Cardinalem Caro-lum"—a group of priests watching on TV thought he meant Cardinal Carlo Confalonieri, who was then eighty-five years old, and they muttered in astonishment "Sono matti!" ("They are mad!"). And when he pronounced the last name— "Woe-ti-wa"—a group of tourists thought the new pope was Japanese, and an Italian journalist started checking quickly through the list of African cardinals to get the name spelled right. Then someone screamed, "E' il Polacco!" ("It's the Pole!") and pandemonium broke loose.

That crowd of a hundred thousand Romans cheered as if they did not care that the long Italian monopoly on the papacy had been broken. They were thrilled at the historic novelty of the moment. In fact it was a great turning point in the history of the modern Church when this particular path to the papacy led to Rome not only from the East but also from the Communist world, where the Christian community till only recently had been referred to by popes as the Church of Silence. Many remembered that at the election of Pope John XXIII two cardinals—Mindszenty and Stepinac—had been kept from attending the conclave by Communist oppression. Now the Church of Silence had sent one of its own to the See of Peter.

The crowd became more exuberant by the minute as the handsome, youthful new pope stood on the loggia and warmed them with his relaxed humor. He spoke so long that a worried protocol official was heard to whisper to him "Basta!"

("Enough!"), but Wojtyla ignored him and continued, though by tradition papal remarks at that moment should be brief and formal. He also pleased the crowd with his command of their language; the Polish pontiff spoke in fluent, though accented, Italian. At one point, in mock reference to the fact that Italian was not his native tongue, John Paul paused to say, "If I make a mistake, you must correct me!"

An Italian dignitary watching the scene wondered aloud if this "foreign" pope would be "corrected" and totally subdued by the long-entrenched Roman Curia. To this, a Catholic politician quickly responded, "Not this man. He will end up transforming Rome."

2

A TRIPTYCH OF DIVERSE PAPAL STYLES

John XXIII: The Triumphal Entry

There are parallels and precedents. When the cardinals met to elect a pope in 1585, they found themselves hopelessly deadlocked between two powerful rival factions. The only way out in the end was to choose an interim pope, one so infirm that he would be able to rule only a short time while the cardinals sorted out their differences and decided on a permanent candidate. The interim pope chosen was the scholarly but aging Felice Peretti, who had lived in retirement for many years and arrived at the conclave bent, limping, and leaning on a cane. But as soon as he was proclaimed pope, he stood erect, threw away his cane, and told the conclave, "Now I am Caesar."

Sixtus V, the "interim pope," surprised everyone with his energetic administration. He arrested thousands of brigands and restored internal security to the Papal States, put order into the state's finances by levying more taxes and building up a cash reserve, and launched a program of public works that included a plan to drain the Pontine marshes south of Rome (a project finally completed in Mussolini's day). In short, the man who was elected to do nothing became one of the most dynamic popes in history.

To many Romans the choice of John XXIII in 1958 was a reminder of the election of Sixtus V. Angelo Giuseppe Roncalli admittedly was a compromise choice, selected mainly because, at the age of seventy-seven, he could be expected to reign in docile fashion for only a short time while the "real" personality emerged who could eventually command a majority of the College of Cardinals.

It is true that John's reign was short—less than five years—but in that brief reign he demonstrated, as few popes ever have, the impact that an individual pontiff can make on the Church and on the world. As *Time* magazine reported, this old man chosen as a bland compromise between liberals and conservatives "did not tiptoe into his reign; he stomped in boldly like the owner of the place, throwing open windows and moving furniture around." This interim pope brought such change into the Church that his three successors spent most of their time coping with forces that he set in motion. And he achieved all this not by teaching or lecturing but primarily through the impact of his unique and charismatic personality.

About a year after John's death, the amiable Cardinal Richard Cushing of Boston on a visit to Rome referred to the late pontiff as Good Pope John in the presence of Cardinal Alfredo Ottaviani, the conservative who then headed the Holy Office.

"Why do you say 'Good Pope John'?" asked the bristling Ottaviani. "Aren't all popes good?"

Perhaps. But probably never before in history had a pope had the quality of exuding goodness as did old Roncalli—despite an unimposing personal appearance. He had neither the majestic figure of his aristocratic predecessor Pius XII nor the magnetic smile and good looks of John Paul II. He was dumpy, overweight, wide-mouthed, plain-faced. Once, as he stood before a mirror to put on his vestments for a ceremony, he chuckled and said to his secretary, "Eighty years ago the Good Lord knew I was going to become pope one day. Why didn't he make me more handsome?"

This aging peasant who at the age of ten was laboring from dawn to dusk in wheat fields and vineyards near the northern Italian village of Sotto il Monte brought to the baroque splendor of the Vatican the folksy, intensely human tenderness of an indulgent grandfather, a tenderness that he projected to those of all ages. Whenever he received groups of families, inevitably one or two little children would have climbed up onto the papal knees before the audience ended.

The aristocratic and reclusive Pius XII had ordered that visitors be barred from the dome of St. Peter's when he walked in the Vatican Gardens so that he could stroll in total privacy. John happily allowed the visitors to stay there, from where they could easily watch the strolling pope. When a protocol official objected, John answered with a chuckle, "Why not let them watch me? I am not doing anything scandalous!"

Even on his deathbed, John showed characteristic tenderness. Just before he lost consciousness for the last time, he whispered to his longtime personal secretary, Monsignor Loris Capovilla, "When all is finished, don't forget to go see your mother."

John's reign is remembered as an era of good feeling that not only stirred Catholics but also won the good will of Protestants, Orthodox, atheists, Marxists, and Jews around the world. By 1962, John had already met more Anglican and Protestant leaders than any other pope in history, and his excessive attention to all those non-Catholics irritated some old Vatican staffers. One conservative growled, "It seems easier to see the pope if you are a Methodist." The good-humored John replied to such complaints with a typically tolerant remark, "Let's give them credit for their good intentions—and if they don't have any, I have one eye open to see clearly myself."

This old man who exuded such goodness admittedly had his human weaknesses. An archbishop who once worked closely with Roncalli before he became pope described him to me as "un buon uomo, si, ma non era santo!" ("a good man, yes, but he was no saint"!). Certainly he was not a saint in the manner of Saint

Anthony, who withdrew from the world to a limestone cave, or Saint Simeon, who renounced the world and spent many years atop a lonely pillar in the desert. John's goodness was an earthy, this-worldly goodness, that of a human being who loved the world and enjoyed the good things of it.

Although born and raised in the world of the land-tilling laborer, John was introduced to the sophisticated pleasures of life as secretary for ten years to the aristocratic bishop of Bergamo, Giacomo Radini-Tedeschi, a gourmet of exquisite tastes. Young Roncalli developed what Italians call *una buona forchetta* (a good fork), and years later as papal nuncio in Paris he became one of the most popular diplomats in the French capital, at least partly because of the conviviality and good food at his table. Far beyond the simple pasta and pizza usually associated with the Italian diet, Roncalli loved the more sophisticated Italian dishes—raviolini, polenta with small birds, hare in salmi, *pollo alla diavola*, tripe Bergamasque.

John did not lose his very special interest in good eating after becoming pope. He once telephoned personally to the Vatican City grocery to explain to those Romans just how to order the best parmigiano cheese. The pope knew that around Reggio Emilia, heart of the parmigiano country, the hills are numbered, and he also knew that the finest cheese comes from hills with numbers below 999. He instructed the grocer never to buy cheese from hills numbered 1,000 or higher. John also insisted that the grocer order his cornmeal, for making polenta, from one of two special zones, one near Bergamo, the other near Mantua.

"Non era santo" in the traditional sense, but even while he was dying the public attributed to John XXIII some qualities of sainthood. A few days before his death, the pope was sinking so fast that his doctors had given up hope. The physicians were surprised when the powerful peasant constitution rallied yet again, and those of us maintaining a deathwatch were amazed to see the dying pope appear at his bedroom window one more time to bless the crowd in the piazza down below. All around me in the piazza I heard shouts of "Miracolo! Miracolo!" and when the news of that appearance was transmitted around the world, millions of Catholics instantly assumed that an authentic miracle had taken place.

A few years after John's death, Pope Paul formally opened the process for his canonization, which normally may take several generations. But already during the first Vatican Council session after John's death a serious move was begun to have the council proclaim him a saint by acclamation, bypassing the normal lengthy process. (It was Pope Paul who squelched the idea, reminding the council fathers that "the Church must honor virtues, not the person.") In any case, John has received what might be called a popular canonization from the public. In the homes of simple Italian Catholics it is common to see little shrines set up with John's picture between candles, and his old home in Sotto il Monte has become an unofficial pilgrimage center.

The impact of that old man's spirit was never felt more strongly than on the evening of his death. His illness had been a long and painful one, periods of recovery interspersed with days and weeks in which he hovered between life and death, between awareness and unconsciousness. Through even that dark period, John warmed the hearts of the public with his calm, uncomplaining, good-humored acceptance of his fate. At one point he told his doctors with his usual chuckle, "They say I have a tumor. *Ebbene* [very well], may God's will be done. But don't worry about me, because my bags are packed and I am ready to go."

To his secretary, Monsignor Capovilla, he spoke with serenity: "I have been able to follow my death step by step. Now I am going sweetly to the end."

The end came sweetly. On that warm June afternoon, a sunset mass for John was celebrated on the front steps of St. Peter's Basilica, situated so that the thousands of worshipers could look on the right to see the window of the apartment in which their pope lay dying. The service ended, and the people began moving across the square to return home and listen for news on their TV sets. Before they could get out of the piazza, those of us watching the papal window were frozen in the grip of a sudden tension. Television cameramen and news photographers stopped chatting and smoking and trained their long lenses on the window of the pontifical apartment. We could see the curtains being drawn and a blaze of artificial light inside, as if photographs were being taken. Then it came. A voice from a public address system floated over the piazza with the announcement: "It is with the most profound emotion that we must announce that the Supreme Pontiff of the Universal Church, Pope John the Twenty-third, is dead."

There was a moment of stunned silence. Then a woman standing beside me began to weep softly. A trio of nuns in black dropped to their knees to pray. Soon almost everyone in the square was on his knees. The bells of St. Peter's began to toll. Through the columns of Bernini's colonnade we could see the great bronze doors of the Vatican Palace slowly closing, to remain shut until the Church would have another pope.

It was my duty to rush to a studio to make a news broadcast, and rarely in my professional life have I been so moved by an event that I had to cover. I managed to get through the script until I reached my last line. I tried to say, "The pope of the people is dead," but it was too much. My voice cracked. I couldn't go on. And I knew that around the world hundreds of millions of people were reacting in the same way.

The peasant pope had come and gone in a manner that in some ways could be compared with Jesus' Triumphal Entry into Jerusalem on the first Palm Sunday. As he rode on a donkey into the Holy City over a path of palm branches and the garments of his followers, Jesus awakened in that cheering mob hopes that long had lain unrealized and frustrated. To many of them, Jesus was the long-awaited Messiah, the Christ who would defeat Israel's enemies and restore the Kingdom of David. In that moment of euphoria and hope, the crowd attributed to Jesus a dream that they wanted him to realize, not what he had in fact taught about himself. Many were bitterly disillusioned later in the same week when Pontius Pilate asked Jesus if he was king of the Jews, and he answered, "My kingdom is not of this world."

In somewhat similar fashion John XXIII aroused hopes in the Christian world that went far beyond anything he himself claimed as his intentions. Long after his death, liberal Catholics and Protestants alike often were to say that the move to Christian unity would have gone much faster and farther if only Good Pope John had lived longer. Many progressives were convinced that the old pope favored a democratic form of government in the Church, married priests, liberalization of Catholic teaching on birth control. Nearly five years after John's death his secretary, Capovilla, by this time Bishop of Loreto, had to circulate a pastoral letter denying allegations by Church liberals that John had favored leaving the question of birth control to the individual conscience. Liberal theologians still yearn for the era of John and speak as if he would have permitted something approaching unlimited freedom in Catholic theological speculation.

Pope John was neither theologian nor scholar; in fact, there was little in his past to mark him as a man of innovation. Although he had supported the worker-priest experiment in France when he was nuncio there, he suppressed the movement when he became pope.* It was John who appointed the archconservative Cardinal Ottaviani to head the Holy Office, the watchdog of orthodoxy in the Church. And he spoke the language of conservatism when in his apostolic constitution "Veterum Sapientia" he supported the use of Latin in the Church. He was elected pope not as the candidate of the liberals but as a compromise. Even after his death, some well-informed Vatican experts continued to belittle John's liberal credentials. An astute Protestant theologian who was an observer at the council argued in an interview with me: "John's approach to piety was completely old-fashioned. He was totally innocent of all modern trends in theology. His conception of Christian unity was to invite the 'separated brethren' back to the Catholic fold. His formula for the population problem was to enlarge the banquet rather than reduce the number of guests

---

*Priests in the movement worked in factories as ordinary laborers to make contact with the working class.

through liberalized birth-control teaching. He was far less liberal than his successor, Paul VI. After Paul became pope there was a net shift in the Vatican Council of at least three hundred votes (out of nearly twenty-five hundred) to the liberal side from the time when John headed it up."

Such cynical comments could not dampen the enthusiasm that John had generated in the world. In a vast and diverse array of human activity, there were those who attributed to John qualities that were almost revolutionary. In Czechoslovakia today a movement of Marxist priests—approved and supported by the Communist regime but disavowed by the Vatican—call their organization Pacem in Terris after one of John's famous encyclicals. An ecological conference on the island of Malta called itself Pacem in Maribus (Peace in the Sea), a title inspired by John's "Peace on Earth" encyclical. The Grand Mufti of Lebanon, the leading Sunni Muslim authority in that country, made an impassioned speech praising John at his death, citing passages from "Pacem in Terris" and calling it an inspiring message for the entire human race. An antidrug center in New York is named for John XXIII. After John's death, Athenagoras, the ecumenical patriarch of Constantinople, spiritual leader of the Eastern Orthodox churches, which have been in schism with Rome for nearly a millennium, declared with emotion, "There was a man sent from God, whose name was John."

The optimism generated by Good Pope John fit the mood of the times perfectly. His reign coincided with the most promising era mankind has enjoyed since the end of World War II. Western Europe had recovered from the devastation of war and had embarked on an epoch of unparalleled prosperity; the groundwork was laid for a united Europe that would rival the superpowers in economic strength. In the Communist world, dictatorship was mitigated by the de-Stalinization and liberalization launched by that good-humored character Nikita Khrushchev. In the United States, spirits were soaring with the election of John F. Kennedy as the youngest of American presidents, a leader who inspired dreams of new frontiers, of peace and prosperity without limit. The Cold War seemed to be coming to an end with the two "K's," Kennedy and Khrushchev. I remember at the time visiting Bologna, the heart of Communist strength in Italy, and hearing a Communist official explain that among his fellow party members "we are about equally divided—fifty percent Khrushchev, fifty percent Kennedy."

Pope John was seen by millions as the third man in a triumvirate of détente, along with the two "K's." He was looked to as the bridge between the rival empires, the catalyst who would bring the "K's" together in understandings that would make "Pacem in Terris" a reality in our time. And the pope's nature fueled this hope. He once said, "Men have come and gone, but I have always remained an optimist, because that is my nature, even when I hear around me deep concern over the fate of mankind."

The old pope was everyone's ideal, perhaps in part because as a rule he avoided taking strong positions on issues and so allowed others to assume that he supported their favorite causes. His emphasis was always on the human relationship, not the theory, the heart rather than the head, intuition rather than intellect. In conversation, he often rambled without focusing on a specific point. Among his favorite audiences were those with Italian families from his native region in northern Italy, with whom he spoke in the local dialect and whom he regaled with local wit and humor totally incomprehensible to outsiders. He would meander from one folksy platitude to another, rarely coming to any conclusions—and never failing to charm his guests totally and absolutely.

To some extent, John dealt with the rest of the world the same way. Instead of bluntly taking a position and promoting it with vigor, John simply created a situation in which things would happen of their own momentum. Typical of this tactic was his summoning the Second Vatican Council, the greatest achievement of his reign.

Throughout Church history, popes usually called councils to deal with very specific matters; the First Vatican Council (1869–1870), for example, was summoned by Pius IX to declare the infallibility of the pope. John's council had no such precise agenda. He only knew intuitively that there was need for *aggiornamento*, or renewal, in the Church. And so he just called in all the bishops of the world, urged them to exercise "holy liberty" in their deliberations, and let events take their course. John even gave the impression that he was rather indifferent to the council's work. He did not attend the sessions personally but watched the proceedings on closed-circuit television. A good friend of his reports that often when he visited the pope during that time the TV set would be on but the council proceedings would be ignored, while John chatted amiably with visitors.

As pope, the old man used the same subtle methods that he had employed as a diplomat in non-Catholic Bulgaria, in Muslim Turkey, and in Gaullist France. One of his most delicate diplomatic assignments came when he was papal nuncio to Paris. De Gaulle accused the Catholic hierarchy of collaborating with the Vichy regime, and he demanded that all thirty bishops in the country be replaced. Instead of fighting about it directly, Roncalli stalled, asked for more information, reported that he was studying the case of each bishop individually, until the French tired of the whole thing. In the end, Roncalli told a friend with a chuckle, he had agreed to remove the bishops, "on condition that we just eliminate one little zero." He subtracted the zero from thirty— and removed exactly three bishops.

John's favorite maxim of administration was "Omnis videre, multa dissimulare, pauca corrigere" ("To see everything, to turn a blind eye on much of it, to correct a little"). Certainly as head of the outmoded and often sluggish Vatican bureaucracy he preferred to turn a blind eye rather than try to correct it all. When a visitor once asked how many people worked in the Vatican, the pope answered, "About half of them."

The subtle, indirect approach had been typical of John's behavior from the beginning of his ecclesiastical career. Always a stickler for neat personal appearance, John set up in a youth center in Bergamo a mirror inscribed "Know Thyself" as a discreet reminder to students to take care of their dress. While serving as secretary to the bishop of Bergamo, he became disturbed at the slovenly appearance of priests from his native village who called at the bishop's residence. Instead of bluntly telling them to spruce up, John put the point across with his usual subtlety. For a priest who shaved too rarely he produced a razor, explaining that it was one he didn't need and he wanted to offer it to the priest as a gift. (The priest began to shave every day after that.) Another cleric turned up regularly wearing a dirty collar, and Roncalli made him a gift of a set of collars "which are too small for me now that I have gotten fat." The priestly collars henceforth were clean.

While he was patriarch of Venice, Cardinal Roncalli deftly coped with the annoying problem of tourists swarming into the city, and even into its churches, scantily clad. Instead of railing against a habit that conservatives termed immoral, Roncalli with his usual humor noted that "Venice is not on the equator, but even on the equator lions wear their coats, and crocodiles are adorned with their most precious hides."

This "pope of the people" may have been "innocent of modern trends in theology," but liberal theologians got a great stimulus during John's reign. He didn't take a position on modern theological issues, but he called to the council as experts some of the most advanced Catholic theologians of the time—liberal thinkers like Hans Kung and Karl Rahner and Yves Congar—many of whom in subsequent years have been curbed in one way or another by the Holy See. Their presence at the council had a tremendous influence on its decisions.

Paul VI: The Via Dolorosa

Pope John lived long enough to preside over only the first of four sessions of the great council he had summoned. He died in June 1963, and in retrospect it seems that the era of good feeling died with him. Within a few months Kennedy was assassinated, and the following year Khrushchev was ousted by the Brezhnev clique in the Kremlin. Optimism gave way to the dark era of the Vietnam War, and liberalization in the Communist world was crushed by the Soviet invasion of Czechoslovakia. Characterized by the hippies and Maoists, a storm of protest spread over the West that challenged not only political systems but also the moral and social structures of modern society. Crisis struck inside the Church itself. Authority was challenged, tradition flouted. Vocations declined precipitously; the confessional was almost empty. The Triumphal Entry had given way to Gethsemane and the Via Dolorosa. And the man on whose shoulders rested the massive cross to be borne along that Way of Sorrows was a frail successor to Saint Peter, Pope Paul VI.

Both John and Paul were born in villages not far from Milan, but beyond that the two could hardly have been more different. John's optimism and laughter gave way to Paul's pessimism and suffering. It would have been a formidable task for any pope to follow the charismatic John, but it was especially hard for the introverted, reflective Giovanni Battista Montini. Columnist Giuliano Zincone summed up the problem in an article in the Milan daily *Corriere della Sera:*

"When Pope John looked out from the balcony and seduced the multitude with his sweet voice, Cardinal Montini already knew that he would be the next pontiff. And perhaps he knew fear, because his mind, that of the intellectual, was full of doubts and fine distinctions. . . . Montini knew that no theological subtlety, no profound analysis of social and moral problems, would make him popular (and therefore useful to the cause), as did those simple words of his predecessor: 'Kiss your children, and tell them that the pope sends this kiss.' Montini spoke with the head, and the head is the enemy of the heart."

Like the hopes that Jesus stirred in Jewish nationalists on that first Palm Sunday, many of the aspirations that John had aroused were dreams far beyond the possibilities of the time. In Jesus' day there came the moment when the one proclaimed Messiah was scourged and forced to walk the Via Dolorosa, The Street of Sadness, while his disciples huddled together in a mood of despondency. It fell to Pope Paul to lead the Church through a similar period of disappointment, to promote change without revolution and progress without the triumphalism inspired by John's reign. It was Paul who had to explain that the Christian world could not be reunited by the stroke of a pen, that papal power could not be transformed into a democratic system overnight, that Christian doctrine could not emerge from common law. Under Paul Church renewal did come, but often with pain instead of joy, with bitterness instead of applause.

Montini projected an image of pessimism, as if he expected to suffer and almost welcomed it. His secretary, Monsignor Pasquale Macchi, released an unpublished document by Paul after his death, in which he commented on his election to the papacy: "The position is unique. It suffices to say that it puts us into an extreme solitude. . . . I must not look for external support, which would exonerate me from my duty, which is to will, to decide, to assume any responsibility, to guide others, even if that appears illogical and perhaps absurd, and to suffer alone."

The Italian intellectual Carlo Jemolo wrote, "I consider Paul VI a martyr who accepted . . . one of the most painful pontificates that history records." Others found his pessimism excessive. A Jesuit who knew the Vatican well complained, "I sometimes wonder if Paul isn't lacking in the virtue of hope." An American priest described Paul as "a man of anguish who communicates his anguish to others."

While it was obvious that Paul was a "suffering servant," few realized just how much he took on his shoulders in lonely agony. Symbolic of his behavior was an incident during his visit to Bombay on December 2, 1964. As he stepped down from the Air India craft, the top executive of the airline, following Indian custom, placed a garland of flowers around the papal neck. Paul thanked him warmly and moved on, to be greeted by the archbishop of Bombay, who also placed a garland around his neck. A moment later, a top official of the Indian government added yet a third garland. The pope then went through the extensive airport reception ceremonies, delivered an arrival address, heard welcoming speeches, and was driven slowly through the streets of the city in an open car while millions cheered him. It was more than two hours after the airport arrival when he reached the residence, where he could relax a bit. Monsignor Paul Marcinkus, the athletic, six-foot-three American who organized the papal trip, offered to help the pope by removing those garlands. "I first tried to lift them with one hand, but they were much too heavy," Marcinkus told me later. "I finally had to use both hands to move those garlands, and I am no weakling. They felt like they weighed a ton. The Holy Father's cassock was soaking wet, and he was exhausted from bearing that heavy load. But through it all he had smiled and never showed to anyone that he was suffering."

And there was the time in Manila, on November 28, 1970, when we arrived on the papal plane after a thirteen-hour flight from Rome, with stops in Tehran and Dacca. Looking amazingly fresh after such a tiring flight, Pope Paul stepped down from the Alitalia plane to meet a long line of clergy moving up to shake his hand and kiss his ring. One of them, a man in the gray costume of a Jesuit, was in fact a Bolivian painter named Benjamin Mendoza, a man of Indian origin and culture who resented fanatically the imposition of European culture on Indian civilization in Bolivia and blamed the Catholic Church for it as much as the Spanish conquistadores.

At the airport that morning, Mendoza was carrying a crucifix, as if he wanted it blessed by the pope, but under it was a curved dagger. He dropped the crucifix and lunged at Paul, the blade of the dagger flashing in the sun. Monsignor Pasquale Macchi, the papal secretary, threw himself between assailant and pontiff, Mendoza fell backward against Korean cardinal Stephen Kim, and big Paul Marcinkus grabbed the Bolivian by both arms, all in the midst of panic and confusion. Filipino police hustled the assailant away quickly, and in an amazingly short time the diminutive pope, wearing his gentle smile, was proceeding along the red carpet to the podium, where he made his arrival speech. From there he traveled in a motorcade to the Manila cathedral to celebrate mass before an overflow crowd.

The official word went out quickly that the pope was unhurt and undisturbed by the incident. But I had some perplexing doubts. Immediately after the incident, I spoke with Cardinal Kim, who had caught Mendoza as he fell backward and had picked up the crucifix the man had dropped. On the sleeve of the cardinal's ivory-colored soutane was a spot of blood. Only when I asked him where the blood came from did the cardinal notice it at all. He had no idea whose blood it was. He himself had not been hurt. It was certain that Mendoza had not been wounded. The official announcement said that the pope had not been touched. Where, then, did that blood come from?

Not until a year after Paul's death in 1978 did the truth emerge. The spot on the cardinal's soutane was indeed the pope's blood. At a memorial service in the Milan cathedral in September 1979, Monsignor Macchi revealed that in Manila the pope had in fact been wounded slightly in the chest. Mendoza's dagger had nicked him and had drawn blood. The drop of blood on the dagger had fallen onto Cardinal Kim's cuff.

Again, Pope Paul had suffered in silence. Macchi said that "he frowned only once, when he gestured to me not to treat his assailant too roughly. And then he began to smile sweetly, and he continued smiling." At that moment, only the pope knew that he had been wounded, and it was in his character to keep that fact to himself.

Paul's spirituality had a deeply mystical quality, and he even induced suffering as a penitential act. One of his best-kept secrets was that he sometimes wore a hair shirt with metal points that dug into his flesh. On Christmas night of 1974, during the ceremony opening the 1975 Holy Year, many in the audience were disturbed that the pope had trouble moving around. They assumed it was because his health was deteriorating. In fact, it was because under his cassock he was wearing the hair shirt, a clumsy garment that made walking difficult.

When John opened the Second Vatican Council in 1962, it was a triumphal moment filled with promise of happy things to come. What a contrast when Paul took over! There was almost a note of sadness when the final session of the council began in the autumn of 1965. It was inaugurated with a half-mile penitential march by all the bishops—with Pope Paul walking in the rear—from the Church of the Holy Cross to St. John Lateran, all the bishops responding to a litany with the phrase "Pardon us, O Lord."

Paul was a traditionalist who never tampered with the body of Christian doctrine for which he was custodian as successor to Peter. At the same time, his sense of his awesome responsibility before God, his intense intellectual honesty, required that he reexamine every issue. And while he went through this agonizing reexamination, the Catholic world was left to drift in the greatest uncertainty it had known since the Reformation.

The fact that Paul ordinarily came out on the traditionalist side of doctrinal questions in the end embittered Catholic liberals, whose hopes had been so buoyed up by the Triumphal Entry of John. After Paul issued his encyclical banning the contraceptive pill in 1968, a very liberal moral theologian at the Vatican remarked somewhat sadly, "Paul is determined to go down in history as a conservative pope." The papal style gave rise to widespread accusations that Paul had turned back the clock to the pre-council era, that he and a team of reactionaries in the Vatican were "chipping away" at the achievements of the council, an accusation that was most unfair.

All the uncertainties, the disillusionment of the liberals, and above all the inability of Paul to communicate to the public obscured the fact that this frail little pontiff presided over more changes in the Church than had occurred at any time since the Council of Trent. Dr. Albert Outler, the brilliant Methodist theologian who was an observer throughout the four years of the council, insisted that Paul had transformed the council into a "Reformation, Roman Style." In an interview in late 1965, Outler explained what he meant (as I paraphrased his comments at the time):

"Unlike Luther's drastic break with the medieval past, it is a reformation which is often so subtle that it sometimes does not seem like change at all. It is a reformation in which radical ideas blossom in traditional Latin garb, in which new ways are inevitably coupled with warnings against imprudent excess. It is a reformation not of acts but of attitudes, whose distant goal is the ultimate reconciliation of the Church with other faiths in the modern world. It is, in fact, the kind of reformation precisely suited to the temper of the lonely, sensitive, cautious, and puzzling man who guides it."

And yet, with all this, Paul died in 1978 still projecting the image of a weak, indecisive, and essentially conservative pope.

Though he often was misunderstood by the public, Paul's personal, individual relationships were strong. Because of his delicate health, Paul ate little (an occasional saffron-colored risotto Milanese, thinly sliced and very tender veal, a glass or two of white wine, breakfasts of coffee and milk with a bread roll), but he rarely dined alone and enjoyed tremendously the intellectual give-and-take with chosen friends across the table. He was a tireless letter-writer, at one time corresponding with as many as a hundred persons. He insisted on answering all letters himself, usually in his own handwriting, because, as he once said, "a father doesn't write to his son with a mimeograph!" The day after his election to the papacy, Paul remembered that it was the name day of a priest who had worked with him in Milan. He personally telephoned the priest to congratulate him.

Paul established his authority over those working with him through example and integrity, never playing the role of slave-driver but making great demands on his staff by making even greater demands on himself. With his intimate team he was informal. While John affected a quaint Renaissance mode of dress and made a big thing of neatness of attire, Paul rarely wore anything more elaborate than a simple white cassock. When work began to pile up, he would meet his staff with his collar open and sometimes would throw back his cassock and work in his shirt-sleeves. Now and then he would be seen pecking out a memo on a battered Olivetti portable. He never asked more of his staff than he asked of himself, and through this informal, considerate, and totally dedicated style he won the infinite loyalty of those who worked with him.

At the Vatican there is a strict rule that no visitor ever smokes during a private audience with the pope. Paul made an exception when he received the president of the Soviet Union, Nikolai Podgorny. The pope learned beforehand that Podgorny was a chain-smoker who suffered when he couldn't have a cigarette. And so Paul asked which brand Podgorny preferred and had a pack on the desk when the two met in the papal library. It was characteristic of Paul's kindness and consideration for others.

Montini's diffidence toward crowds and his preference for the private contact probably was traceable to his frail health, which plagued him from childhood to the end of his life. As a boy he had to drop out of school in Brescia because of sickness and for years had to do his studies alone at home. He was rejected for military service because he could not pass the physical examination. In the early years of his career, he was sent to Warsaw as a diplomat but had to return to Rome after a few months because the cold Warsaw winters were too much for his delicate constitution. Thereafter, instead of following the career of a diplomat abroad—as had John—he spent thirty-two years inside the Roman Curia, an environment that stressed the bureaucratic rather than the practical, where discretion was more important than innovation, where there was minimum contact with the public and maximum contact with other bureaucrats.

Being thus sheltered from the public may have contributed to Paul's introversion and bookishness, as well as to his spiritual depth, introspective intellectualism, and mysticism. As a boy growing up in Brescia, he attended mass every morning at seven and regularly prayed at three in the afternoon, traditionally the hour when Jesus died on the cross. As pope he suffered from insomnia, and it was common for late-nighters in Rome to see the light still burning in the papal apartment as they drove through St. Peter's Square in the wee hours of the morning. As he reached old age, he suffered terribly from an arthritic hip. Those who criticized him for resuming use of the *sedia gestatoria* (the sedan chair in which the pope was carried on the shoulders of men, and which he earlier had discarded) did not know that he did so because his arthritic pains made it impossible for him to attend audiences on foot. The arthritis also forced him to cancel all international travel after 1970, another barrier to contact with the public.

Though he lacked the robust appetite and worldly tastes of Pope John, the introverted Paul did have some interests beyond the purely spiritual and ecclesiastical. Perhaps to compensate for his own physical inadequacy, Paul enjoyed sports as a spectator. When time permitted, he liked to watch championship soccer matches on TV. He was a special fan of cycling and once persuaded his mentor Pope Pius XII to grant an audience to two Italian cycling champions. He could enjoy a good drama on TV; when Italy's state television network screened Manzoni's classic *I Promessi Sposi (The Betrothed),* Paul enjoyed it so much that he telephoned lead actor Nino Castelnuovo to congratulate him. Scientific discoveries absolutely fascinated the pope. His eyes were glued to the TV screen for that first moon landing. He loved classical music and sometimes relaxed by listening to Brahms or Mozart.

Above all, the pope's great passion was that particularly private form of diversion, reading. He began his day by carefully perusing the morning press, sometimes underlining errors or misconstructions in the Vatican daily *L'Osservatore Romano* and sending a note to the editor: "You should use your pencil more heavily." He was a ravenous reader of books. When he moved to Milan as archbishop in 1955, the books he carried along filled ninety cases. Although he covered a wide range of material, the pope's favorite reading matter was the work of modern French Catholic philosophers.

These peripheral diversions and amusements were not nearly enough to ease the pain for such a sensitive person in presiding over the Church in those troubled years. Paul's secretary, Monsignor Macchi, once described the pain Paul felt whenever he had to sign approval of a request for laicization (a priest's dispensation from his holy vows). According to Macchi, the pope inevitably would say, "This is my heaviest cross." Always at the end of his long, long days his last act before retiring was to go alone into his unlit private chapel and kneel in prayer.

As the years passed the pope often spoke of his impending death in gloomy and fatalistic terms, even though he did not suffer from any ailment likely to be fatal. On the Feast of the Assumption in 1977, he told an audience, "I see the end of my life drawing near. I see myself approaching the hereafter. It may be that we shall not celebrate this feast together again."

On one of the last Sundays of his life, he told a group of the faithful, "I would wish to give you an appointment. The threshold of the afterlife is near, and therefore I take this occasion to salute you all. . . ."

Within a month he was dead. It was as if Paul had taken the occasion to bid farewell to the world, and he did it with his characteristic pessimism.

John Paul II: The Resurrection

Papal pessimism was replaced dramatically by optimism. After the interim reign of John Paul I, the "smiling pope" who lived just thirty-three days after his election, there came the Polish pope, John Paul II, who burst onto the scene like an explosion of light blasting away the gloom of the Pauline papacy. From the moment he stood on the balcony of St. Peter's to give the city and the world his first blessing and then shocked his protocol officials by joking with the crowd, this man made such an electrifying impact as to prompt one veteran Roman Jesuit to observe: "Pope Paul constantly reminded people of how hard it is to be a Christian in this world. Pope John Paul reminds them of how wonderful it is to be a Christian in spite of all the difficulties. Pope Paul was the Way of the Cross; John Paul is the Resurrection."

This "resurrection" moved the Church away not only from the gloom of Paul's Via Dolorosa but also from the messianic euphoria of John's Triumphal Entry. With John Paul II there was happiness without impractical dreams, joy with realism. He proved to be a stern taskmaster, a tough, no-nonsense disciplinarian who aimed at restoring absolute values after the vagueness of John and the agonizing of Paul. But he administers the medicine with the sugar-coating of good humor and humanity. A priest who has spent many years at the Vatican expressed the feeling that "this pope says the traditional thing, but he says it with such an exquisitely personal touch."

That personal touch has taken unpredictable and even bizarre forms that shocked traditionalists in the Roman Curia. This man from Poland differed from his predecessors even more than Paul differed from John. He was the first non-Italian to become pope since 1522, the youngest pope to be elected since 1846. Unlike his two predecessors, he was not brought up in the shelter of the priesthood. John and Paul both opted for the priesthood when they were boys (John when he was only eleven), but Karol Wojtyla worked as a factory laborer and miner, as an actor and a playwright, before taking holy orders.

Wojtyla is handsome and athletic, even in his sixties. He has a strong face with square jaw, stands above average height, and sports a rugged frame, has twinkling blue eyes and a charming smile. His only physical defect is a slightly deformed shoulder, the result of an automobile accident in his youth, which gives him a somewhat hunch-backed posture. In his youth he had enjoyed the company of women and even when a cardinal still loved the outdoor life. How different he is in appearance from the homely and overweight John or the frail Paul of the hook nose and sunken eyes. And with his physical good looks, the Polish pontiff brought along a style that was very much his own, based on a humanity approaching that of John but carefully crafted by skills mastered in the theater.

His humanity showed in a remarkable moment during John Paul's first trip abroad, in a working-class suburb of Guadalajara, Mexico, in February 1979. The happy crowd was whooping it up when the pope stood to speak, and before he could begin they drowned him out with the lusty singing of that old Mexican favorite "Cielito Lindo." Suddenly over the public address system there boomed a beautiful baritone joining in with their "hi-yi-yi's." It was beyond belief but true; the pope was singing "Cielito Lindo" with the crowd.

You have to live in Rome to understand how unthinkable it was for a pope to sing a secular song in public. When I reported the incident to an old Jesuit at the Vatican, he simply refused to believe me, explaining bluntly that "popes don't sing."

This pope does. During his visit to Poland in 1979, he told a crowd of students, "Some say you sing because you have a voice. I say you have a voice because you sing."

Blessed with a good voice, John Paul is full of song. Sometimes when he rolls up his sleeves to work on an encyclical or other official document, he will punctuate his labors by bursting spontaneously into some old Polish folk hymn. Once, from his apartment window overlooking St. Peter's Square, he thanked a group of young Catholics for singing a Polish song for him at a mass earlier in the day. As if on the spur of the moment, the pope said, "Let's sing it again!" and they all sang along with him.

One Easter Sunday evening, after the sun had gone down and the pope's apartment window was dark, a busload of students arrived in the square and began chanting for John Paul to appear. In a few moments the papal head in fact emerged at the window, and the youngsters could see John Paul setting up his microphone and testing it expertly. He had had a long day of many speeches and ceremonies, and now his voice was slightly hoarse as he reproached the young people for arriving so late, after Easter festivities had ended. But he wound up singing "Ave Maria" with them and giving them his blessing. As the singing finally died away, he could be heard to say wearily, "Now the account is settled."

At one time during his Tokyo visit in 1981, the pope was entertained by a rock quartet called the Dark Ducks. Very soon the Ducks realized that they had become a quintet. The pope had picked up a microphone and was singing with them.

The Polish pontiff demonstrated that personal, human touch

when he visited Rio de Janeiro in 1980. The schedule called for a look at a favela, one of those impoverished shantytowns found on the outskirts of most Brazilian cities. John Paul went to the favela of Vidigal, where twenty thousand persons live in shacks of wood or mud lining narrow streets that are quagmires of mud and fetid water, where most of the population lack running water or sewage facilities or electricity and live under constant threat of eviction. As the pope climbed the hill through that filth he stopped at least five times to kiss impoverished children. He then turned abruptly into a three-room shack to embrace an aged woman, who was so moved by the appearance of the pope in her hovel that she pulled the tablecloth off the kitchen table, buried her face in it, and wept.

This pope underlined the values of the marriage sacrament the day he received in audience the street sweepers of Rome and their families. The daughter of one of them seized the chance of her lifetime and boldly asked the pope if he would perform her wedding ceremony. To the horror of his protocol-conscious aides, the pope agreed. Within a month, there was the unprecedented scene of the head of the Universal Church performing the marriage ceremony of a street sweeper's daughter in St. Peter's Basilica.

There is no doubt that the John Paul "resurrection" gave the Church a special kind of stimulation. In the first year of his reign, he attracted pilgrims to Rome in numbers unmatched except during a Jubilee Year. Vendors and shopkeepers around St. Peter's sold more photos of John Paul in six months than of Pope Paul in fifteen years. The vast crowds at papal audiences create massive new traffic problems in traffic-plagued Rome. Street sweepers complain that it takes them more than two days to clean up St. Peter's Square after a general audience. Equally weary are the penitentiaries in St. Peter's Basilica. They estimate that in the first year of this pope's regime confessions at their booths increased at least twenty-fold. Recordings of the pope singing folk songs and hymns had brisk sales all over Europe. After John Paul's trip to anticlerical Mexico, sales of his photos, tape-recorded speeches and masses, and books soared. In the United States and parts of Western Europe, his conservative stand, especially on sex-related issues, including the ordination of women, attracted widespread hostility, but even his critics could not ignore him. He is still one of the rare leaders in the world who can draw a crowd of a million. And certainly no other pope in history has been covered so completely by the media. In the first six years of his reign, *Time* magazine did nine cover stories on John Paul, compared with three on Paul in fifteen years. Many networks have devoted special documentaries to him. By now, he has probably been seen by more people than any other individual in history.

Perhaps because of his easy informality and innovative style, there was initially a widespread assumption that John Paul would be a liberal pope who might ease up on priestly celibacy, birth control, and divorce. He very quickly disabused those who thought so. The election of John Paul II brought an end to the experimentation, uncertainty, and indecision that characterized the era of John and Paul. From the beginning, John Paul II set out to enunciate Christian doctrine in absolute clarity.

We newsmen who flew with John Paul on his first international trip—to Mexico in 1979, barely more than three months after his election—learned at first hand how blunt and clear this pope can be. On his first foray into the press section, he spent more than an hour in intense conversation with one newsman after another, answering the toughest and most delicate questions frankly, and lacing it all with a bit of humor. (When someone asked if he didn't find his many audiences tiring, John Paul answered, "The most tiresome of all was the one yesterday afternoon." It was only after some minutes that we realized he was referring to an audience with Soviet foreign minister Andrei Gromyko.)

There has been so much debate about what is called liberation theology that it is hard to believe John Paul could have so easily summed up his attitude toward that movement when on the flight to Mexico. When we asked him about it, the pope looked down at the floor, collected his thoughts, and answered, "Liberation theology, yes, but which liberation theology? A liberation theology based on a non-Christian ideology is not acceptable."

That said it all more clearly than any encyclical or theological treatise. The Church is for liberation but rejects the Marxist approach to liberation.

During the eighteen international trips I have taken with this pope, I heard him sum up his views with such clarity that I wondered why there is still any uncertainty about the Holy See's teaching on those issues. We were flying back from Africa shortly after the pope had ordered Father Tom Drinan, a Jesuit, to give up his seat in the U.S. Congress (canon law forbids priests to hold political office). During our African stay the pope had called on Christians to become deeply committed to political and social action. When I asked him about this seeming contradiction, John Paul answered, "I was speaking of laymen, not priests. It is the apostolate of the laity to become deeply committed to political action."

The pope then started to walk away from me but abruptly turned around, wagging a finger to stress the point, and added, "And the priest should assist them."

There it is. Priests should not participate in political parties or hold public office, but they must stimulate Catholic laymen to do so.

On another trip to Africa, I asked the pope about the possibility of easing the priestly celibacy rule in black Africa, given the cultural differences between Africans and Europeans. He answered, "No. The difficulties are as great in every culture."

In other words, celibacy is as tough for a Pole as for an African.

While John Paul adopts a relaxed affability in communicating with the world, he makes sure that this style is not interpreted as indulgence of confusion or weakening of discipline in the Church. He is a tough and demanding boss. The Polish pontiff comes from a country where authoritarianism has been the rule, ecclesiastically as well as politically, and he expects total obedience from bishops, priests, and nuns.

The grandfatherly Pope John won the cooperation of his underlings through diplomatic, and sometimes indirect, hints and suggestions. Paul often accepted disobedience, while suffering because of it. John Paul gives orders bluntly and expects them to be obeyed. Vatican ceremonial officials learned who was boss just before a very formal occasion right after John Paul was elected. They were insisting that he follow the traditional rules and alter some of his planned actions because "this is the way we do it here in the Vatican."

"Excuse me," answered John Paul. "You seem to misunderstand something. It is I who am the pope."

Only a few weeks after Wojtyla was elected, a Vatican official told me, "I dread ever crossing this man. If you get in his way, he will run a bulldozer over you. Then he will back it up and run it over you again."

John Paul has used the bulldozer in some famous cases: ordering Father Drinan to give up his congressional seat; informing Swiss theologian Hans Kung that in his teaching role he would no longer be considered a Catholic theologian; defrocking four Nicaraguan priests who disobeyed the Church in accepting posts in the Sandinista regime. At times this seemingly amiable man with the mischievous twinkle in his eye can be almost brutal in enforcing obedience. He was especially unhappy about the lack of discipline in the Society of Jesus. Some Jesuits were publicly rejecting Church teaching on birth control and sexual morality, were questioning papal authority, and were advocating violent revolution in Latin America. John Paul decided to take matters into his own hands.

The Basque general of the Jesuits, Father Pedro Arrupe, was bedridden after suffering a massive stroke, and day-to-day administration was being handled by the senior assistant general, Father Vincent O'Keefe. Out of the blue the Vatican secretary of state, Cardinal Agostino Casaroli, arrived at Arrupe's bedside and without further ado read a message from the pope. The message was that Arrupe was being suspended from his post, and the pope was taking the unprecedented step of appointing his own *delegato* to take charge of the society pending its reorganization and the election of a new general. When he finished reading the message, Casaroli stuffed it back into his briefcase and left the sick man's room.

John Paul cracked his whip again immediately after his return to Rome from his 1983 visit to Poland. As that trip was nearing its end, the Vatican daily, *L'Osservatore Romano,* carried an article that in effect repudiated Lech Walesa and the Solidarity movement, implying that Walesa had served his purpose but that now his time was past. The article could not have come at a less opportune time in terms of Vatican foreign policy. The piece was signed by Don Virgilio Levi, deputy editor of the newspaper, who normally took full personal responsibility for anything written over his name. He assumed it would be understood this time that he was expressing his own opinions, not those of the pope. He quickly learned that the moment was too delicate for expressing such opinions.

Don Virgilio was called in for a dressing-down by Archbishop Eduardo Martinez Somalo, undersecretary of state and one of the pope's most trusted aides. The unhappy priest-journalist proposed putting out a statement explaining that the ideas in the article were his personally and did not reflect Vatican opinion. Not enough, answered the archbishop sternly. He pointed to his desk, on which lay pen and paper. "The Holy Father wants you to write your resignation," said Martinez. "Now."

It caused something of a crisis when those four Nicaraguan priests accepted posts in the Marxist Sandinista government, in violation of the Code of Canon Law. Advised by local ordinaries that this was a very special situation, John Paul at first agreed that they stay in those positions during a transition period, but for that time they must not perform priestly functions and must not wear clerical garb when acting officially for the government. After a while the pope judged that the "transition period" had passed and sent word through his Congregation for the Clergy that they must either resign from the government or be expelled from the priesthood. The four stubbornly remained in their posts and so were "defrocked."

The tough boss gave a demonstration of how unbending he can be on this problem when he landed in Managua in March 1983. A long line of officials and dignitaries awaited the pope at the airport, the queue stretching out in the form of a "U" around the tarmac. All our eyes were on one bearded man in a blue beret toward the end of the line. He was Father Ernesto Cardenal, a priest and former Trappist monk who was minister of culture in the Sandinista cabinet. We all were waiting for the pope's reaction when he reached the priest-minister. When the pontiff finally stood before him, Cardenal dropped to his knees and reached for the pope's hand to kiss the papal ring.

From John Paul there came not the slightest show of warmth, no pat on the shoulder or even a good-natured reproof. Instead he leaned over Cardenal with a look of stern reproach on his face, holding back his hand so that it could not be kissed, wagging both index fingers at the priest as he warned, "You must regularize your position with the Church."

With such rigidity John Paul has broken the pattern set by John and Paul, who both accepted, though sometimes reluctantly, the necessity of the Church's changing enough to adapt to the swiftly evolving modern world. John Paul instead emphasizes preserving the historical identity of the Church as its greatest hope of survival. To preserve that identity, he believes, it is necessary to protect external symbols and forms as well as fundamental beliefs. That is why he not only jealously watches over Church teaching but also insists that priests don clerical garb, that nuns wear distinctive habits, that the clergy not lose their uniqueness by taking on the role of politician or social worker or psychiatrist. Such an approach often puts John Paul at odds with modern Catholics and to gain acceptance this pope counts on his remarkable talents as a communicator.

Perhaps John and Paul were more adaptable because they were products of Western European culture and so were deeply aware of, and often admired, new currents of thought and modes of living. John Paul, by contrast, came out of a society in which the Church and the nation again and again had to fight bitter struggles for survival and won by closing ranks and clinging to a common historical identity. More than once the Polish nation has disappeared, politically and geographically, and Karol Wojtyla personally has lived through an experience in which Poland survived as a nation only by retaining its special Polish Catholic character as a rallying point. Now that he presides over the Universal Church in a period of challenge and crisis, the Polish pope applies his national experience on a worldwide scale.

Though he sits in Rome at the center of an organization that reaches around the globe, though he travels to the ends of the earth, though he speaks many languages, Pope John Paul II remains essentially Polish, and to understand him, his Polishness must be understood. Before his election in 1978, there had been a yearning among modern Catholics to choose a non-Italian as pope in the hope of making the papacy more international. But this non-Italian has turned out to be more nationalistic than any other pope in many decades. His recent predecessors were Italian, but their culture and character reached across frontiers beyond Italy. Pius XII was heavily influenced by German behavior and contacts; John XXIII had spent much of his career outside Italy and had developed a genuinely international outlook; Paul VI was immersed in French intellectualism. John Paul II, make no mistake about it, is a real Polish patriot.

A man who cares little for physical possessions, John Paul added only one item to the furnishings of his private apartment in the Vatican Palace, a replica of the Black Madonna of Częstochowa, the focal point of Polish nationalism. Likewise, his only addition to the furnishings of his summer palace at Castel Gandolfo was a simple painting of snow-covered mountains in Poland, the kind of scene he loves so dearly. When I saw that painting, it reminded me of a day in June 1979, during his first return home to Poland after his election. He sang along with a crowd of Polish students a melancholy folk song that reflected his homesickness for his native land. The song was about "the highlander," who clearly represented Wojtyla himself to those who were present:

> Don't you miss the country you came from,
> Don't you miss the mountains, the pastures?
> Return to your pastures and valleys and streams.
> But the highlander cannot return, because he has been
> Called away by the Lord and is on his way to heaven.

That song drew tears not only from the pope's eyes, but from the eyes of everyone there, including me.

Around the Vatican John Paul sometimes is criticized for giving excessive attention to his native land. He traveled three times to Poland in his first eight years as pontiff, even though his desk is piled high with invitations to other countries. After martial law was declared in Poland in late 1980, John Paul personally took over Vatican-Polish relations, which normally would be handled by the secretary of state. When he addressed those massive crowds during his visits back to Poland, John Paul obviously was a national leader as much as a Catholic pontiff—a fact not lost on the leaders of the Soviet Union.

John Paul's confidence that Polish-style Catholic unity will guarantee ultimate triumph over the Gates of Hell came across once when I asked him about plans to visit his country for the six-hundredth anniversary of the Madonna of Częstochowa. I specifically wanted to know if he would visit Poland while martial law remained in force. He paused for a moment of reflection and replied grimly, "Poland. Martial law. Our Lady. Martial law has been in existence since last December. Our Lady has been with us for six hundred years."

A newsman asked if this meant that, in fact, the pope planned to go to Poland.

"I have answered the question" was the papal reply.

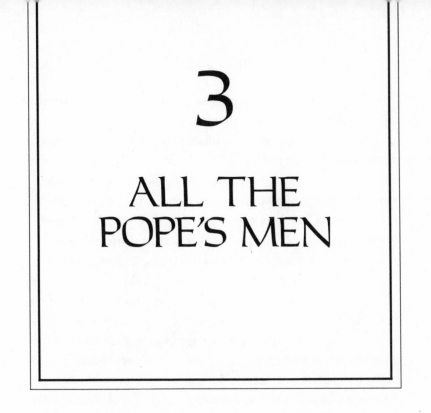

3

ALL THE POPE'S MEN

Papal Advisors, Official and Unofficial

When a new pope emerges from the conclave, he immediately moves into the papal quarters in the Vatican Palace. There is no going back home to pick up his belongings or to put personal affairs in order. Along with settling into unfamiliar surroundings, the pope has to begin working at once with a vast team of advisors whom he has inherited from his predecessors, advisors who often are total strangers to him. Since each pope has his own personal inclinations and style, it is natural that he may not be able to work effectively with the official counselors surrounding him, and so many a pope has built up his own "Kitchen Cabinet," an intimate group of persons whom he can trust completely and whose opinions he seeks regularly, regardless of their official status. The choice of those informal advisors is one of the most significant expressions of papal individuality. It is most revealing to compare the official advisors that a pope inherits with the "real" team that each sets up for himself, a team that obviously wields massive power in the everyday business of governing the Church.

The newly elected pope inherits a governmental bureaucracy that includes not only a secretary of state and the equivalent of ministers of such areas as finance and education but also a theologian, a media man, a Vatican banker, a confessor, a team of scientific counselors, a valet, and an *elemosiniere,* who advises the pontiff on personal charities, and countless others. The government of the Church is called the Roman Curia, in which the Vatican secretary of state acts as the pope's prime minister; beneath him are the ten sacred congregations, somewhat comparable to ministries in a secular cabinet, each dealing with a specific area of church activity such as Catholic education, doctrine of the faith, divine worship, candidates for sainthood, bishops, clergy, and so forth. In addition to the congregations, the curia includes an array of secretariats, councils, and commissions, dealing with peace and justice, the family, the laity, Christian unity, dialogue with non-Christians and nonbelievers. There also are special Vatican tribunals, the best known of which is the Sacra Rota, the supreme court of appeal for cases involving annulments of marriages. When a new pope is elected, all heads of these departments automatically hand him their resignations. He usually reconfirms them in office till he has time to build up his own team.

The secretary of state, prefects of the congregations, and heads of most of the other important Vatican offices are cardinals, a group originally created to serve as the pope's primary advisory body. (The word "cardinal" comes from the Latin "cardo," hinge, because so much "hinged" on the advisors.) The College of Cardinals was created by the twelfth-century pope Eugenius III, who was so plagued by Roman in-fighting that he decided he needed a proper team of powerful advisors. Catholic kings made the cardinals "princes of the blood royal"—they still are often called princes of the Church—and Pope Innocent IV gave them the right to wear scarlet hats and robes. In 1630, Pope Urban VIII decreed that they should be addressed as "Your Eminence," a practice that continues to the present day. (The patriarch of the Egyptian Coptic Catholic community is also a cardinal, which creates some complication regarding the form of address, since as patriarch he should be "Your Beatitude" and as cardinal, "Your Eminence." The present patriarch solved the problem by asking to be called "Your Most Eminent Beatitude.")

Originally all cardinals lived in Rome, to be on hand whenever the pope needed their advice. Today, of the approximately one hundred fifty princes of the church, the majority live abroad; most of them are archbishops of the leading dioceses around the world, such as Los Angeles, São Paulo, Kinshasa, and Manila. As popes developed the Roman Curia as the real government of the Church, the College of Cardinals as a body was used less and less for advisory purposes, although individual cardinals continued to hold the most powerful official positions. For nearly four centuries the College of Cardinals as a body was summoned to Rome for only one reason—to elect a new pope. It was not until John Paul II became pope that the college as a whole was called to Rome for any other purpose. (He summoned them to help the Holy See face a serious financial crisis.)

Rising above all these official advisors there usually are those papal favorites in whom the pope has maximum confidence and to whom he entrusts the really big decisions and most important work of the Vatican. The Borgia pope Alexander VI (1492–1503) leaned heavily on his acknowledged son, Cesare Borgia, whom he made a cardinal but who eventually "defrocked" himself in order to marry a French princess. A series of Renaissance popes adopted what came to be called the cardinal-nephew system, which meant making a close relative a cardinal and using him as top counselor. This system eventually was so abused by papal relatives that it was abolished after the cardinal-nephew of Pope Clement X (1670–1676) provoked a popular revolution in Rome by imposing oppressive and ridiculous taxes. But even after the abolition of the cardinal-nephew system, popes continued to rely on their personal favorites as their most intimate counselors.

The practice has continued into the twentieth century. A woman was the most powerful person on the papal team during the last years of the reign of Pope Pius XII (1939–1958). She was the German nun Sister Pasqualina Lehnert, nicknamed Virgo

Potens (the Powerful Virgin) by cynical Romans. Because of the pope's recurring bouts of severe illness, he came to depend on Sister Pasqualina, officially his housekeeper, to make sure he got the right medicines on schedule, to oversee his diet, and eventually to organize his daily program of appointments. These duties expanded till the pope was dictating to her his most important documents and seeking her advice on vital matters; the word spread that she had the power to veto or approve the choice of new cardinals. Even powerful Italian politicians found they had to deal with Sister Pasqualina to reach the pope.

The Kitchen Cabinet of Pope John XXIII

Pope John XXIII inherited in his curia a team of aging conservatives, most of them traditionalist Italians, men who were totally out of step with his innovative inclinations. John was then seventy-seven and probably felt he didn't have time to remake the Church government, and so he left the old boys in place and spent most of his time circumventing them. John took such far-reaching decisions as making contact with Soviet leaders and calling the Vatican Council without consulting his own curia. By summoning the council, he in effect went over the heads of his cardinals to the "People of God" worldwide. As the first session of the council ended, John said of his conservative entourage, "They are men of zeal, I am sure, but they are not running the Church. I am in charge, and I will not have anyone else trying to slow down the momentum of this council."

The old men of the curia in John's era were most unsuited for the task of opening the windows of the Church to the winds of change. They were an insular group, immune to the rapid social and cultural evolution taking place in the post–World War II era. They saw no need for a council, because they were satisfied with the Church as it was. They still believed that the world had to listen when Rome spoke, still clung to the old concept "Roma locuta est; causa finita est" ("Rome has spoken; the matter is settled"). From Rome they tightly controlled all the major aspects of Church policy—the appointment of bishops, rules for the behavior of priests, missionary activity, seminaries and universities, and the sacraments, including marriage. The powerful Holy Office kept a tight lid on theological speculation; it often harassed modern theologians, sometimes forbade them to publish their works, and at times wouldn't even let them reveal that they had been forbidden to publish. So who needed a council?

The archetype of the team that John inherited was Cardinal Alfredo Ottaviani, who eventually became head of the Holy Office and did his best to shape the council according to the heart's desire of the curial conservatives. When Pope John invited liberal theologians, including Karl Rahner, Hans Kung, and Yves Congar, to attend the council as *periti* (experts), a favorite limerick circulated in Vatican press circles:

> Rahner and Congar and Kung,
> Their praises are everywhere sung.
> But one fine *domani*
> Old Ottaviani
> Will see they're all properly hung.

Ottaviani even looked the very model of the traditional inquisitor. He was almost blind—he had lost the sight of one eye completely and could see only with difficulty from the other—and this gave him a sinister appearance that was belied by the personal charm, good humor, and love for children reflected in his private life. His personal motto was "Semper Idem" ("Always the Same"), and in many ways his life was dedicated to resisting change. Even after the council, he was to attack Pope Paul VI publicly for introducing the new liturgy, which involved use of modern languages instead of Latin. He was probably the most feared man in the Vatican. Immediately following the death of Pope John, Ottaviani told a member of his staff, "All right. The windows of the Church have been opened to the winds of change. Now it's time to close them again."

The old *carabiniere* of the Church, as Ottaviani liked to call himself, was so old-fashioned as to oppose religious liberty and freedom for non-Catholic minorities. These concepts are so widely accepted today that it is shocking to recall that on John's team there were people who still tried to turn back the clock to oppressive state control of religious life and thought. Ottaviani once expressed amazement that anyone could argue for "giving error the same rights as truth." In a public speech in the early fifties, he had said: "It is the duty of rulers of a Catholic state to defend the religious unity of its people from disturbing elements. . . . Reason revolts at the thought that, in deference to a small minority, the faith of practically all the people should be injured by those who would foster schism."

Ottaviani was known to have a sense of humor, but it had its limits. Once I was at the Holy Office discussing with the secretary a planned interview with the cardinal. As we wound up our talk, I tried to be funny by mentioning that "we would also like to get some pictures of the torture chambers." When I left the office, the somewhat embarrassed secretary followed me out the door to whisper, "When you see His Eminence, I suggest you not say anything about the . . . torture chambers. He wouldn't think it funny."

Another of those around Pope John was an Irish Dominican theologian, Cardinal Michael Browne, who worked closely with Ottaviani in the Holy Office. Browne was a kindly man, and I feel eternally in his debt for the courtesy he always showed me when I first arrived in Rome and so badly needed a bit of guidance in covering the Vatican. He would meet me at the Holy Office, leaning on a cane and with a faint aroma of shaving lotion always about him. I remember his explaining to me, "We hear a lot about truth being in a process of evolution, but we insist that certain truths are permanent and unchanging." As if to put the point across, he added, "You may be interested to know that you now are sitting in the very room where Galileo stayed when he came to Rome to face the Inquisition."

An important member of John's official team was Cardinal Domenico Tardini, who for so long had expressed his contempt for Roncalli's abilities as a diplomat. On the first day of his pontificate, John appointed Tardini secretary of state (the office was vacant because the late Pius XII had been his own secretary of state). Though there obviously was little love lost between the two, John realized that to keep peace in his house he needed a secretary of state acceptable to the curial cardinals, and Tardini fit the bill perfectly. He was one of them in every way and later teamed up with the conservatives to try to slow down preparations for the council, perhaps in the hope that it would be delayed so long that the old pope would die before it took place. These men were typical of the "official" corps of John's advisors, but the pope deftly maneuvered to go ahead in spite of them and became the most innovative pontiff of the century.

Pope John regularly managed to sidestep his old nemesis Tardini. As secretary of state, Tardini should have been John's closest collaborator in the Vatican. But John didn't work "officially," preferring instead to operate through persons who were sympathetic to his style and instincts and whom he could trust totally. Often he used people for missions that had nothing to do with their official positions. And so he was able to forge a totally new Vatican policy toward the Soviet bloc—a policy of accommodation rather than confrontation, as was the case under Pius XII—without, as noted, consulting his own secretary of state. For example, some of his first probes beyond the Iron Curtain were made through Cardinal Koenig, archbishop of Vienna, rather than through the Vatican diplomatic corps.

The man who collaborated most closely with John and who skillfully helped him circumvent the curia was Monsignor Loris Capovilla, whose official title in the Vatican was *cameriere segreto partecipante,* an ancient office of the papal court which literally meant being the pope's private cup-bearer. In fact, Capovilla was John's personal secretary; he had to have some other official post because there was no provision for a papal secretary in the Vatican budget.

When he went to Venice as patriarch, Cardinal Roncalli had taken on young Capovilla as his secretary, and the two formed a lasting team in spite of a forty-year difference in age. Capovilla was born in Mestre, the industrial suburb of Venice, and has been described by persons who knew him as "totally modern in outlook." Some say he had Socialist sympathies, a shocking thing to a conservative like Ottaviani, who had signed a Holy Office decree during the time of Pius XII excommunicating Italians who voted Marxist (to Ottaviani there was no difference between a Socialist and a Communist). Right-wingers in Italy accused Capovilla of orchestrating the historic *apertura a sinistra* (opening to the Left), the 1962 decision by the pro-Vatican Christian Democratic party to bring the Italian Socialist party into the government.

Nobody can say just how much Capovilla influenced John's thinking, but it would appear that his views had considerable weight with the old man, who had been very much a traditionalist, conventional in style as well as thinking, for most of his prior career. Contact with this youthful mind no doubt contributed to the remarkably innovative style that characterized John's papacy.

As soon as he was elected pope, John provided Capovilla with an apartment on the third floor of the Vatican Palace, just above his own. Capovilla's loyalty to the pontiff was limitless, and his closeness to John caused some critics to call him Monsignor Pasqualina, drawing a parallel between him and Pius's German housekeeper.

Capovilla no doubt played a vital role in shaping Vatican foreign policy and in the delicate preparations for the council, which had to be done with special dexterity to keep the curial team from taking it over. There were often screams of outrage and threats of resignation from Tardini when he read documents John and Capovilla had drawn up without consulting him. The pope would try to placate his secretary of state by redrafting the document to suit him, only to have Capovilla change the wording later.

Things got a little better for John in 1960, when the powerful Tardini died. The pope replaced him with the amiable, aging Cardinal Amleto Cicognani, longtime apostolic delegate in the

United States. The old pope and Cicognani had a jovial personal relationship, but the cardinal was too feeble to function effectively in his new post. By now, however, John had a man he trusted in an official post—Archbishop Angelo dell'Acqua, undersecretary of state, who cooperated closely with John and Capovilla whenever it was necessary to handle some matter formally through the Secretariat of State.

A prime example of Pope John's way of working with a man unofficially but effectively was his relationship with the German Jesuit Cardinal Augustin Bea. On the surface, Cardinal Bea until that time had not looked like a flaming liberal. A brilliant biblical scholar, he had served for many years as rector of the Pontifical Biblical Institute in Rome and for nearly fifteen years was confessor to Pius XII. After John became pope, he and Bea got to know each other through routine meetings, and a new team was formed. Soon Bea was handling assignments totally outside his official capacity.

John had explained to Bea that the upcoming council should open the way to a reunion of all Christians but that first the Church must renew itself internally. He had earlier told an audience of Orthodox bishops that "the work of the council will be to present the Church as its founder did—'sine macula et sine ruga'" (without spot and without wrinkle). Once this was achieved, John explained to Bea, the Catholic Church might call back to its fold the "separated brethren."

The concept caught fire with Bea, who was assigned by John in 1959 to begin making contact with Protestants, Orthodox Christians, Jews, and Muslims. For more than a year, Bea worked vigorously in the ecumenical field without an official title. Then on June 5, 1960, John announced formation of the Secretariat for Christian Unity, with Cardinal Bea as its head, to serve as one of the commissions preparing for the council. Ottaviani was furious, because he felt that his Holy Office should control any ecumenical activity, to ensure that Catholics gave away nothing in their zeal for unity. Even after the secretariat was established, Ottaviani and his curial team refused to accept any help from Bea in planning for the council. One of his aides told Bea, "We don't need you. We judge you."

Archbishop Benelli, Pope Paul's "Berlin Wall"

Pope John's somewhat haphazard use of his people differed completely from the well-organized regime set up by his successor. Paul VI had spent thirty-two years in the curia and had come to place great value on tidy administration, with duties and responsibilities precisely defined. In 1967 he reformed the curia to streamline it and make it more efficient in the Montini mold. He gave the secretary of state vastly increased powers, making him the prime link between the curia and the pope. In general, the bulk of curial business would be funneled through the secretary of state to the pontiff. This system protected the pope from being overwhelmed with appointments and interviews and gave the introspective Paul the time he wanted to read, study, and pray while his secretary of state dealt directly with the underlings.

The only flaw in this neat organization was that the secretary of state Paul inherited from John, Cardinal Cicognani, was eighty-four years old. In the words of an archbishop who saw him often at the time, he "had moments of lucidity," but once he got through a morning's work, he was finished for the day. And so, sailing in like Superman to fill the vacuum, came the undersecretary of state, Archbishop Giovanni Benelli, a longtime Montini intimate and at forty-six the youngest man in the curia at his level. Though not even a cardinal, Benelli in effect took over the duties of the secretary of state, as defined by Paul's administrative reform, and for a decade ruled the Vatican with an iron hand. His disgruntled colleagues nicknamed him the Berlin Wall because of his habit of blocking off access to the pope. Others addressed him behind his back as His Gray Eminence and His Efficiency.

Benelli's close association with Paul went back to 1948, when his first assignment on entering the Vatican diplomatic service was to be personal secretary to Archbishop Montini, then undersecretary of state. From that time, Montini regarded Benelli as one of a dynamic group that he liked to call men of the elite and whom he moved up as quickly as possible in the government of the Church. After his term as Montini's secretary, Benelli had diplomatic assignments abroad in Dublin, Paris, Rio de Janeiro, Madrid, UNESCO, and as apostolic delegate for all of West Africa.

Along with great capacity for administration, Benelli had a broad and deep general culture, a gift for languages (he spoke French, English, Spanish, and Portuguese, in addition to Italian), an international outlook, and a keen interest in problems outside as well as inside the walls of the Vatican. He had a strong social conscience, specialized in literacy programs for the underdeveloped world, and took a courageous stand against totalitarian regimes, in particular that of Franco Spain. When assigned to the Nunciatura in Madrid, he backed the Young Christian Workers of Spain in their opposition to Franco. When the national chaplain of the group, Father Ramon Torrella, was forbidden by Franco to say mass, Benelli invited Torrella to say mass in the papal nuncio's residence.

Benelli clearly was just the man Pope Paul was looking for to organize what some called the Montini government and to implement his curial reform. The young archbishop quickly moved more than thirty Vatican officials to posts more suited to their abilities. He abolished a mass of petty, outdated rules—and took all important matters into his hands to a far greater degree than had his predecessor. He was proud of the way he introduced new efficiency into the Vatican and once told me in an interview: "Before, no curial congregation ever knew what the others were doing. Today, we are making them coordinate their activities. Of course, we cannot change everything in a day. Old habits are deeply rooted here, and we have to realize that change comes slowly. But we are making progress."

A short, well-built man with a handsome round face and close-cropped iron-gray hair, Benelli always appeared tightly wound, a man perpetually in motion, ready to spring even when sitting in a routine conversation with a visitor. Perhaps because of his excess energy he tended to be irritable and often quarreled with high-ranking officials at the Vatican.

Under Pope Paul's method of governing, each curial cardinal met the pontiff on a fixed schedule, according to a calendar set up at the beginning of the year. The head of the Doctrinal Congregation (successor to the Holy Office), for example, would meet Paul on the first, third, and fourth Fridays of each month, the head of the Congregation for Evangelization on the first Monday of each month, and so on. The cardinals could request other meetings to discuss special problems. But it was Benelli who was in there with the pope *every* day.

The pope got his first dose of Benelli at breakfast, from eight to nine each morning. The archbishop was not there in person, but always on the papal breakfast table was a stack of clippings and notes, underlined in red by Benelli, which Paul carefully perused. Later in the morning Benelli would see the pope, and he often lunched with him and called again after the pontiff rose from his siesta around half past four in the afternoon.

Benelli was intellectually honest and no doubt tried to give the pope a balanced picture of what was going on, but his choice of news inevitably reflected his own rather alarmist feelings. Cicognani, who was not overly fond of his subordinate, occasionally rallied enough strength to complain about Benelli's sending all those documents to the pope, arguing, "It is for me to decide what is important for the pope to see and what is not." But the old man, who was ordained before Benelli was born, lacked the stamina to compete with the young archbishop. A source in the Vatican at the time said, "Benelli has acquired, or has deliberately taken into his own hands, almost every decision made by the Secretariat of State."

One side effect of Benelli's driving style was that when he handed down a decision, no one knew whether it was Benelli's or the pope's. When dell'Acqua was in the same post under Pope John, it was clear that the important decisions were made by the pope himself; dell'Acqua was not strong enough to shoulder such responsibilities. But Benelli could do it, and in fact did. Despite his self-confidence, he was a worrier and often communicated his nervousness to the pope. Many times he went to Paul in a state of agitation and later came out of the papal library to announce grimly to his staff: "The Holy Father is very worried about this." His letters were filled with phrases like "the Holy Father thinks" and "according to the pope," but whether what followed was the pope's view or Benelli's was unclear.

Benelli had the knack of acting quickly, impulsively but always decisively, and he would often catch others off guard. When President Nixon visited the pope in late February 1969, the program called for his helicopter to land on the Janiculum Hill and for the president to be driven from there to the Vatican. At the last minute, Benelli changed all that. There had been some serious anti-American rioting in Rome, with mobs of youngsters chanting "Nixon Boia!" ("Nixon, Hangman!"), and Benelli told American security men that the Holy Father had become deeply concerned about the president's security. He then ordered the presidential helicopter to land not on the Janiculum Hill but right in St. Peter's Square, inside Vatican City territory and only a short walk from the papal palace.

Even inside the palace, Benelli played havoc with the arrangements. The plan was to have President Nixon go directly to the papal library to meet Pope Paul. Benelli abruptly decided to put the president instead into a small waiting room on the ground floor while his entire entourage was sent up first. The archbishop explained that there would be less confusion if all the others were already upstairs waiting for the president. The sudden change of plans sent American security men into a panic when they reached the top floor and couldn't find Nixon.

There were bitter complaints about Benelli's allegedly high-handed, arrogant behavior, not only from the old guard in the curia but also from liberals elsewhere. By this time the disillusionment following Pope John's Triumphal Entry had set in with many Catholic liberals, who now were accusing Pope Paul of betraying the council and who saw Benelli as the killer of their dream. In 1973, liberal Jesuit Peter Hebblethwaite, writing in the

London Observer, launched a savage attack on Benelli, calling him "the Universal Hatchet Man." Hebblethwaite accused Benelli of stifling dialogue, even among the laity, and claimed that he represented "an embattled war-psychosis which sees enemies lurking in every corner" (an accusation at least partly true). The Hebblethwaite attack was so severe that the Jesuit superior general, Pedro Arrupe, apologized for it to Pope Paul. To Benelli, such attacks meant little. He had a tough skin and could slough off personal criticism. Archbishop Edward Heston, who worked in the curia with Benelli, once said, "Benelli is a Tuscan, and he has inherited the traditional Tuscan pigheadedness. He is ruthless."

One man who refused to knuckle under was Archbishop Michele Gonzi of Malta. Since Pope Paul had decreed that at seventy-five all bishops should offer their resignations, Gonzi dutifully presented his resignation to Paul when he reached that age at the beginning of 1968. The pope rejected the resignation and asked the archbishop to carry on. Benelli was unaware of this exchange, and about a month later wrote to Malta that the pope wanted Gonzi to step down within two weeks. The outraged Gonzi stormed in to Rome for a showdown but was kept waiting for two weeks by Benelli. The archbishop finally went directly to the pope, who was surprised that Benelli had asked him to resign and again told him to carry on. Benelli said nothing else on the matter, and Gonzi kept his post.

As he grew older and more infirm and could see the end of life approaching, Pope Paul apparently wanted to guarantee that his right-hand man would not suffer the same fate he himself had endured under Pope Pius. In 1977 he named Benelli archbishop of Florence and made him a cardinal, thereby ensuring that his protégé would be *papabile*. It looked very much as if Paul was dropping his mantle onto the Benelli shoulders. It was not to be. Benelli missed his chance in 1978, when the old enmities he had created as curial top sergeant kept him from being chosen pope. He never had another chance. In 1982 he died of heart disease.

Benelli's influence over the pope was significant in administration and, to a lesser extent, politics, but not in theology or spirituality. In the purely religious sphere, Paul found guidance primarily in the French Catholic philosophers who had developed what was known as the New Theology in the prewar era but who had become old hat among liberals after the council. Pope Paul was so enamored of French thought and culture that critics accused him of setting up a French Mafia in the Vatican. In a Roman Curia that for centuries had been an Italian preserve, Paul introduced some French faces. When Cardinal Cicognani finally retired in 1969, Paul named as his new secretary of state Cardinal Jean Villot, former archbishop of Lyons. As prefect of the important Congregation for Catholic Education, he appointed the scholarly French cardinal Gabriel-Marie Garrone. As number-two man in the Doctrinal Congregation, he named French archbishop Paul Philippe. As head of the Pontifical Family (formerly Papal Court), Paul chose the French bishop Jacques Martin.

In addition, Paul thoroughly internationalized the Roman Curia. He appointed the first black African to a top curial post—Cardinal Bernardin Gantin of Benin, as president of the Pontifical Commission for Justice and Peace. He named Yugoslav cardinal Francis Seper to replace Ottaviani as prefect of the Congregation for the Doctrine of the Faith; this was the first time anyone from a Communist country had headed a curial body. And Paul brought in the first Latin American to preside over a congregation—the Brazilian cardinal Angelo Rossi, as head of the Congregation for Evangelization of Peoples. He also named an American, Cardinal John Wright, prefect of the Congregation for the Clergy, and an Austrian, Cardinal Koenig, as president of the Secretariat for Non-Believers.

John Paul's Vatican, a Team Without a Top Sergeant

All this internationalization prepared the way for the election of a pope who was not only non-Italian but also non-curia. Except for his short-lived predecessor John Paul I, the pope from Poland was the first pontiff without curial experience to be elected since 1903, a marked contrast with Paul, the veteran Roman bureaucrat.

This difference was quickly reflected in John Paul's obvious dislike for administrative routine, a trait most unlike Paul's penchant for tidy organization. In some ways Paul as an administrator resembled Jimmy Carter, whereas John Paul resembles Ronald Reagan.

Pope John Paul is a man who establishes priorities, and early on he made it clear that administering the curia was low on his list. Pope Paul had tried to keep his finger on every detail of Vatican activity; he pored over all the curial documents that came his way and inevitably sent them back covered with handwritten comments. John Paul seldom annotates papers. One curial official told me, "This pope makes marginal notes so rarely that if he ever does, he scares us to death. We are sure it must be something tremendously serious."

Pope Paul had given the curia a thoroughgoing reform in 1967, but he had not stopped there. He named Bishop (now Cardinal) Edward Gagnon to work on a further reform of the reform. Shortly after John Paul's election, Gagnon showed him where the reform plan stood. The cardinal recalls that "for a month or so, the pope seemed to be interested. But then he forgot about it, obviously preferring to concentrate on projecting the Christian message through his international trips, his audiences, his pastoral activity in the diocese of Rome." Years passed before he got around to doing anything about Gagnon's curial reform. John Paul again showed his indifference to administration when he waited more than six months after his election before taking his first look at the budget of the Holy See, a matter that was screaming for attention, since the Vatican was running deeply into the red.

John Paul has a good personal relationship with his curial cardinals, but he interferes little in their day-to-day work. Given his priorities, he simply does not have the time to get involved in the bureaucracy. He makes an average of four international trips a year and must prepare as many as fifty speeches for each. The great majority of those speeches are meaty, delivered with specific objectives in mind, and therefore require a massive amount of work and care. He also studies intensively the languages of the countries he is to visit and spends an enormous amount of time in contact with bishops, Catholic laymen, diplomats, government officials, and experts before taking a trip.

As bishop of Rome, John Paul tries whenever possible to visit a different parish of his diocese each Sunday, and he does his homework in minute detail: he must know the physical layout of the parish, the rate of literacy and general education, the average attendance at masses, social problems, unemployment rates, how the people voted in the preceding election. He also uses his weekly general audiences as a teaching platform; instead of simply greeting the crowd amiably, he delivers a lecture to drive home vital religious points. John Paul is one of the most political of popes and spends many hours every week keeping in touch with the political situation in Poland, Nicaragua, the Philippines.

While he does not try to control every detail of the Vatican in the manner of Paul, neither does John Paul turn a blind eye to much of it, as did John. He expects high-quality work from his curial cardinals, but he leaves the job to them to do; he is accessible, regularly lunches with them individually, often invites one or the other in to extend greetings to him on his birthday or other anniversary—but he does not expect them to ask him what to do in their areas. This system frees the pope for what he considers his fundamentally pastoral role. He has tried to put the best possible men, by his standards, in the top jobs, and he demands competence. If any curial head fails to meet his standards, John Paul rolls out the old bulldozer.

Two once-powerful cardinals learned this after the Polish pope took office. They were Sebastiano Baggio, who then headed the tremendously important Congregation for Bishops, and the Argentine Eduardo Pironio, then prefect of the Congregation for the Religious. Both men had been considered *papabili* in 1978, but John Paul didn't hesitate to demote them when he found their work unsatisfactory.

A close friend of the pope told me that downgrading Baggio was "one of the hardest decisions John Paul has made." Not only did the pope have warm and cordial relations with the cardinal, but also Baggio was acknowledged to be one of the strongest men in the curia. He had built up worldwide contacts in his long term as head of the Congregation for Bishops, had been a major influence in shaping Vatican policy in Latin America, and was the leading supporter in the curia of Opus Dei, the powerful lay religious order of which John Paul so heartily approves. It was not surprising that in 1978 he was among the top four or five *papabili*. But John Paul weighed Baggio and found him wanting. The cardinal had to go.

The chief reason for Baggio's demotion was John Paul's displeasure at his handling of appointments of American bishops. The pope was disturbed at reports that some bishops in the United States were failing to impose discipline on the clergy and were not speaking out clearly on birth control, abortion, and divorce. And the pope was irritated by Baggio's laxity in following the established norms in choosing new bishops, and by his proposing candidates from a pool so limited as to exclude certain men that John Paul especially liked.

One the pope favored was Cardinal Joseph Bernardin, a candidate to become archbishop of Chicago. Yielding to pressure from archconservatives in the United States, Baggio had tried to veto Bernardin's candidacy—and found himself on a collision course with the pope. Wojtyla and Bernardin had had a long friendship, dating back to the time when the two served together on the permanent council of the World Synod of Bishops. While he was secretary of the American Bishops' Conference, Bernardin had been a great help to John Paul in keeping him informed on the inner workings of the American episcopate, information passed on during long, intimate luncheons at the papal table. In the end Bernardin got the Chicago post and Baggio got the ax. John Paul gave Baggio the consolation prize of the presidency of the Commission for Vatican City. Some sympathetic Italian journalists tried to report Baggio's transfer as a promotion, but the cardinal knew that he had been demoted. When he met a close friend shortly after the move was announced, he hung his head and murmured, "I am nothing in the curia now—nothing!"

Pope John likewise used the bulldozer on the highly respected Cardinal Pironio, who as prefect of the Congregation for the Religious wielded vast power in the Church all over the world. When Pope Paul died in 1978, there was widespread speculation that if the cardinals wanted a non-Italian pope, their choice would be Pironio. But the Polish pope, who put so much stress on discipline in religious orders, considered the liberal Argentine far too indulgent to handle that job. (Pironio's critics labeled him the protector of the Jesuits because of his leniency toward the Society of Jesus, which at the time seemed to be breaking all the rules.) In early 1984 the pope transferred Pironio to the less controversial and far less important presidency of the Pontifical Council for the Laity.

Unlike most popes, John Paul has no "top sergeant" like Paul's Benelli, no general staff, no proper Kitchen Cabinet. At any given time, the Vatican official closest to the pope will be the one responsible for the problem to which John Paul is giving priority at that moment. Of course, he has his own personal secretaries, who by the nature of their jobs must be at the papal elbow every day, all day. His number-one secretary is Monsignor Stanislao Dziwisz, who came with Wojtyla to Rome from Kraków.

When he accompanied Cardinal Wojtyla to that historic conclave of October 1978, Dziwisz never dreamed that his life would be so drastically changed. Along with a hundred thousand other people, he was in St. Peter's Square as the white smoke appeared, and when, from the balcony, Cardinal Felice pronounced the first name, "Carolum," Dziwisz's knees began to shake. When he heard the last name, "Woj-tyla," he fell in a faint and would have hit the ground if two friends hadn't held him up. It meant that for the lifetime of the pope Dziwisz would not live in his beloved Kraków.

John Paul uses his secretary not only for keeping track of his appointments but also as a sounding board. Dziwisz is no scholar or theologian, but he is practical and down-to-earth and has a delightful Polish sense of humor. When mulling a problem, the pope often tries out a decision on his secretary and listens carefully to his opinion.

Because he was determined not to be overburdened with office duties, John Paul early on handed over day-to-day Vatican administration to his secretary of state, Cardinal Agostino Casaroli, a dumpy, balding, bespectacled Italian with a beguiling Mickey Mouse smile. A veteran of half a century in the Vatican's Secretariat of State, Casaroli had been Pope Paul's "foreign minister" (officially secretary of the Council for Public Affairs), and theoretically he and Benelli had the same rank. In fact, Benelli assumed the role of superior and, speaking in the name of Pope Paul, unabashedly barked orders at Casaroli. It must have been difficult and frustrating, but Casaroli never complained, accepting Benelli's bullying in a spirit of humility and resignation. The day came when Benelli was moved out of the curia to Florence, and Casaroli soared to prominence in the Vatican. Pope John Paul's first top curial appointment was to make Casaroli secretary of state.

A subtle and never-failing sense of humor no doubt has helped Casaroli bear the burdens of serving with the likes of Benelli. The humor showed through one evening when I had the pleasure of playing host to him at dinner in my home in Rome. Someone told the story of how Winston Churchill had made a pet of a goose, which was eventually served to him on a platter, prompting Sir Winston to push it away with the sad comment, "I cannot eat him. He was my friend!"

As the punch line was being delivered, Casaroli was served a delectable boiled bass with freshly prepared mayonnaise. With knife and fork poised, Casaroli said, "This fish is a total stranger!" and dug in with gusto.

The outwardly gentle Casaroli demonstrated his reliability after John Paul was shot and very nearly killed by a Turkish gunman. On May 13, 1981, the Vatican's secretary of state had flown to the United States to receive an honorary degree from St. John's University and heard the shocking news when he landed at Kennedy Airport. He took the first return flight to Rome, saying simply, "My duty is to be with the Holy Father," and was the first Vatican official to enter the intensive care unit where John Paul lay between life and death; for several days he was, indeed, the only one allowed to visit the pontiff (except for a single brief call by the president of the Italian Republic, Sandro Pertini). Church law does not provide for an "acting pope," and Casaroli never pretended to be playing that role. But during those critical days of the pope's incapacitation, the man who held the Holy See together was Agostino Casaroli.

Though the pope has tremendous confidence in Casaroli, the two are not intimate friends in the personal sense, although their close acquaintance goes back to Casaroli's first visit to Poland, in 1967. (A short time later Pope Paul made Archbishop Karol Wojtyla a cardinal, on the recommendation of Casaroli.) John Paul is an outspoken Pole, Casaroli a subtle Italian whose speech is flavored with quotations from Dante and Manzoni. In describing the difference between the two men, someone once said, "The pope will tell you to jump out the window. Casaroli will talk with you for two hours and persuade you to jump out."

John Paul rarely backs away from a confrontation; Casaroli always looks to compromise. Perhaps because he values Casaroli's diplomatic skills, the pope has entrusted to Don Agostino (as he affectionately addresses him) some of the most delicate tasks involving relations with the temporal world: negotiating a new and more liberal concordat with the Italian Republic to replace the one that had been worked out with Mussolini in 1929; settling the claims of more than one hundred foreign banks after the great Vatican Bank scandal of 1982; dealing with a newly formed labor union in Vatican City; mediating the dangerous quarrel between Argentina and Chile over the Beagle Channel.

Even while he was a student back in his native Piacenza in northern Italy, Casaroli's superiors assigned him to the Secretariat of State, and he has stayed there through his entire career. His first job (at the age of twenty-three) was to work in the archives. "It was like being a government bureaucrat," he later recalled, and the idealistic young priest yearned for some kind of pastoral activity. When a Jesuit spiritual advisor suggested that he moonlight as an unofficial chaplain to teenage delinquents, young Agostino took the suggestion seriously and began spending his evenings in prisons for young offenders. Even after he became a prince of the Church as cardinal secretary of state, Casaroli would whenever possible make the last appointment of his busy day a visit with his boys, to whom he became known as the *sacerdote amico* (the priest friend). Few knew it at the time, but one of the prisoners he befriended was Giuseppe Pelosi, who when only seventeen had murdered the Italian writer Pier Paolo Pasolini.

Casaroli has held important Vatican posts under four popes (John, Paul, John Paul I and John Paul II) and some cynical persons sneer that he is primarily a survivor. One said, "He does only what he is told to do, and he does it with rare ability." Casaroli is so self-effacing as to give currency to this view of him. When a newsman once asked him if he was the architect of the Vatican's "Ostpolitik," he answered: "That is not true. I am only the man who implements to the best of his ability the policies of the Holy See. These policies are decided by the pope and it is he who is the architect. I am the instrument."

It is true that Casaroli never promotes publicly a policy different from that of the pope, but in private meetings with John Paul he speaks his mind without inhibition. He has quietly sold the policy of accommodation with Eastern European regimes to a succession of popes, each of whom then promoted that policy as if he had originated it himself.

Though he takes prime responsibility for Vatican administration and diplomacy, Casaroli has never tried to be the boss of the curia or to dominate his colleagues in the Benelli style. It is not his inclination to play that role, but in any case it would be impossible because John Paul has set up in his curia a team of individuals so strong that no one cardinal can dominate the others.

The Polish pope has introduced a group of conservative and tough Northern Europeans, best personified by the German prefect of the Congregation for the Doctrine of the Faith, Cardinal

Josef Ratzinger. The soft-spoken but coldly efficient Ratzinger has attracted more attention than other curial cardinals mainly because of his tough disciplinary actions against progressive theologians like the American Charles Curran, the Swiss Hans Kung, and the Brazilian exponent of liberation theology Franciscan Leonardo Boff.

Another of John Paul's Northern European group is the Belgian Dominican Jean Jerome Hamer, named prefect of the Congregation for Religious in place of the more liberal Pironio. The rather dour Belgian had trained for the job in eleven years as number-two man in the Congregation for the Doctrine of the Faith, the watchdog of Catholic orthodoxy which one Vatican wag noted "is no training ground for wimps." Hamer is sometimes called The Hammer because of his toughness. A liberal American Catholic publication even compared him to a wife-beater because of his rigid disciplinary stance toward nuns. A third Northern European, the German cardinal Augustin Mayer, now head of the Congregation for Divine Worship, likewise drew the ire of American feminists when, as secretary of the Congregation for Religious, he was instrumental in launching an investigation of U.S. religious orders.

Well known as the most powerful person in the Northern European group, Cardinal Ratzinger is much admired by John Paul, who chose him after a minimum of consultation with others. The pope often seeks his advice, and not only on doctrinal matters. John Paul will sometimes call in Ratzinger to discuss political problems. A Polish friend of the pope's says Ratzinger is "the kind of man who has the pope's ear, a professorial type with great competence in his field, and at the same time a pastor who has proven himself in the pastoral field. The pope continually is struck by Ratzinger's theological ability."

A slightly built man with a diffident, self-effacing appearance, Ratzinger has none of the sinister look or overpowering manner of his onetime predecessor Cardinal Ottaviani, but his gentle style conceals a Teutonic toughness. Vatican specialist Giancarlo Zizola aptly wrote of him, "With his pallid and sad appearance, his white hair well groomed and combed, his blue eyes, Cardinal Josef Ratzinger has brought back into the fortress of orthodoxy an air of Gothic rigor."

His pastoral experience was limited to four years as archbishop of Munich, one of Europe's most important dioceses, where, according to a German critic, he "tended to treat his priests as university students sitting at the feet of the great Professor Ratzinger."

Ratzinger was indeed a professor of theology for most of his career, and he is the first theologian in modern times to head up the Holy Office. When he was a young theologian attending the Vatican Council as an expert, he was publicly rebuked by Cardinal Ottaviani for a document he had helped draft which contradicted the Holy Office. In the years since the council he has become increasingly conservative and is now uncompromisingly traditionalist. As a young man, he was one of the founders of the extremely liberal journal *Concilium,* which continues today as a thorn in the side of the Holy See. When a journalist jokingly asked Ratzinger if he considered his connection with *Concilium* a "sin of his youth," he answered in dead seriousness, "Not at all. I have not changed. Those who took over *Concilium* after me have changed."

Ratzinger is a much-quoted man. He grants interviews to the press, publishes articles, and almost always provokes controversy. He has complained in print that the Vatican Council failed to produce the "new Pentecost" that Pope John had hoped for; he argues publicly that all those bishops' conferences set up by Pope Paul have no doctrinal basis, and he bemoans the fact that the Church has slipped from the "sacred into the profane," that there is too little understanding of the existence and the power of the devil, that the Church has given away too much to accommodate ecumenical movements and Marxism. When Ratzinger was appointed to his Vatican post in 1981, a somewhat irreverent Roman remarked: "It would be hard to imagine a Catholic scholar now choosing a book title like that of the liberal Belgian theologian Edward Schillebeeckx's *Jesus: An Experiment in Christology.* From now on such a work would be entitled *Jee-sus! An Experiment in Christology?*"

Those who assume that Ratzinger runs the Vatican also assume that his conservative and somewhat negative statements reflect precisely the opinion of John Paul. This is not so. Ratzinger often speaks for himself. When the pope was returning from a trip to Africa in the summer of 1985, a newsman asked him about a controversial Ratzinger comment on the council, and John Paul surprised everyone by answering, "That is his opinion, and he is free to express it."

In fact, the pope has given Ratzinger the right to express his own opinions. Ratzinger accepted the doctrinal congregation post on condition that he be allowed to write and speak in his personal capacity as a theologian, a function paralleling his duties as prefect of the congregation. It was an unprecedented request, but the pope readily agreed. This does not mean that Ratzinger will disagree with the pope on fundamental points of doctrine. It does mean that Ratzinger's negativism and pessimism do not necessarily reflect the mood of the pope. Nor are Ratzinger's initiatives and style of work necessarily prompted by papal orders.

To balance the tough Northern Europeans, John Paul has appointed some progressives to top posts. The black African cardinal Bernardin Gantin, a man who has amply demonstrated his progressive social consciousness, was named prefect of the Congregation for Bishops to replace Baggio; as head of the tremendously important Congregation for Catholic Education, he named a self-effacing American, Cardinal William Wakefield Baum. Dutch cardinal Jan Willebrands, John Paul's president of the Secretariat for Christian Unity, openly supported the liberal Edward Schillebeeckx when he was under investigation by the doctrinal congregation. Moreover, John Paul broadened geographical representation in the curia by naming Indian cardinal Simon Lourdusamy head of the Congregation for Evangelization of Peoples—the first time an Indian has ever held high curial office. All this demonstrates that John Paul's team, far from being a conservative club dominated by a "Ratzinger clique," represents in fact a wide range of viewpoints, cultural backgrounds, and personal styles.

Overall, the best description I have heard of John Paul's Vatican team came from a veteran curial official who summed it up: "The papal government today is divided between the 'flexible ones,' typified by Casaroli, who are willing to compromise when necessary but are saddened at having to compromise, and the 'rigid ones,' typified by Ratzinger, who reject compromise totally."

It should be noted that the pope has put the flexible ones in charge of areas where compromise seems possible to him, such as diplomacy and ecumenism. In those areas where John Paul is least likely to compromise—doctrine and discipline—he has installed the "rigids."

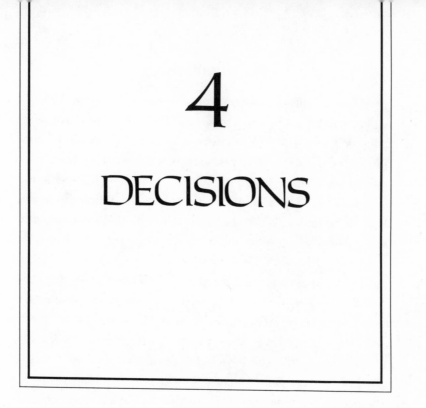

4

DECISIONS

Summoning the Council

Although the secular power of popes has shrunk to the vanishing point, pontiffs must still make decisions that affect human beings all around the globe. Some years ago I met a devout Catholic in Beirut who had four children and lacked the means to support any more. For nearly four years he had been exercising self-discipline while he waited for Pope Paul to pronounce on whether the contraceptive pill is licit for Catholics. There are innumerable Catholics in analogous situations: couples waiting for annulments that would allow them to have a Catholic marriage; priests asking to be laicized; divorced and remarried persons yearning for a relaxation of Church law so that they can be readmitted to the sacraments.

The most important papal decision of the century transcended all such purely personal problems. In 1962 John XXIII called the Second Vatican Council, an action that would alter almost every aspect of the life of the Church.

In nearly two thousand years of Church history, there have

been only twenty-one general, or ecumenical, councils. The first eight were called by emperors; only thirteen popes have dared take such a decision. The most recent council before John's time met in 1869, and it was the first in three hundred years. John's two immediate predecessors, Pius XI and Pius XII, both seriously considered calling a council but backed off. John's successor, Paul VI, on one occasion told Cardinal Silvio Oddi that his greatest achievement was bringing to a close the council John had summoned, but Paul would have been the first to admit that he lacked the resolve to call a council. Cardinal Koenig said to me that Paul "might have felt a council was needed, but he never would have been able to make up his mind to do it. He once told me he felt that he was in a railway station where many trains were leaving all at the same time, and he couldn't decide which train to take."

John had no such problems. Less than three months after he was elected supreme pontiff, John XXIII summoned the Second Vatican Council.

A general council is the supreme legislative body of the Church, and its decisions, when ratified by the pope, are binding unless modified by a later council. Councils usually have been summoned to deal with specific crises confronting the Church.

The First Vatican Council, called by powerful and stubborn Pius IX in 1869, proclaimed the doctrine of the infallibility of the pope, declaring that the pontiff is infallible on matters of faith and morals when he speaks "ex cathedra" (from the chair of Peter) and announces that he is doing so. Before that council could be adjourned, the troops of King Victor Emmanuel stormed into Rome to abolish the Papal States and absorb the Eternal City into the modern secular kingdom of Italy. In protest, Pius IX locked himself in his palace. The visiting bishops packed up and went home.

For decades afterward there was speculation on whether the council should be reconvened and brought to its proper conclusion. In 1925 Pius XI spoke of reconvening the First Vatican Council, but his closest advisors dissuaded him. They pointed out that the "Roman question" was not yet solved: the pope still did not recognize the legitimacy of the secular monarchy that had replaced the papacy as sovereign in Rome. Moreover, some conservative advisors insisted that, since the pope had been proclaimed infallible, there no longer was need for a council; the pope alone could do all the legislating necessary for the Church. And so Pius XI dropped the idea.

His successor, Pius XII, spent several years preparing for a council that never took place. It was not to be a simple reconvening of the First Vatican Council but an entirely new gathering to meet the challenges of the twentieth century, though in a rather negative fashion. The idea was given to the pope by two of the most conservative personalities in the curia, Cardinals Ernesto Ruffini and Alfredo Ottaviani, two men who later were to lead the fight against freedom of conscience and religious liberty at John's Vatican council. Ruffini first discussed the project with Pius in 1939, shortly after his election. The pope shelved the idea until 1948, when he began serious planning for the project with Ottaviani. A preparatory commission was appointed, and intensive, though secret, work went on until 1951, when the idea died out.

One suggestion was that the council should convene during the 1950 Holy Year and proclaim the Assumption of the Virgin a dogma of the Church. (Eventually, Pius XII, without the assistance of a council, proclaimed the Assumption a dogma in the Holy Year; this is the only time since the First Vatican Council that a pope has spoken infallibly.) Ottaviani argued that a council was needed primarily to combat "the great accumulation of errors which are being diffused in philosophical, theological, moral, and social fields." Proposals of the preparatory commission recommended action "against existentialism, against false concepts of the relation between revelation and theology, against multiple errors in the field of scriptural studies, against the various forms of materialism, of pagan humanism, of naturalism, against errors involving the primary aim of matrimony, birth control, artificial insemination, against those who support Communist doctrine, against those who propagate the class struggle, against those who support the idea that any 'sincere' man, even without baptism and without visible dependence on the head of the Church, is a true and proper member of the Church, against those who argue that the dissidents differ only in name from the faithful. . . ."

Such proposals were a reverse-image of much that eventually was done at John's council, but in a negative way they reflected the need to confront modern issues. And some of the proposals were positive: the commission also pointed out "the necessity of proclaiming the social doctrine of the Church, of speaking out against those who would go to war to settle disputes, of proclaiming the Catholic doctrine of love toward all creatures."

The Pius council plan died partly because of disagreements within the commission on whether to seek the opinion of bishops outside the Vatican, but the fundamental reason was probably that given by an unidentified bishop quoted in the Jesuit journal *Civiltà Cattolica:* "To bring the council into being, a man like John, with his courage and decisiveness, was needed. Perhaps Pius XII never convoked the council because his character was such that he could not adapt to having near him an organism of this type, with the powers and the influence of a council."

It is a little-known fact that the work of Pius's preparatory commission made it much easier for John to convene a council, and to do so in such a short time. The commission finally handed its documents to Pius on January 4, 1951, and the work of nearly three years was put away in secret Vatican archives, there to lie for the rest of that pope's life. John knew that he had inherited this treasure trove of preparation. Although it did not coincide with the mood of his council, it served as a launching-pad for his own preparatory commissions, which initially took an extremely conservative view of what a council should do. By April 1959, John gave permission to release from the archives the material prepared for Pius. His men found there a mass of extremely useful studies, especially on marriage and the family, international problems, and social justice.

In the Vatican there are certain procedures for helping a pope pass judgment, but John bypassed them all in calling his council. Pius's approach had been to study the problem with his curia, to appoint a commission to come up with detailed proposals, and then to make a decision. John, however, made his decision first, and only afterwards tossed the problem to the curia and preparatory commissions.

The first indication that he would call a council emerged during a meeting between John and his secretary of state, Cardinal Tardini, on January 20, 1959. They were discussing problems relating to the Cold War. The pope later wrote that he asked himself at that moment, What should the Church do?

John's account of the moment continues: "Our soul was illuminated by a great idea which we felt in that instant and received with indescribable trust in our Divine Master. A word, solemn and binding, rose to our lips. Our voice expressed it for the first time: 'A council!' To tell the truth, we feared we had aroused perplexity, if not dismay . . . but a clear expression appeared on the cardinal's face. His assent was immediate and exultant, the first sure sign of the Lord's will."

Later events were to prove that Tardini was not quite so enthusiastic as John assumed at the time, but the pope's mind was made up. Only five days later, at a meeting with his curia in the Benedictine monastery at St. Paul's Outside-the-Walls, John stunned his team of old cardinals by announcing formally that he was summoning the twenty-first ecumenical council in the history of the Church.

In view of the great caution shown by John's immediate predecessors, it is incredible that he should make such a momentous decision less than three months after his election, and with almost no consultation with his curia. While there is good reason to believe he had thought of the idea before that famous meeting with Tardini, there is little doubt that it was an intuitive decision, perfectly consistent with the man's character. In his "Journal of the Soul" John wrote: "Above all I am grateful to the Lord for the temperament which he has given me and which protects me from anxiety and from troubling confusion. I feel myself in obedience in everything, and I observe that keeping myself in this way, 'in magnis et in minimis,' confers on my smallness such a power of audacious simplicity . . ."

John quite clearly had no idea what he was setting loose in taking his decision. Unlike Pius, who hoped to have a neat set of proposals to be rubber-stamped by a gathering of bishops, John had only a vague hope that the council would somehow open the way for a new descent of the Holy Spirit. He wrote in early 1962, a few months before the council opened, "The council must produce a new Pentecost of faith, an apostolate of extraordinary grace, for the prosperity of men, for peace in the entire world . . . like the dawning of a new day, a living dawn of the Catholic Church." He often used the phrase "new Pentecost" as he awaited the council's opening, but he was vague on just what form that Pentecost would take.

His preparations for the council showed that John may well have underestimated that great event. One of the Vatican functionaries pointed out to the pope that there would be a considerable cost in providing 2,500 visiting bishops with necessary equipment, including kneelers and chairs. The functionary suggested it would be more economical to buy this equipment than to rent it, as had been planned.

"Why buy it?" asked the pope. "The council will be over in a few weeks."

In fact, the council lasted four years.

The pope was not alone in his vagueness about what lay ahead. When the bishops of all the world were asked to send to Rome their suggestions as to what the council should do, many of the replies were superficial. An archbishop who later became a cardinal suggested that the council discuss ways to shorten episcopal ceremonies, "especially in hot climates, where there is a problem of changing vestments so frequently during the service."

John's own intimate entourage had doubts about the project. His intensely loyal personal secretary, Loris Capovilla, was sympathetic with the spirit of the proposal but feared it would be too much for a man of John's age to undertake. Tardini was frankly skeptical, and in his usual blunt fashion once told the pope that summoning his kind of council "would mean creating chaos from pole to pole!" Even his close ally Cardinal Bea at first had doubts. He reminded John that Pius had thought of calling a council but had given up the idea. Bea asked, "What forum can we possibly provide to bring together a torn and disunited Christian world?"

The more conservative elements around the Vatican were positively opposed to calling the council. A longtime associate of Pius XII insists to this day that John's calling the council was "a courageous, but imprudent, decision." Cardinal Ottaviani, who had pressed Pius to call a council, very much feared the kind of council summoned by the intuitive, unpredictable John. American cardinal Joseph Ritter told a journalist at the time that the old guard in the curia "couldn't see any need for a council. They thought everything was all right with the Church. They had a kind of closed corporation inside the Vatican and were satisfied with it."

At first the Ottaviani clique tried to kill the idea with procrastination. After all, John was an old man who had serious health problems; he certainly would not live many more years. If they could manage to drag out the preparations for a bit more than four years—as history demonstrated—Pope John's hopes for a council would have been filed away in the Vatican archives along with those of Pius XII. But every time the curial cardinals suggested delaying the opening, John insisted on moving it forward. When one cardinal went to the pope to complain, "We cannot possibly get ready for a council by 1963," John answered, "Very well, we will have it in 1962."

When they realized that delaying tactics would not work, the Ottaviani clique tried to mold the council in their own image. They persuaded John to allow the heads of the various curial congregations to serve as presidents of all the preparatory committees. They prepared sixty-nine "schemata," or documents, reflecting the curia's own somewhat narrow view of the Church; they naïvely believed that they could present these proposals to the council for rubber-stamp approval with a minimum of debate.

John went along with all this in the interest of getting the council opened as soon as possible. He knew that once the bishops of the world got together, a little curial clique would be powerless to stem the tide of renewal. However diplomatic he might be with his cardinals, however much he sought to avoid conflict with them, Pope John had made his decision to open the way to a new Pentecost, and he would not be deterred.

John lived through only the first of the four sessions of the council, but in a historical sense that did not matter. The important thing was the decision, the fact that he had the will and courage to call in his bishops from the ends of the earth to a meeting which had such far-reaching consequences for the Catholic world.

Paul and "the Pill"

Good Pope John's resolve in calling the council contrasted totally with the approach used by his successor, Pope Paul, in making the great judgment of his reign—his pronouncement on birth control. It was a decision forced on Paul, one that he did not seek out and would have preferred to ignore. John Paul II later told me that "the hardest decision any pope has had to make in this century was Pope Paul's decision on birth control. The great problem for him was that his own birth control commission was divided." (John Paul knew what he was talking about. As Archbishop Wojtyla of Kraków, he was a member of that commission.)

Paul had always accepted the traditionalist Catholic position banning all artificial means of contraception, and he expected no problem with the issue. But times were changing and the Catholic world was demanding a new reading of this old problem.

By the time Paul became pope, the worldwide population explosion was seen as a danger to the human race comparable to the Hiroshima atomic explosion. Leading Catholic population experts were demanding that the Church take a stand. Father Arthur McCormick, who served as a population expert with the pope's Commission for Peace and Justice, pointed out that "when

God told man to be fruitful and multiply, the population density was two persons per square world." And at the prestigious Catholic Louvain University in Belgium, two leading professors of moral theology gave cautious approval to the new birth control pill. Other liberal Catholic clerics reasoned that the pill might be licit, although they rejected purely mechanical birth control devices.

During the Council, British cardinal John Heenan told a group of newsmen in Rome that "the Church already approves of birth control." Pope Pius XII had decreed that it was licit to use the rhythm method, reasoning that it was a "natural" method, as opposed to artificial methods. Some Church thinkers wondered out loud if the new contraceptive pill was not just an extension of the rhythm method.

Perhaps most important of all, on the floor of the council itself bishops were raising questions about the issue. Cardinal Bernard Jan Alfrink of Holland spoke of "honest doubts" about Catholic teaching on birth regulation. Cardinal Paul Emile Leger of Canada warned against "a certain pessimistic and negative attitude about human love." The patriarch of the Greek Catholic Church, Maximos IV Sayegh, attacked the "celibate psychosis" and the tendency of many to see only evil in sex. The highly articulate Belgian cardinal Leo Joseph Suenens, in referring to the birth control issue, warned the council, "Let us avoid a second Galileo case—one is enough for the Church!"

In its document *The Church and the Modern World*, the council used some phrases that aroused hopes for change among the innovators. The document declared, "This council realizes that often [married couples] find themselves in circumstances where at least temporarily the size of their families should not be increased," and it stated that "marriage to be sure is not instituted solely for procreation."

All this showed that the time had come for the Church to make a clear pronouncement on whether or not there was any evolution or alteration in its teaching on contraception. Paul could not avoid the issue, because if he had not taken it on himself, the council would have acted on it. The pope feared that the council fathers were too subject to pressures of current public opinion and might yield to relativistic impulses in altering an eternal truth. Hence, he not only withdrew the issue from the council but also refused to allow his own birth control commission to make the final decision.

Paul's determination to take on his own shoulders this awesome responsibility was made official in October 1964, when Italian bishop Emilio Guano came out of a meeting with the pope to announce: "The Holy Father has established a proper commission of doctors, biologists, sociologists, psychiatrists, and theologians to study the problem of conjugal morality. He has reserved to himself the final decision in the matter."

Accepting the responsibility to make the decision alone put the pope under terrible pressure from all sides. A Vatican journalist wrote at the time: "Rivaling each other's ingenuity to find secret channels through the Byzantine court structure, opposing groups inundated Paul with petitions, studies, theories, and warnings. Laymen and priests, Catholics and non-Catholics, grew progressively more outspoken in calling for change."

By his own admission, Paul took more time than most in making up his mind on even minor issues, and on a major problem like birth control he was determined not to be hurried. A priest who once worked with him complained, "Before saying a piece of paper is blue, Montini has to lift it up to see that it does not turn gray." Some critics sneered that he had led the Church into a "holy sea of howevers," that Paul's statements amounted to nothing more than a series of "Yes, buts . . ."

Barely a month after his election, Paul wrote, "There are those who deliberate from instinct, or who are content with an empirical examination of the circumstances to be studied. For me, a certain rationality is necessary, which, of course, impedes the speed of my decisions."

Paul opted to "suffer alone," as he had when he wore those heavy garlands in India or when he secretly endured the hair shirt. An overpowering sense of papal responsibility would not permit him to let this bitter cup pass to others. He revealed something of the weight of the decision in a speech to a general audience shortly after the encyclical "Humanae Vitae" eventually appeared:

"Four years devoted to the study and the elaboration of the encyclical . . . brought us no small spiritual suffering. Never have we felt the weight of our office as in these circumstances. We have studied, read, discussed as much as we could, and we also have prayed a great deal.

"How many times have we had the impression of being almost submerged by the mass of documents, and how many times, humanly speaking, have we realized the inadequacy of our poor person for the formidable apostolic duty of having to pronounce on the matter. How many times have we trembled before the dilemma of an easy condescension to current opinions, or of a decision poorly supported by present-day society, or which would be arbitrarily too grave for conjugal life!"

Paul's tendency to agonize over the problem perhaps gave rise to hope that in the end he would opt for change. In hindsight it is somewhat surprising that there was such widespread expectation that he might possibly alter the teaching. On this point, he always had been a traditionalist and had often reaffirmed "Casti Connubi," the 1930 encyclical of Pius XI which ruled that "any use whatsoever of matrimony exercised in such a way that the act is deliberately frustrated in its natural power to generate life is an offense against the law of God and of nature, and those who indulge in such are branded with the guilt of a grave sin."

The pope dramatically reaffirmed his commitment to the traditional teaching when he addressed the United Nations General Assembly in New York in the autumn of 1965. He urged the nations of the world "not to favor an artificial control of births, which would be irrational, in order to lessen the number of guests at the banquet of life."

But even though he made such unequivocal statements at times, Paul seemed indecisive enough to sow confusion and give rise to false hopes among the liberals. In his 1967 encyclical

"Populorum Progressio" he had given a hint of his concern about the problem when he said that nations should control their populations. Many wishful thinkers erroneously interpreted this as a pontifical endorsement of all forms of birth control. Shortly after the encyclical was published, B. R. Sen, director-general of the U.N. Food and Agriculture Organization, summoned a press conference to thank the pope publicly for approving birth control as an answer to the population explosion. Similarly, when Pope Paul told a meeting of cardinals that he had formed a commission to study the birth control problem but added that in the meantime the norms given by preceding popes must be considered valid, "at least until we feel obliged in conscience to change them," that seemed to open the door to the possibility of a change.

Another glimmer of hope for the pro-change group was the makeup of the birth control commission. Paul had inherited from John a six-man (three priests and three laymen) Commission for the Study of Population, Family, and Birth Problems, which came to be called simply the papal birth control commission. Pope Paul enlarged the group, first to fourteen and later to sixty, and the experts he appointed were open-minded persons. The fact that he had not weighted the commission with traditionalists gave rise to new hopes that a change was in the making.

By 1964 the pope was pressing his commission to treat as a matter of urgency the question of whether scientific advances in contraceptive pills altered the teaching enunciated by Pius XI in "Casti Connubi." After a meeting in June 1964, the commission came up with an ambiguous response: The pill indeed was a contraceptive agent—not simply an extension of the rhythm method—but there were doubts that contraception itself was intrinsically evil. Since Pius XI was not speaking *ex cathedra* when he issued his encyclical, that document was not infallible and therefore could be put on the table for discussion.

Things got more confused the following May, when the commission, after a heated session, came up with an eighty-three-page report that left the whole question in doubt. More than forty commission members were undecided, six favored all forms of contraception, and seven took the traditionalist line that only the rhythm method was licit. The majority did advise the pope, however, not to take a stand on specific methods of birth control.

Although the commission's meetings were secret, word spread to conservatives like Cardinals Ottaviani (who still headed the Holy Office) and Browne, who weighed in with dire warnings to the pope. Ottaviani told the pope his commission was "dangerous" and "confusing the faithful by saying that the Church has been wrong all the time."

The commission seemed to be confusing Paul as much as the faithful. He could not accept the group's conclusions (or lack of conclusions), and yet in good conscience he could not make a decision without further examining the question. And so in late 1965 he once again enlarged the commission by adding a kind of watchdog group that came to be known as the supercommittee: sixteen cardinals and bishops who were expected to keep the commission more nearly in line with traditional Church teaching. (One member of the supercommittee was Archbishop Wojtyla of Kraków, who was not yet a cardinal.)

If the pope thought this supercommittee would guarantee a traditional stance by the commission, he again was disappointed. In mid-1966, the commission asked the nineteen theologians in their group to draw up what became in effect their final say, and it differed spectacularly from traditional teaching. The theologians concluded that contraception was not intrinsically immoral or a violation of natural law. They recommended "the regulation of conception by using human and decent means." Even this recommendation was not totally clear, because the group did not define what it meant by "human and decent" methods of birth control. What was more amazing was that the pope's own supercommittee of cardinals and bishops looked with some favor on the theologians' rather ambiguous recommendation, though with considerable reservations. (Archbishop Wojtyla was absent from that discussion.)

The commission concluded its work on June 28, 1966, when it handed its conclusions to Paul. The report offered the pope an easy way out. He could have declared that he had altered Church teaching on birth control as a result of the intensive work of dedicated experts, theologians, and members of the Church hierarchy. But he would not take the easy way.

On the other hand, the windup of the commission's work offered Paul the chance to bring his agonizing to an end by simply rejecting the conclusions and reaffirming traditional Church doctrine. Again, he made it harder for himself by doing more thinking. Almost incredibly, he asked for more information. He had his staff and close associates dig up for him the very latest information on contraceptive pills, including an advanced study that was being conducted at Ohio State University. He sought data on the population problem from points as diverse as the United States, France, and the Soviet Union.

Meanwhile, the pope was being buffeted from the Left and from the Right. Cardinal Ottaviani pulled together what he called a "minority report" of the commission and personally told the pope, "It is my duty to warn the Holy Father of the grave danger to Catholic doctrine." In more subtle fashion, the traditionalist view was supported by certain French intellectuals who for so long had influenced Paul's thinking: philosopher Jean Guitton, theologian Henri de Lubac, sociologist Paul Poupard. On the other side, powerful cardinals like Leo Joseph Suenens of Belgium and Julius Doepfner of Germany, old friends of the pope, weighed in with all their strength to persuade him to liberalize Church teaching. (Their only success was to persuade him to delay his decision even longer.)

While fundamentally committed to the traditionalist view, Paul obviously was shaken deeply by the strong arguments on the other side. During the long months of agonizing, he told an Italian visitor: "It is a strange subject for men of the Church to be discussing, even humanly embarrassing . . . and in deciding we are alone. We must say something—but what? God must truly enlighten us."

Altogether Paul hesitated for two full years after the commission handed him its report—two years in which the Catholic world was left in confusion on the subject, two years in which the pill became ever more widely diffused and increasing millions of Catholics began using it. More delays were caused by the pope's prostate operation in November 1966. At long last, the Rome corps of journalists was advised that on the morning of Monday, July 29, 1968, a news conference would be held in the press office of the Holy See to announce the papal verdict on birth control, in the form of the encyclical "Humanae Vitae." Until the press conference, the document was top secret, and the Vatican went to great lengths to make sure that it did not leak.

The document in fact did leak. On Friday before the Monday of the press conference, an unknown man dropped into the Rome bureau of *Time* magazine with a copy of the encyclical, which he offered for sale. Our bureau staff did a bit of discreet checking with the Vatican's Polyglot Press (where official documents always are printed) to make sure the item was genuine. We then offered the stranger 300,000 Italian lire (about $500 at the time), which he gladly took and scampered away. Who that person was we have no idea to this day, and yet his casual sale gave *Time* a spectacular exclusive. The magazine went to press Saturday night. On Sunday its promotion department issued a press release announcing the news, which would appear in detail in the weekly newsmagazine Monday morning. And so in that way the world learned that, as most newspapers headlined it, the pope had said no to the pill. He had taken a completely traditionalist position, rejecting all forms of artificial birth control.

John Paul's Decisiveness

If John Paul II had been involved instead of Paul VI, *Time* would have had no scoop because everybody in the world could have predicted his decision. The Polish pope is no hand-wringer or agonizer. On the surface, his decision-making recalls the spontaneity of John XXIII, but the resemblance is only superficial. Vatican official Monsignor Diarmuid Martin says John Paul's decision-making technique "is a mix between spontaneous ideas and concrete understanding. He has a much clearer vision of where he wants the Church to go than did John. He doesn't just open it up and let it roll as John did."

Memories of John's intuitiveness were evoked on January 25, 1985, when John Paul, in a speech at St. Paul's Outside-the-Walls, announced he was calling an extraordinary meeting of the World Synod of Bishops in November of that year, to mark the twentieth anniversary of the close of the Second Vatican Council. It was the same place where, exactly twenty-six years before, John had stunned his curia and the world with his announcement that he was summoning a council. John Paul's decision was equally surprising. He had not discussed the question officially with anyone. Only two days before the announcement, he had held a three-hour meeting with his curial team and had not mentioned a synod. Archbishop Jozef Tomko, who then was secretary-general of the World Synod of Bishops and the man who would have to organize the meeting, had learned of the plan from the pope only three days before.

As impetuous as the announcement seemed, a great deal had gone into John Paul's decision. It started when his Commission for Peace and Justice had proposed holding a seminar, in which the pope would participate, to discuss what had happened to the social message of the Church in the two decades since the council. Soon other curial departments were making similar proposals, each suggesting a specific conference or seminar to take a look at what had happened in its own field in those twenty years. The pope examined all these suggestions carefully and came up with his own decision, an extraordinary synod of bishops from all over the world which would wrap everything up in one meeting. One of his curial team explained: "In that short announcement at St. Paul's, John Paul included all the elements of what he expected the synod to do. He had a specific program in mind, but he had no idea of how it would be carried out. He left the mechanics of it to the synod secretariat. It was a very typical John Paul decision."

Since papal decisions are so important, obviously there is

tremendous pressure on the pope when a question is to be decided. Every day letters pour into the Vatican calling on the Holy See to take action on this or that problem. One of the great sources of such letters is the United States, with its tradition of "writing to your congressman." After John Paul was elected, a Polish-American priest in the Middle West organized a system of regularly sending by courier on Trans World Airlines packets full of documentation on the condition of the Church in the United States. When the packet reached Rome, it was taken by special arrangement immediately to the pope's secretary for transmission to the Holy Father. A high-ranking Vatican official explained "We have our faithful" around the world who regularly write the Vatican to call attention to special problems, "and most of them are laymen, not priests."

Letters that reach the pope normally are sent back to the Secretariat of State, from where they go to the curial department concerned. If the matter is of top priority to the pope, of course, he may act on the letter himself, but he usually prefers to hand ordinary problems to the congregation involved and to leave it entirely to that authority to handle. At times curial officials, assuming the pope was indifferent to a problem, have showed indifference themselves, only to be embarrassed some months later when he abruptly asked what they had done about it. He has a long memory.

One problem with all those letters that pour in from the United States is that the majority of them come from conservatives. A person who knows the Vatican very well says, "The liberals ignore Rome. It is the discontented conservatives who most often write to the Holy See. And many of them are right-wingers not only in religion but also in politics. They often go after religious liberals mainly because of their political liberalism."

Pope Paul was a man who always liked to have things written down and tried to keep track of every detail in the Vatican. John Paul prefers to deal through personal contacts, working out problems with those concerned, leaving it to them to come up with proposals, and then refining the solutions himself. He is a good questioner and a good listener, capable of soaking up massive amounts of detail in conversation. Before he made his 1979 trip to the United States, he missed no opportunity to discuss America with anyone informed on the subject. A few months before he made the trip, a Polish-American priest telephoned to the pope's secretary Monsignor Dziwisz to fill him in on Catholicism in the United States. As he finished the conversation, he said; "And please pass on my greetings to the Holy Father."

"The Holy Father is right here beside me," said Dziwisz. "Why don't you speak to him yourself?"

The priest found himself speaking to the pope, who grilled him on what was happening in the United States.

John Paul knows that he cannot make every decision for the Church and so he has developed his priorities. These priorities explain why he gets into some problems and leaves others to his curial team. He took upon himself the case of the four priests who disobeyed the Vatican by holding ministerial posts in the Sandinista government in Nicaragua. John Paul had become personally involved in the Nicaraguan case during his trip to Managua in March 1982, and so the problem of those priests in government was one he wanted to handle himself, and it was he who made the decision to defrock them.

Typical of John Paul's decision-making process was his handling of the revision of the Code of Canon Law. Work on the code began under John XXIII, who appointed the original commission in 1963. The group did not get down to serious deliberations till the end of the council, but in the following seventeen years they put in more than six thousand hours of work, involving fourteen subcommissions and at least one thousand experts. After John Paul was elected, he showed the same indifference to this commission as he had to that for reform of the curia. But it was a different story when the pope got the first draft of the new code in late 1981.

Once he had the draft in hand, John Paul moved in on the project with hurricane force. Overnight, the Code of Canon Law became papal priority number one. Although he knows Latin perfectly, the pope had a group of Polish experts translate the more technical passages into Polish to make doubly sure he understood the text perfectly. He formed his own team of half a dozen experts (not members of the original commission) to go through the draft, and he drove this team pitilessly, calling them in for daily meetings that dragged on for hours, often lasting through long working lunches. In a matter of weeks the pope had a document that he was ready to approve.

One of John Paul's most characteristic decisions was a very personal one, involving his own health. Because he gives high priority to taking the Christian message to the world in person, making direct contact with human beings everywhere, the pope faced the greatest crisis of his pontificate when he was hospitalized and unable to travel after the assassination attempt of May 1981. While still convalescent and partially incapacitated, the pope managed a few appearances at his balcony window, made a television broadcast to pilgrims at Lourdes, and delivered a major speech in St. Peter's Basilica. But for the most part he was restricted to reading documents and meeting with Casaroli and his other curial aides, almost in the manner of those earlier popes who had been "prisoners of the Vatican." That kind of paper-pushing, bureaucratic administration was not the style of the extroverted John Paul II.

The five-hour abdominal operation that saved the pope's life after the shooting left him with a temporary colostomy, which was to be reversed with a relatively simple operation a month later. In the meantime, John Paul developed a stubborn lung infection which so weakened him that he had to return to the hospital. Doctors began to speak of postponing that second operation for a few months. Rumors spread that the pope would never recover fully. The European press speculated that he might abdicate.

That was when John Paul took control. The pontiff demanded that a panel of physicians get together and decide when he could have that second operation. And he, the pope, insisted on sitting in on their conference, telling them, "I am the subject of this situation, not an object." For those conservative physicians, it was unthinkable that a patient should sit in on their consultations, but they couldn't argue with the pope and so agreed to have him present.

Eight of the nine doctors on the panel voted to postpone the operation for many weeks. Only one was ready to proceed at once. The pope himself made the final decision. He ordered the doctors to go ahead with the surgery immediately. He told them bluntly that he was not going to accept being "half-alive and half-dead," that he wanted a showdown with his health. The doctors operated.

His decisiveness paid off. Within a few weeks, John Paul was resuming a normal schedule. On November 22, 1981, he left the Vatican to visit Todi in Central Italy. The following February, he was in the air again, this time on a seven-day trip to Nigeria, Benin, Gabon, and Equatorial Guinea. And he has been traveling ever since.

5

PROPAGATING
THE MESSAGE

Papal Propaganda in the Past

The French revolutionary leader Jean Paul Marat was soaking in his bath on a July afternoon in 1793 when his servants rushed in to announce that a young woman had arrived to see him. She claimed to have information on a counterrevolutionary conspiracy. Marat told the servants to usher her into the bathroom. The woman, Charlotte Corday, entered the room, walked to the tub, and stabbed Marat in the heart.

Riders on fast post-horses set out from Paris at once to carry the story of the spectacular assassination to all the capitals of Europe. But the first European sovereign to get the news was Pope Pius VI in Rome.

The pope was informed so promptly because of a remarkable system of communications called the semaphore of the Holy See, set up by the papal superintendent of posts in the fifteenth century. It involved flashing messages from one hilltop to another with mirrors by day and flares by night, using a special code and spelling system. The semaphore served not only for ecclesiastical purposes but also for secular news. The pontifical "scoop" on the Marat killing, for example, was of tremendous value to a pope deeply concerned about the anticlerical revolution that had engulfed once Catholic France.

From its very beginnings, the Church has given high priority to communications. It is one of the prime duties of each pope to propagate the Christian message, and the way he does so is yet another reflection of the impact made on the office by the style and personality of each pontiff. Popes John, Paul, and John Paul all recognized the tremendous value of communicating, but they have communicated in vastly different ways. Pope John depended on his personal charisma for getting his message across and entirely neglected the Vatican's mass communications structures. Pope Paul put the emphasis on systems and organizations but was a weak communicator in person. Pope John Paul II combined aspects of both—he improved on the structures while demonstrating an incomparable ability to communicate through the impact of his personality.

The word "gospel" originally meant "good news"—news that was to be taken to all corners of the earth and preached to every creature. During the period of martyrdom in the first three centuries, Christians used symbols—like that of the fish, representing Christ—to maintain contact with each other. Umberto Eco, author of *The Name of the Rose* and probably the world's greatest expert on semiotics, once told me that the Gothic cathedral "was the pop art of the Middle Ages," speaking to an illiterate public with its soaring arches, its picture stories in stained-glass windows and frescoes, its dramatic and sometimes frightening sculpture. It was the Catholic Church that invented the word "propaganda"; in 1599 Pope Clement VIII established a congregation named De Propaganda Fide, for propagating the faith.

The Church today has the benefit of ultramodern media to get its message across. The late Archbishop Edward Heston, then the Vatican's top media man, commented to me: "The gospel first was spread by word of mouth, then by images, then the printed word. In modern times there came the radio and now television, cassettes, communications satellites. We have to adapt our 'preaching' to this era. We must understand that we now are dealing with a generation that cannot remember a world without television. There is a great and growing interest in what the Church is doing, and woe to us if we fail to realize it."

The Holy See indeed has managed to keep abreast of the times reasonably well with regard to technical developments in communications. In the nineteenth century, the telegraph replaced the mirrors and flares of the semaphore, and the papacy established its own daily newspaper and periodicals. No less a personage than Guglielmo Marconi, inventor of wireless transmission, in 1931 set up Vatican Radio, a powerful broadcasting system which today puts on the air 430 programs a week in 32 languages, reaching as far as the South Pacific. The Holy See does not operate a television station, but it does have a unit for producing TV films. There is a Vatican press office and a Pontifical Commission for Social Communications (the Holy See's term for mass media), headed by John Foley, the only archbishop to have graduated from the Columbia School of Journalism.

With all this technical progress, popes in recent centuries have often adopted a somewhat less than enlightened attitude toward the free flow of information. When the open-minded, forward-looking Pope John XXIII was elected, he found himself surrounded by Vatican officials who seemed still to suffer from the trauma of the French Revolution and the 1848 Republican uprisings and remained obsessed with fears of sedition, fears which in the past outweighed arguments for freedom of the press.

At one time the authorities of the Papal States imprisoned in the grim Castel Sant' Angelo on the Tiber anyone caught committing the crime of disseminating news. Through most of its history, in fact, the government of the Papal States was a tyranny, and it has been hard for entrenched powers in the Vatican to understand that the public today has to be persuaded rather than commanded. Until very recently, the Vatican attitude, basically, was to suppress news, or at very least to control it, rather than to encourage its free flow. The obsession with secrecy—often without any obvious purpose—has died hard in the Vatican.

Excessive papal secrecy once cost the Holy See a pile of money. Pope Leo XIII, toward the end of the nineteenth century, established the Vatican Bank, then known as the Administration for Religious Works, a highly secret organization that answered only to the pope. The bank was hidden away in an office called *il buco nero* (the black hole), so named because it formerly housed the headquarters of censorship of the Papal States. Even inside the Holy See few knew of the existence of the bank. It so happened that in 1900 Italian police were tipped off that there was about to be a major robbery at the Vatican and assigned special guards to all papal offices and buildings where money and valuables were kept. But no guards were put on *il buco nero* because even the police had not been told that the bank existed, and burglars easily carried off all the bank's liquid assets.

Some feeble attempts were made by twentieth-century popes before the council to set up an organized system of dealing with the mass media, but their efforts continued to reflect the old Papal States mentality. After Pius XII became pope, his undersecretary of state, Montini, persuaded him to open the first Vatican press office. It was located in a former tailor shop on the outer edge of Vatican City. Journalists accredited to the office were strictly forbidden to make any direct contact with offices inside the Roman Curia or to approach directly any resident of Vatican City. They had to depend entirely on briefings by a monsignor, who inevitably began with the phrase "Having gathered from the august lips of the Holy Father . . ." The old obsession with secrecy remained so deeply ingrained that even as late as the middle fifties a Vatican press officer was refusing to "reveal" to newsmen the number of audiences the pope had granted that year. As recently as the early years of the reign of John Paul II, a Vatican press officer avoided mingling with journalists because "they might ask some questions."

The difficulty of breaking through that kind of press setup was a challenge to journalists. Tom Morgan, a correspondent of

United Press during Pius's reign, beat the system by getting himself a top hat, frock coat, and pair of striped trousers, the costume of the typical diplomat of that time. When there was a big occasion at the Vatican to which (as usual) journalists were not invited, Morgan would don his diplomatic outfit and walk with determined strides right up to the line of gendarmes blocking the way of unauthorized persons. He always had a rather modest-looking little man follow behind him, and with an air of authority he would jerk a thumb back at the little man, bark to the gendarmes, "It's all right. He's with me!," and then stride right on through while the gendarmes saluted smartly and clicked their heels.

An even more remarkable bit of journalistic enterprise in the Pius era was dug up a few years ago by that tireless Vatican historian, Jesuit Father Robert Graham. For nearly a decade (1939 to 1948) an Italian journalist named Virgilio Scattolini made a steady income out of selling fake "exclusive" information about the Holy See to foreign journalists, embassies, and intelligence services. Scattolini simply sat in his apartment on Rome's Via Bocca di Leone and ground out such convincing imaginary news that for years his customers included both the Associated Press and the United Press, Goebbels's D.N.B., Japan's Domei, the old International News Service, and many leading newspapers. His false reports found their way not only into the world's press but also into the archives of many an embassy and government ministry. At least one of his fictitious "scoops" landed on the desk of Hitler himself. A Soviet agent in Switzerland sent the Scattolini dispatches to Moscow via a clandestine radio transmitter. Had the Holy See been more open with its information, the Scattolini fake news could not have been fed to the world.

Pope John—the Impact of Personal Goodness

Even after the election of the tolerant and forward-looking Pope John XXIII, the Vatican's public relations system showed little improvement. On the eve of the historic Second Vatican Council, a Holy See official wrote to a Paris journalist, "We don't need the press." Robert Kaiser, in his book *Inside the Council* (written in early 1963), complained: "Since the Reformation, since Trent, the curial mind had developed some strange mental quirks that could best be called totalitarian, obscurantist, closed. They are now largely unconscious in the average curial mind, but they are nonetheless real."

Though he was a great communicator in direct personal contact, Pope John did not even try seriously to combat those "strange mental quirks" in the curia that he inherited when he became pope. This jovial old man could work only on a personal, unofficial basis, depending on his instincts more than on organization. He was so inept an administrator, so incapable of working through tightly organized structures, that he made no real effort to overhaul the Holy See's public relations machinery. His failure to meet the needs of the modern media contributed to a lasting distortion of the first session of the Vatican Council in the eyes of much of the world.

Hundreds of newsmen from all over the world poured into Rome to cover the council when Pope John inaugurated it in the autumn of 1962. This was an unprecedented opportunity for the Church to send its message to all the earth, but instead, officials at the Vatican acted as if the council were their private affair. Pope John left media arrangements in the hands of the secretary-general of the council, Archbishop Pericle Felici, an old-school curial functionary who was aligned with the Ottaviani clique. Felici did his best to keep the world in the dark about the council. He issued regulations forbidding newsmen to enter Vatican offices or to talk with Vatican officials or employees without special permission from proper authorities.

Newsmen were barred from council debates and were expected to depend for information on a bland daily communiqué written by Monsignor Fausto Vallainc, head of the council press office. Officers who briefed the various groups set up on the basis of language had strict orders to translate only what Vallainc had written and to say nothing more. This daily handout faithfully reported exactly who enthroned the Book of the Gospels on the altar each day and announced exciting news such as: "The Pontifical Commission for Vatican City will distribute to each council father an envelope containing a card indicating postal and telegraph rates to all the nations of the world and also two series of stamps issued on the occasion of the council's inauguration, one already canceled, the other new." The daily Vallainc bulletin carefully concealed the fact that behind the High Renaissance façade of St. Peter's a historic confrontation between conservatives and liberals of the Catholic Church was taking place.

While the conservatives thought they were keeping a lid on news of the council, they were in fact playing into the hands of the liberals. Newsmen soon learned that the liberals would speak to them, and unofficial press offices and briefing panels popped up all around Rome. Briefings and background interviews were easy to get from liberal cardinals like Suenens and Koenig and Alfrink or from the theological experts brought into the council by Pope John. Because the news was filtered through the opinions and hopes of the liberals, the media by and large got a much too optimistic view of what the council was doing. From those briefings by liberals, one would have thought the council would produce radical changes in Church teaching on birth control, abortion, papal elections, papal powers. When these things did not happen—because a majority of the council fathers never intended to go that far—Catholic liberals complained that a conservative clique in the Vatican had "turned back the clock."

While Pope John can be faulted for thus neglecting the structures of Vatican public relations, there is no doubt that he introduced a dramatically new style in papal communications. The old pontiff communicated mainly through his personal image, an image of goodness and love, which was refreshing in a world that still remembered the horrors of two world wars and the ominous threat posed by the Cold War. Instead of relying on Vatican public relations machinery, he depended on the world's secular media to report his acts of humanity, whether he was exchanging birthday greetings with a Soviet leader or welcoming a Jewish delegation to the Vatican. Through acts of warmth and friendliness, John sent waves of good will throughout the world, as far as Moscow, the Bible Belt of the American South, and black Africa.

Pope John ended the concept of the pope as a "prisoner of the Vatican" that had been inaugurated by Pius IX in 1870 and instead went out to the people. The vast difference between John and his immediate predecessor, Pius XII, can be seen in a simple thing like the speed of their motorcades. On the rare occasions when Pius XII left the Vatican, his automobile raced so fast through the streets that the public got only a blurred glimpse of the pope, and many who saw him were not even aware it was the Holy Father. To Pius XII, traveling by automobile was a matter of moving from one point to another; it simply never occurred to him to use the occasion to communicate with the masses. When John circulated around Rome, he insisted on going at a slow pace so that he could catch the eye of bystanders, wave to them, hear their shouts, laugh with them. Now and then he would stop the car, hop out, and walk along the streets, patting children on the head and embracing the elderly. He won the nickname Johnnie Walker because of his habit of going out to visit those who might need help—to hospitals, schools, prisons.

The Old Guard in the Vatican was shocked at John's behavior and argued that it would be more in keeping with papal dignity for him to wait in the Vatican for the public to come to him, to attend his weekly audiences. The old pope replied: "How can a man in jail come to my audience? How can an invalid in a hospital come to the Vatican? Since they cannot come to me, I must go to them!"

On Christmas Day, 1962, "Johnnie Walker" turned up at the children's hospital Bambino Gesù on Rome's Janiculum Hill, his first visit outside the Vatican after a severe illness. He made it a point to speak to each sick child in turn, and he spoke in a folksy way of his own sickness, telling one of the children, "Oh, I am not yet ready to run any races, but all in all I am feeling well."

John was the first pope in modern times to visit a prison. He made history by embracing and kissing on both cheeks a man serving a sentence for murder. It was a totally human gesture of Christian love, done without preaching or lecturing. Of course, it was not possible for John to visit every convict in the world, or to call on every orphan or hospital patient. But the shrewd old pontiff knew that each time he made such a symbolic visit it would be covered thoroughly by the secular news media, and prisoners and invalids all over the world would see it on television or read about it and might be reminded of Christ's words "I was sick and you visited me; I was in prison and you came to me."

In mingling informally with people, Pope John communicated a message of humility and apostolic simplicity aimed at erasing the image of the "imperial papacy." Until his day, the office maintained some of the pomp and ceremony of the Caesars. John deliberately removed the crosses embroidered on his slippers as a way of discouraging the old habit of many faithful of kissing the papal feet. He showed obvious irritation when overzealous Catholics insisted on kneeling in his presence. A devout editor at the Vatican daily, *L'Osservatore Romano,* used to drop to his knees when the pope spoke to him on the phone. I once watched an incredible scene when Pope John was doing one of his walks, followed by journalists. Each time he paused and began to say something, the *L'Osservatore* editor would drop to his knees while taking notes, and John would reach over, take him by the shoulder, and lift him to his feet. Then he would turn away to speak to someone else, and while he was not looking, the editor would again drop to his knees. When the pope looked back, he repeated the exercise of reaching down to lift the man up to his feet again.

Pope John not only took his message of humanity and warmth to the people in the streets and prisons and hospitals of Rome; he also became the first pope since 1870 to visit the small towns and the countryside of Italy. On October 4, 1962, John made a whistle-stop trip from Rome to Assisi, the home of St. Francis, and Loreto, one of the most beloved Marian shrines in the country. He thus became the first pope in the twentieth century to travel by train.

The first pope ever to ride a train was Pius IX; in 1860 he inaugurated a new Vatican railway by traveling from Rome to Civitavecchia in a special, luxurious papal coach. On that trip, Pius IX rode in the style of a European monarch. Pope John made his train trip as a pilgrim.

Pius IX reigned over a temporal kingdom that still covered much of central Italy. Pope John's "kingdom" was reduced to the 108.7 acres of the State of Vatican City. His state was too small to have a railway system, but it had a railway station, its rails linked to the Italian state railroads. The station is still used regularly, though normally not for passengers. Twice a day, a massive gate in the Vatican walls is opened to admit a freight train, which brings supplies of food, mail, and other necessities into the world's smallest sovereign state. When John took his trip to Loreto, the Italian state railways provided a train, which backed into the Vatican station to pick him up.

Pope John opted to take the train on his pilgrimage because it gave him maximum opportunity to make contact with the people along the entire route. He insisted that the train stop at every station on the way, where he would stand on the rear platform and talk and joke with the public. It was an era before international terrorism had spread over the world, and security was lax enough so that the pope easily could lean over to pat children on the head or to embrace the elderly or infirm.

Watching the pope on those whistle-stops gave you a full understanding of his way of communicating. He was not a great orator, nor did he try to be. He was not expert in the technique of handling a large crowd. He didn't know how to exploit applause and sometimes appeared even a bit bewildered or disturbed by it (in contrast with John Paul II, whom I have seen encouraging applause with a subtle wave of his hand while delivering a speech). On that train trip John didn't work from a prepared text and did not try to deliver a profound message. His message was himself, his humanity and his warmth, goodness and love. He would ramble along, but he rambled in such good humor that the crowds invariably loved it. It was not what he said but what he was that charmed them, his personality, his charisma. At one point the train started to pull out of the station while he was still talking. With a wide-mouthed laugh and good-natured wave, he shouted back to the crowd, "On a train, there is only one pope—the man with his hand on the throttle!"

That show of papal humor went a long way to compensate for John's failure to set up a proper Vatican press office.

Pope Paul Modernizes the Structures

Ever eager to improve the organization, the superbureaucrat Pope Paul presided over a major evolution in the Church's relations with the mass media. But he sadly lacked Pope John's ability to communicate as a person. He never mastered the art of personally stirring the masses.

Pope Paul could not project his finer qualities perhaps because he could not love a faceless mass labeled "humanity." Pope John could just love everybody, even those he didn't know. Paul could respond only to individuals. He was at his best in what Italians call *a quattr'occhi* ("four eyes"), a one-on-one encounter. More than any other recent pope, Paul was a man who treasured individual human relationships and deep, abiding friendships, so much so that his associates sometimes accused him of practicing "the cult of friendship." He was a brilliant conversationalist with persons who stimulated him, but he had to know them as individual human beings, not just as an anonymous segment of the human race. Partly because of this he often came across before large crowds as what one American woman called "a blah personality." He also lacked the physical attributes for projecting to a crowd. Slightly built (five feet ten inches, 154 pounds), he had a weak voice that sounded like that of an old woman when he read a speech. When he waved to a crowd his arm looked like the fin of a fish fluttering in water.

Although he was a sincere liberal with an anti-Fascist background, Paul had to struggle with himself to overcome a longtime mistrust of the mass media. Even for him, it was hard to accept the modern concept of a press that publishes both sides of issues, that claims the right to criticize even the most sacrosanct people and concepts.

Often, in speaking to journalists, Pope Paul would remind them that he understood their problems because "I am the son of a journalist." (His father founded and edited the Catholic newspaper *Il Cittadino.*) But he had to struggle within himself against the old Vatican attitude of "help us win our case"—a deeply rooted view that newsmen should print only the "truth," which meant the Vatican viewpoint; anything else was considered immoral. The normally gentle Paul sometimes lost his temper when the press published things he didn't like. At a general audience in April 1970, he denounced Italian newspapers as "no longer journals of information but of defamation" because in their coverage of his trip to Sardinia they reported that protestors had thrown rocks at the papal motorcade. In September 1971, he publicly attacked RAI, the Italian state radio-television network, for presenting a program on the priesthood featuring a debate between Father Ernesto Balducci, a critic of the Church position on priestly celibacy, and Paul's close friend Jesuit Father Jean Danielou. Instead of showing appreciation that Danielou had been allowed to have his say, the pope was furious that the "opposition" had been given equal time.

The pope's worries about the press no doubt were provoked to some extent by his alarmist right-hand man, Archbishop Benelli. As late as 1969, the Holy See press office ruled that Vatican press cards would be withdrawn from any journalists who showed "an incorrect attitude toward the Holy See." An official in the press office told me at the time that this rule had been inserted on orders of Benelli, who "believes journalists should be handled more strictly than in the past . . . because today the journalists try to write like theologians."

But despite his reservations about the media, Paul introduced a new and enlightened Vatican policy toward the press. The change began to be noticed as soon as Paul took over the Vatican Council in the autumn of 1963. Archbishop Felici still tried to keep the lid on, but it no longer was possible. Encouraged by Pope Paul himself, a square-jawed American priest from Ohio, Father Edward Heston, acted as English-language briefing officer at the second session of the council and opened things up. The Felici rules forbade his identifying speakers but allowed him to mention topics discussed. Heston began numbering the bishops who had spoken that day and numbering, paragraph by paragraph, the material discussed. Newsmen soon learned that by matching the number of the speaker to the number of the paragraph, they could tell what each bishop had said. For the first time, the media were getting an official account of debates and disagreements within the council.

The pope personally called in Father Heston to encourage him to open up more to the press. When Heston mentioned that conservative Felici had scolded him for going beyond the rules, the pope told him to ignore Felici. Then, slapping his desk with his right hand, the pope almost shouted; "And if you have any more problems, come to me!"

After the council, Pope Paul established a Pontifical Commission for Social Communications, whose aim was not only to help the Holy See in propagating its message but also to guide bishops' conferences around the world to establish their own structures for public relations. Significantly, Paul named as president of the commission none other than Father Edward Heston.

Another structural innovation was setting up a proper Vatican press office. Admittedly, this office functioned with almost ludicrous incompetence in its early years. Head of it was Monsignor Fausto Vallainc, and his usual procedure was to meet the press each Friday, write down whatever questions newsmen asked, and promise to deliver the answer the following Friday, exactly one week later. A great deal of the time, the answer was "no comment." Vallainc had to struggle with many layers of heavy-handed bureaucracy between him and the pope, and most of those old bureaucrats still believed that Vatican affairs were none of the media's business. But it was a beginning, and over the years, sometimes by trial and error, the Holy See's press relations have improved to the point of matching those of most modern governments.

Vatican media men have learned, often through bitter experience, that it is impossible to suppress news, that it is far better to release it themselves than to have it come out from other sources in distorted form. At one time certain Vatican functionaries augmented their meager salaries by selling to newsmen purloined "top secret" documents of the Holy See. That problem was solved when the Vatican press office learned the system of releasing documents to the press in advance, for publication on an agreed date.

It was Pope Paul who promulgated an extremely progressive document laying out the Church's policies toward the media. Drawn up by his newly established Commission for Social Communications in response to a council directive, the document, issued in June 1971, included statements such as "If public opinion is to be formed in a proper manner, it is necessary that ... the public be given free access to both the sources and channels of information and be allowed freely to express its own views." As *Time* magazine observed at the time: "About three centuries after the concept of a free press was first postulated, the Vatican got around to endorsing it."

Perhaps Paul's greatest contribution to papal communications was the introduction of international travel as a pontifical pastoral activity. Although Pope John broke out of the "prison" of the Vatican, he was too old, too ill, and too preoccupied with the council to travel abroad. That was left to his successor, whose choice of the name Paul implied that he would be an apostle on the move, following the example of Saint Paul, who traveled all over the Mediterranean world to take the Christian message to all cultures.

International travel is a highly effective form of papal communication because, as Pope Paul well knew, when a pope travels abroad, his every move and every utterance are carried around the world by the mass media. While it is true that in the centuries after Peter established his See in Rome popes traveled a great deal, they usually did so for purposes other than communication with the people. Pius IX fled from Rome during the republican revolution of 1848 and stayed in exile until the revolution was crushed in 1850. When Napoleon's army invaded Italy, the French carried Pius VI away by force and kept him in France till he died. In the sixteenth century, the pope-soldier Julius II traveled at the head of his army to conquer Bologna, and in the fourteenth century, because of fears of the hostile Roman nobility, Pope Clement V moved from Rome to Avignon, where popes kept their headquarters for seventy years. When Constantinople was still considered the capital of the Roman Empire, popes often traveled there from Rome to confer with the emperor or to be confirmed by him. But the concept of papal travel as a means of meeting the people and reaching out to the world is a totally new idea.

It was in his speech closing the 1963 session of the council, less than six months after his election, that Paul announced his historic first trip abroad. As he began his discourse, texts were made available to the press. I had agreed to cover the closing session for Voice of America that day, and the text of my broadcast was to be translated into several Eastern European languages for voicing by correspondents from those countries. We were pressed for time, and so I did my broadcast from the advance text, followed by half a dozen correspondents in their languages. After we had recorded and transmitted all those reports to VOA headquarters in Munich, I casually took a look at the Italian news agency ticker—and turned pale. We had missed the big news of the day. Pope Paul had read another page, appended to the text of his speech but not previously distributed to the press, announcing that he planned a trip to the Holy Land on January 6, 1964. In early January he was fastening his seat belt in response to instructions from an Alitalia hostess, the first pope in history to fly.

The public by now has become so accustomed to watching television reports of popes visiting aborigines in Africa or meeting heads of state in India that it is hard to understand what a revolutionary decision Paul announced when he revealed his plan to travel. After all the decades during which popes had remained almost cloistered in the Vatican, the Supreme Pastor of the church would be jetting around the world.

Papal travel very quickly came under criticism, of course. It was inevitable that some would complain about the cost of such trips, that many would argue it would be better to distribute the money to the poor (without stopping to consider that the money would not be distributed to the poor if the pope didn't travel). It is a fact that trips by popes are expensive, sometimes running into many millions of dollars for a single voyage, but the cost to the Vatican itself is minimal. To carry the pontiff, the Holy See charters an airliner (normally Alitalia going and a local airline coming back), but the sixty or so media correspondents and cameramen aboard pay their own way and thus absorb much of the cost of the aircraft. Most other expenses are borne by the host countries, often with local governments paying for special security and logistics and the local church picking up the tab for the specifically religious arrangements. This expense is paid voluntarily by those who have invited him and often begged him to come to their country. As a Catholic layman told me while we looked out over a crowd of several hundred thousand at a papal rally on the island of Cebu in the Philippines, "It is cheaper to bring the pope here than to take all these people to Rome to see him!"

Vatican diplomats and local bishops worry about the diplomatic problems that papal voyages often create. Pope Paul had to walk a razor's edge diplomatically when he visited the Holy Land in 1964, because at the time Jerusalem was still divided between Israel and Jordan. The people of Portugal were furious when Pope Paul announced he was going to India in 1964, because only three years earlier the Indians had invaded the Portuguese colony of Goa and annexed it. To show their resentment of the trip, the Portuguese press did not print a word about it. Even the Catholic media in Portugal "boycotted" the pontifical voyage.

The personal security of the pope is another problem created by travel. The papal cloak of holiness does not protect the pope from assassination attempts or terrorism, and there inevitably is a tug of war between security men who try to build a wall around him, and the pope, who insists on getting as close to the people as possible. Experience has shown that no security arrangements can guarantee papal safety. Security men are human and can never close all the loopholes. I was horrified at lax security on a papal trip to Libreville, Gabon. While the pope was making his farewell speech at the airport before departure, what looked like a whole army of police and plainclothesmen swarmed all over the airport and the departure terminal, watching from towers and balconies all around. But nobody was looking while sixty newsmen climbed onto the papal plane without being checked. They didn't collect our boarding cards, didn't inspect the hand luggage (and some networks men have baggage big enough to hold a Kalashnikov), didn't even count us. An armed terrorist could easily have gotten onto that aircraft and hijacked the pontifical plane.

In Manila in 1970, an embittered Bolivian artist narrowly missed killing Pope Paul in what was essentially an insane and totally unpredictable act. Before Paul's trip to India in 1964, the government had to arrest leaders of the Mahasaba Hindu sect because they had threatened demonstrations against the "leader of the alien, Western religion." (They were released on the personal intervention of the pope.)

Sometimes the pope is endangered not because of hatred or terrorism but because of the excessive enthusiasm of his audience. A mob in Jerusalem almost killed Pope Paul out of sheer joy. Paul had planned to follow the steps of Christ along the Via Dolorosa in Old Jerusalem (then under Jordanian sovereignty) and to pause to pray at each of the fourteen Stations of the Cross. As soon as the slightly built, simply clad pope entered the Old City, pandemonium broke loose. At least a hundred thousand screaming Arabs swarmed into the narrow, flagstoned Via Dolorosa, chanting "El baba! El baba!" ("The pope! The pope!"), and fought tooth and claw to get close enough to touch him. Even some Muslim policemen left their posts and plunged into the crowd to reach the holy man. Cardinal Eugene Tisserant, a member of the papal suite, was shoved to one side. When he tried to force his way back to the pope, shouting to a policeman, "I am a cardinal! I am a cardinal!," the policeman replied by hitting him across the head with a bamboo truncheon. Jordan's King Hussein hovered over the mob in his personal helicopter, trying to direct a restoration of order. The pope was pushed back and forth, twice stumbled, and would have fallen had there been space to fall. Arab policemen saved him only by grabbing him by the arms on either side and frog-marching him to safety. The pope was lucky to come out of that ordeal alive.

Given all the dangers and complications involved in Pope Paul's travels, the question naturally arose as to whether it was worthwhile. In fact, people can get a better look at the pope on television than from the far edge of a crowd. So why not depend simply on TV to project the message to the world?

The answer is that the message gets across better when delivered on the spot. I remember an early morning in 1970 when Paul's aircraft moved across the broad blue Pacific Ocean and the feeling I had when at last we sighted our destination—the little speck of land called Samoa. I wondered why a pope would take the trouble to fly halfway around the globe to land at such a remote spot with its tiny Catholic community. When the same question was raised by his staff, Paul answered, "I want to show the world that the pope cares about people no matter how far away they are, no matter how isolated and lonely they may be."

Paul communicated an ecumenical message on the Mount of Olives during his visit to Jerusalem. The ecumenical patriarch of the Eastern Orthodox Church, Athenagoras, met Paul there, and the two exchanged a historic "kiss of peace"; it was the first meeting between pope and patriarch in many centuries. In Medellín, Colombia, in 1968, Paul delivered a speech on human rights and social justice that became almost a charter for advocates of liberation theology in Latin America. Had he delivered the same speech back in Rome, it would not have had such a direct application to Latin America.

Apart from communicating these specific ideas, Paul's trips

demonstrated that there are some things that television cannot do. To hundreds of millions of people around the world, there is a value beyond logical explanation in being physically in the presence of the living, breathing pope. Though Pope Paul was lacking in charisma, still he was a "holy man" and the mere fact of his presence triggered an incredible response from crowds in the Third World.

I remember once in Manila looking from a point behind the papal altar at a crowd in an open park stretching out almost as far as the eye could see. There were perhaps a million people in that audience, and to someone out there on the very edge of the crowd the pope would be only a tiny spot of white. Why did that person bother to come there and stand for hours through the ceremony? He or she could have seen it all, and much more clearly, on television. Obviously it was tremendously important to be in the physical presence of the pope, to receive a special blessing of a kind that cannot be transmitted over the ether waves. I thought of those crowds in the New Testament who struggled to get to Jesus, to touch the hem of his garment or at least to see him.

The episode on the Via Dolorosa reminded me of the Arab concept of *baraka*, an untranslatable word that refers to a special aura that holy men—of any religion—have about them, an aura that transmits a blessing to those in their presence. A pope has *baraka*, and the blessing can be transmitted to Muslims or Hindus or unbelievers as well as to Christians. It was significant that in that mob scene on the Via Dolorosa, tens of thousands of those fighting to touch the hem of the papal garment were Muslims. A pope who was not naturally gifted in dealing with the public thus found in papal travel a great vehicle for reaching people.

John Paul II, the Great Communicator

By a remarkable turn of the "papal tombola," the man who found it hard to communicate was succeeded by the greatest communicator of them all. Whether with a turn of phrase or a deft gesture before a crowd of a million, or with a touch of the hand or pat on the shoulder in a personal meeting, Pope John Paul II projects his message more powerfully than any other public figure I have encountered in all my years as an international journalist.

The Jesuit Avery Dulles has written a book entitled *The Church Is Communications.* You could almost say that John Paul II is communications. He combines the personal charisma of John XXIII with the organizational shrewdness of Paul VI. He has greatly improved the public relations structures he inherited from his predecessor. He brought into the Commission for Social Communications and the Vatican press office a real professionalism. As president of the commission he named Archbishop John Foley, who had spent most of his career practicing journalism. As head of the press office—and, in effect, the Vatican spokesman—he appointed Joaquín Navarro-Valls, a Spanish correspondent who for many years had worked shoulder-to-shoulder with his colleagues in the Rome press corps and understood fully the needs of the modern mass media. John Paul also set up a Vatican television unit, which supplies film to the secular networks. The pope works closely with these elements in his tireless campaign to spread the Christian message, a campaign in which his own theatrical talents and personal charisma are the centerpiece.

John Paul's skill as a communicator is enhanced by a remarkable gift for languages. When he mingles with the international press on papal flights, I have watched him hear and respond to complicated questions in Polish, English, Italian, French, German, and Spanish with ease and fluency. It is impossible to say how many languages this pope knows, because he is almost always in the process of learning a new one.

Before traveling to Mexico in 1979, the pope for many weeks spent an hour every morning improving his Spanish. When preparing for his trip to Papua New Guinea in 1984, he enlisted two Divine Word missionaries to teach him enough Pidgin to utter some phrases of greeting to the indigenous population. Before going to Japan, the pope engaged a Japanese Franciscan, Father Nishiyama, to tutor him in the Japanese language and to draft his speeches in Japanese (though in the Latin alphabet). For many weeks before the trip, the pope said his early morning masses in Japanese, usually with some Japanese nuns participating. Before his trip to Guam in 1981, John Paul spent many hours listening to tape recordings of greetings in Chamorro, the local language; in Guam he pronounced the phrases so well that an amazed Guamanian remarked, "His Chamorro is better than his English!"

In addition to his deft handling of words, this pope has a very special knack for symbolic action. I have seen him don a wolverine parka and ride a dogsled across the snow in Alaska. I have seen him establish rapport with crowds by putting on Indian headdress, Mexican sombreroes, workers' hard hats. And there was that unforgettable scene when John Paul danced in Africa. We had flown over the vast rain forest of the Congo basin, a jungle untamed by man, to land at the upriver town of Kisangani. Awaiting the pope was a band beating out Christian hymns to African rhythms while two lines of beautiful girls in green-and-golden garments swayed back and forth and sang. When the door of the plane opened and the pope surveyed the scene, he succumbed to the magic and instantly made contact with the crowd as he, the successor to Peter, began to swing and sway the African way.

In the conservative atmosphere of Rome, not surprisingly, some are disturbed at what they call the "exhibitionism" of this Polish pope, his "showmanship" and artful use of the media. Defenders of John Paul reply that he considers his theatrical talent a charism, a special gift from God, which he believes he must use to the maximum to communicate the Christian message. As a high school student back in Poland, young Karol Wojtyla developed a passion for the theater. He became producer and lead actor with a high school troupe that toured southern Poland, staging modern Polish plays and Shakespearean drama. Later, during the German occupation, Karol organized an underground group, called the Rhapsody Theater, which featured anti-Nazi dramas and appealed to Polish patriotism.

This love for the theater stayed with Wojtyla even after he entered the priesthood. In 1960, when he was already auxiliary bishop of Kraków, he wrote and published (under the pseudonym

Andrzej Jawien) a drama on married love called *The Goldsmith's Shop*. First published in the Polish Catholic monthly *Znak*, the play was shown in 1979 on Italian television.

With that theatrical background, it is no wonder that this actor-pope is at his best when he stands before a crowd. I will never forget a day in Brazil when he mounted the platform of the altar before a crowd of more than a million. He walked slowly but deliberately to the far right corner to look at the people in that direction, lifting his hand as if to wave or give a benediction, a subtle smile playing about his lips, his eyes almost squinting but at the same time twinkling. He touched off an explosion of applause on that side of the audience. John Paul then moved slowly around the platform, reaching out with eyes and smile to those in front of him, and the applause followed his eye contact like waves in the wake of a ship. By the time he had turned to the far left, the entire crowd was cheering, chanting, clapping, and singing. Then the pope stepped to the microphone to call out "Silenzio!" and a million people became quiet.

Jesuit father John Navone, a theologian who has lived in Rome nearly a quarter of a century, once sat at his typewriter and without preparation jotted down a set of notes that aptly describe John Paul's style of communicating: "Extrovert—social—a mixer. Natural habitat the stage. People-oriented. Thrives on improvisation. Much eye contact. Feedback—essential for every good actor's performance. At home with feedback as constitutive of life. Thrives on its challenge."

Response from his audience is so important to John Paul that when he delivers a speech on television, with only the camera in front of him, he is not effective. And this explains why he has traveled all over the globe, to establish eye contact with Eskimos and black Africans and Argentines and Filipinos.

John Paul has experienced many times a kind of crowd ecstasy, mobs numbering in the hundreds of thousands pressing through security lines to touch the pope. After moving through a mass audience in Kaduna, Nigeria, in 1982, John Paul told a congregation in a small church: "Before I begin this heavy speech"—and he lifted the manuscript with both hands to show that it indeed was heavy—"I must tell you of a dream I had. I dreamed I was back in Rome, and Saint Peter asked me where I had been. I told him I had been to Nigeria, but he would not believe me—until I showed him the dirt on the sleeves of my cassock."

And he lifted both arms to show how his white sleeves had been smeared almost black by the many dusty hands that had touched him that day.

On that day in Kaduna, a Nigerian journalist explained to me why the crowd was so enthusiastic: "To many of our people, the pope is a spiritual figure who lives in Heaven and comes down to earth in Rome every day to perform his work. Just think what it means to them to see him in real life, to understand that he is a real person who cares enough to come to see them."

To John Paul, an international trip is an indispensable technique for communicating. Pope Paul's travels abroad were largely symbolic. He made nine trips in his fifteen-year reign, and most of them had a single destination. But John Paul wants to get as deeply involved in Church problems at the local level as possible. He makes an average of four international trips a year, and by the time he had been pope seven years he had traveled the equivalent of going to the moon and back. Whereas Paul would fly to Bombay and return, a one-point trip, John Paul would visit fourteen cities in ten days in Spain, or thirteen cities in a twelve-day trip to Brazil. He tries on each trip to deliver a message with a universal meaning but with a very precise local application.

The former actor from Poland stages his trips like a master theater director. He first softens up his audience with seemingly spontaneous touches of personal warmth and good humor. At Shea Stadium in New York he broke up the crowd when with mock seriousness he began his speech: "Anyone visiting New York cannot fail to be impressed!" A long pause. Then: "Sky—scrappers!"

Anyone who has watched this pope's trips on television is familiar with his use of kissing to establish rapport with crowds, whether it is kissing the ground as soon as he gets off the plane or kissing babies or girls or men. He shows great tenderness when a toddler wanders away from his parents to the papal feet—he picks up the little fellow, tosses him in the air, gives him a kiss, and hands him back to his mamma. I have seen women weep at the sight of the pope kissing their babies. But he doesn't discriminate against those a bit older. In Częstochowa, Poland, a choir of teenage girls entertained John Paul with a concert, and he rewarded each of them with a peck on the cheek. In Kraków, where he spent so many years as bishop, I saw John Paul throw his arms around priests who were his old friends, sometimes good-naturedly roughing them up a bit and planting a kiss on the scalp.

There were fears that the kissing habit would cause complications in Japan. Priests and bishops on the scene warned the pope ahead of time that it would be better not to kiss the ground at Tokyo airport or to kiss Japanese babies, acts that would offend the Japanese concept of hygiene. But when the pope arrived in Tokyo on a cold, wet day, he knelt and kissed the soggy tarmac, and wherever he went he reached out to pick up little Japanese children and give them his usual tender kiss. A Jesuit with long experience in Japan told me, "To my amazement, the people seemed to love it."

Let's face it. Sometimes the show of warmth and humanity is not entirely spontaneous. As the shadow of terrorism becomes ever more threatening, security demands make it increasingly hard for the pope to reach out to the crowds as he would like to do. And so, if necessary, he stages it. Only two days after a deranged priest tried to kill him in Fátima, Portugal, John Paul frightened the public with his seeming disregard of security in the agricultural area of Vila Viçosa, about a hundred miles east of Lisbon. As he walked down a long path, the pope was tightly protected by cordons of police standing shoulder-to-shoulder on either side of his path. All of a sudden the charismatic pope turned to the right, broke through the cordon and began to shake the hands of peasants in the nearby field. Soon it looked as if he were immersed in peasants and security had broken down. It was only much later that I learned from security sources that this little incident had been carefully planned and coordinated with the police. A similarly staged incident took place the following day in Oporto, when the pope broke through a police cordon to kiss a paralytic child in a wheelchair.

There was also a bit of staging during a youth rally for the pope in Tokyo. As John Paul sat in an armchair on the stage, a group of little Japanese girls—surely the sweetest that God ever created—dressed in Polish costumes sang Polish songs and did Polish folk dances for their visitor. As they danced, two of the little girls abruptly broke ranks and, holding hands, timidly approached the pope to ask, "Won't you come and dance with us?" The pope looked surprised, seemed to hesitate, and then, with a shrug of the shoulders and a broad grin took one of the little things by the hand and walked into their circle, and they danced around him. It was indeed a touching scene.

It just happened that I was present in that same hall a few hours earlier as the little girls were rehearsing. An old American Jesuit sat in the armchair as a stand-in for the pontiff. While the girls were dancing, two of them broke ranks and, holding hands, timidly approached the old Jesuit to ask, "Won't you come and dance with us?" The stand-in looked surprised, seemed to hesitate, then shrugged his shoulders and stepped into the circle while the children danced around him. . . .

This may be a bit disappointing, but again, it is John Paul using his theatrical gifts to the full to communicate a message. Sometimes he uses the technique of repeating words or phrases that have a special meaning in the country he is visiting, and linking his message to those phrases. In France, he spoke of "Liberté, Egalité, Fraternité" and called them Christian virtues. In his trip to Latin America in early 1985, he preempted the advocates of liberation theology by peppering his speeches with words like "liberation" and phrases like "the option for the poor," which are part of the vocabulary of liberation theologians. It took vast courage for a pope to denounce birth control in Bombay, one of the world's most overpopulated cities; but he tried to make the message palatable by quoting Gandhi and the Indian Nobel Prize-winning poet Rabindranath Tagore. One of his strongest denunciations of the nuclear arms race was delivered in Hiroshima, in the presence of many who still suffered the physical effects of the first atom bombing.

John Paul had to travel to the United States to convince Americans that he was a traditionalist in doctrine, and an uncompromising traditionalist at that. Before he visited the United States in October 1979, his image in the media was dominated by his humor and his warm, informal personality. Somehow vast numbers of American Catholics assumed that his informal style implied that he was "easy" on Church doctrine and discipline, a kind of indulgent uncle who would overlook deviations from Church teaching. Many Americans had come to believe that it was only their own mossback, old-fashioned bishops who were holding the Church to a conservative line. The pope disabused them of such notions, beyond the shadow of a doubt, in a speech to American bishops in Chicago. He demonstrated his full support of the conservative bishops by building his speech around a pastoral letter, "To Live in Christ Jesus," which the U.S. Bishops' Conference had issued three years earlier. The pope quoted the bishops on almost every point of Church moral teaching that he brought up—divorce, abortion, permissive sex—and supported an unmitigated traditionalist line on every issue. He had said the same things many times before in Rome, but somehow it didn't get across to the American public until he stood among them.

Because of his strong attacks on the Marxist variety of liberation theology in Latin America, the pope often is thought to be a supporter of reactionary regimes in Central and South America. But during his visit to Brazil in 1980, he made clear that he strongly endorsed social involvement by militant Catholics. He got the message across by his acts more than by his words. In an emotion-filled moment in São Paulo, a Catholic layman, law professor Dalmo Dallari, arrived at a papal mass in a wheelchair. The pope embraced him, and Dallari read the Lesson during the mass. The hundreds of thousands in the audience knew that Dallari had been arrested during a forty-one-day strike of steelworkers earlier in the year and only the night before had been badly beaten by four men presumed to be supporters of the right-wing government. Later, in Recife, the pope gave a warm, emotional public embrace to aging Archbishop Helder Camara, whose name for years had been censored out of the Brazilian press by right-wing authorities and who had often been called the red bishop because of his zeal for social action. Among those assisting at the mass at Recife was Dona Isairas Periera, mother of a priest who had been assassinated because of his deep involvement in campaigns for human rights. Such actions communicated papal support for human rights more effectively than a hundred sermons.

Just as Jesus used the parable, and the medieval church used the stained-glass window, so Pope John Paul uses the modern mass media. He knows how to orchestrate his trips so as to give the press a new headline each day, the TV correspondents a new spot in every cycle. On his trip to India in February 1986 he made news the first day by praying at the tomb of Gandhi. The second day he met with Mother Teresa among the dying in Calcutta. Another day held a meeting with the Dalai Lama, and he made yet another front-page story by speaking out on the Bhopal tragedy, in which two thousand persons had died and three hundred thousand were injured from a leak at a Union Carbide pesticide plant a year and a half before. And he wound up his trip with more headlines when he dared to denounce birth control in over-populated Bombay.

No doubt John Paul's most spectacular exploitation of the mass media was achieved not on a voyage abroad but in Rome itself—his meeting two days after Christmas, 1984, with the man who had gunned him down three years before, Mehmet Ali Agca. In mid-December the pope decided to pay a Christmas-season visit to Rome's Rebibbia prison, following the example of his predecessors Paul VI and John XXIII (the only previous pontiffs who had visited prisons). Agca was one of the inmates of Rebibbia, where he was serving his life sentence for the near-fatal shooting of the pope. When the Turk heard that the pope would visit the prison, he told the chaplain, "I would like him to come to me, because I am sorry." A meeting was arranged.

The encounter took place in Agca's bare white-walled cell in the maximum-security wing of Rebibbia, a large penal complex on the outskirts of Rome. Four persons entered the cell with the pope—his secretary Monsignor Dziwisz, two security men, and a cameraman of the Vatican television service. These four stood far back near the door while pope and assailant sat on black plastic chairs in a corner of the cell with their heads together. Agca bowed to kiss the pope's hand as they met, and John Paul's first words were "Do you speak Italian?" Agca does. The conversation was conducted in Italian.

During the meeting, the pope often held one hand to his forehead with eyes tightly closed while Agca spoke to him. At times he grasped the Turk's arm in what looked like a gesture of support. The unshaven Agca laughed now and then, but the smile would fade quickly. Nobody ever revealed the full text of that conversation, but the TV tape picked up faint phrases:

Agca: "First of all, I wish to ask your forgiveness."

Fragments from what the pope said: "Jesus . . . Perhaps one day . . . We remember . . . The Lord give you grace . . . A small gift . . ." (a rosary in silver and mother-of-pearl).

This scene was shown on television screens around the world. Photos ran on front pages of newspapers everywhere, and on the cover of *Time* magazine. Luigi Accattoli, Vatican correspondent of Milan's *Corriere della Sera,* observed: "The decision of the pope to meet Agca was audacious. But even more audacious was his wish to have the meeting photographed and filmed."

John Paul easily could have met Agca privately, with no press or cameramen around. It was his decision to make the meeting a media event, a decision that showed he meant to use this dramatic meeting to communicate to all the world, more effectively than words could, the message he had chosen for 1984, which he had proclaimed a Holy Year. The theme of that Jubilee Year: "Penance and Reconciliation."

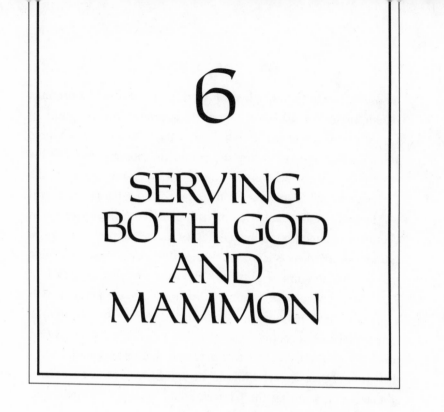

6

SERVING BOTH GOD AND MAMMON

Papal Poverty and Avarice

Renunciation of wealth has been considered a Christian virtue since Jesus told his disciples, "Ye cannot serve God and Mammon." In modern times, Pope Paul VI echoed the spirit of Christ's teaching when he declared that "the Church must be poor, and must be seen to be poor." The Church at the same time has a mission to carry out within the framework of this world, and it needs money to perform its task. This paradox has troubled the Christian community from the early centuries of its history right down to the present; the necessity of administering vast wealth to serve as "the patrimony of the poor" inevitably has involved the risk of corruption, whether in the ostentation of Renaissance popes or the Church financial scandals of the twentieth century.

The style with which individual popes have handled this touchy problem has a great impact on the public image of the Church. There have been ascetic popes whose lives embodied an apostolic ideal of poverty, and there have been avaricious popes who lived in luxury rivaling that of kings and emperors, and

147

whose behavior certainly blackened the image of the Church. In recent times, we have seen pontiffs approach the question of Church finances in ways that were characteristic of each one: John XXIII trying to ignore the whole question and to leave the system very much as he inherited it; Paul VI trying to reform the Church's financial structure and to lower its profile in the world of Mammon; John Paul II trying to put the best men possible in charge of finances so that he would be free for his pastoral chores. No one of the three succeeded in working out a financial policy that did not in some way tarnish the image of the Church.

The Church first became a financial power in the fourth century, when the emperor Constantine made Christianity the state religion. The emperor gave the Church vast holdings, which provided enough revenue to guarantee that priests could have their living, that Church buildings could be maintained and new edifices built, and that the Church could perform its mission of caring for the poor. Wealthy Romans followed the imperial example by privately endowing places of worship and convents and giving a tenth of their income to the Church.

By the time of Gregory the Great at the end of the sixth century, the papacy had become the leading landowner in Italy. The collapse of the Roman Empire in the West had left the Church as not only the prime civil authority but also as the great financial power of that chaotic age. Pope Gregory proved to be a conscientious custodian of the vast wealth that accrued to the Church. On the first day of each month he distributed wheat, clothes, and gold to the needy; the nineteenth-century historian Gregorovius says that once, "hearing that a beggar had died in the streets, he shut himself up, filled with remorse, and did not venture to approach the altar, as priest, for several days."

After the empire collapsed, no state in Western Europe was strong enough to protect the wealth of anyone. The only safe havens were the churches and monasteries, considered by all to be inviolable sanctuaries. Sometimes people deposited their savings with the churches simply for safe-keeping, and sometimes against a guaranteed income for life, a kind of primitive annuity system. Receipts issued by the Church against these deposits came to be among the most widely distributed commercial paper in Europe, often issued in the smallest denominations to accommodate the poorest investors. Such practices drew the Church ever more into the field of finance and, eventually, into banking.

The tension between Church wealth and Christian poverty led to a savage confrontation in the early fourteenth century, when four dissident Franciscans, known as Spirituals, were excommunicated and burned at the stake in Marseilles. Their crime was teaching that Christ and his disciples did not own property, either individually or in common, and that the Church should follow their example. This obviously did not go down well with the reigning pope, John XXII (1316–1334), who was called the Midas of Avignon because of his vast wealth. Historian Gregorovius writes that Pope John XXII lived "without any other love than money." To counter the Spirituals, and many other poverty movements of the time, John issued a document declaring that Christ and his disciples in fact were property-owners. He and other popes of that era carried out a crusade against the poverty-advocates, using the most horrible methods of torture and execution to crush those heretics who dared to teach that the Church should be poor.

During the era of the pope-kings of the Renaissance, the papacy vastly increased its wealth, but all too often popes sought wealth as a means for holding and expanding their personal power rather than as a trust for the poor. Alexander VI, the Borgia pope, did not hesitate to confiscate the lands of great families when in dispute with them. He auctioned off cardinal's hats, making cardinals of those who offered him the highest bids. When he needed more money to finance a military campaign of his son Cesare, Pope Alexander proclaimed a Jubilee Year to attract thousands of wealthy pilgrims to the country and sold them absolution for cash.

After the Counter-Reformation, papal finances were established on a more legitimate basis, founded on taxation, customs receipts, and income from papal properties, but right down to the latter part of the nineteenth century popes possessed wealth comparable to that of many secular kings of Western Europe.

A great change came in 1870, when the papacy lost its temporal power and vast landholdings to the new Italian state. To survive, pontiffs then had to look for new sources of funds. One of the prime new fonts of income was the charity of the international Catholic community. Church people in France and Belgium launched a campaign for the annual collection of special offerings for the pope, called in Latin *Denarius Sancti Petri* but generally known in English as Peter's Pence. This international collection went directly to the pope, with no regulation or control by anyone else.

The Peter's Pence habit spread from the Continent to Britain, the United States, and most other Catholic countries and in the late nineteenth century gave the popes the capital they needed to establish Vatican finances on a secure footing. To this day the Peter's Pence is a vital item in the Vatican operating budget. It is not a constant sum, of course, and in some years it has fallen off seriously. But during the reign of the charismatic and much-traveled John Paul II there has been a big increase in this annual offering. In the early eighties it averaged around $25 million a year but rose to more than $35 million in 1987.

It is convenient for the financial welfare of the modern Church that the teaching on usury has changed over the centuries. The early Church considered the practice illicit. The Church councils of Arles in 314 and Nicaea in 325 declared it unlawful for the clergy to charge interest on loans. In 1311 the Council of Vienne proclaimed that anyone denying that usury was a sin should be punished as a heretic. In 1745, Pope Benedict XIV changed the rule. In his encyclical "Vix Pervenit" he approved the principle of charging interest on loans, defining usury only as "an exorbitant rate of interest."

Pope Leo XIII, who reigned from 1878 to 1903, took advantage of the change in the teaching on usury to invest much of his Peter's Pence in stocks and bonds and to get the Vatican involved in banking. He was given valuable assistance by a group of the

"Black Nobility" (those Vatican noble families who wore black as a sign of mourning when the Italian army occupied Rome and brought the Papal States to an end), who organized the Banco di Roma mainly to serve the pope. At one point, still in the time of Leo XIII, the Vatican held at least one fourth of the shares of the bank and had three seats on its board of directors. Also during Leo's reign (in 1896), the Holy See for the first time took majority control over an important industrial firm, the Pantanella flour-milling company. It was the same Pope Leo who established the Administration for Religious Works, the Vatican's own bank.

The Holy See came into big money in 1929, when Pius XI and the Mussolini regime negotiated what is known as the Lateran Pacts, the peace treaty that finally settled the 1870 war between the Papal States and modern Italy. At last the Black Nobility could remove their mourning dress and reopen the doors of their great baroque palaces. The pacts established the present-day State of Vatican City, thereby guaranteeing papal sovereignty over a remnant of territory. The agreements also gave the Holy See a major infusion of money, the equivalent of $80 million, as compensation for the Papal States' lost properties. In the monetary context of the time, it was a massive sum.

The Vatican has kept such a tight lid of secrecy on its financial affairs that it is difficult to trace just what was done with that $80 million. But from interviewing reliable persons close to the Vatican I have concluded that most of the cash was invested in three areas. About one third went into real estate, mainly to replace buildings lost in 1870. Another one third was invested in gold to serve as a financial reserve. Although this investment must have appreciated many times over since then, it is still a reserve and not an asset usable to meet current operating costs except in extraordinary circumstances.

The last third was invested in stocks and bonds to render a return to be used in the operating budget of the Holy See. To oversee this capital, known as the Special Fund, the pope established what is known today as the Administration of the Patrimony of the Holy See (APSA). Popes continued to seek the financial counsel of members of the Black Nobility, men like Marchese Giovanni Battista Sacchetti, longtime president of Rome's Banco di Santo Spirito (the Bank of the Holy Spirit), and Count Enrico Galeazzi, an architect and financier who was an intimate of Pius XII.

Vatican Finances and Italy's Boom Under Pope John

In personal style and moral qualities there is little similarity between Good Pope John XXIII and his antecedent Pope John XXII, the fourteenth-century "Midas of Avignon." But they had one thing in common: Both presided over the Church when it projected an image of considerable wealth. When John XXIII, the man from a peasant background, was elected in 1958, the Vatican was deeply involved in vastly expanded investments in Italian securities.

That was the period of the "Miracolo Economico," that unprecedented boom for Italian business and industry. Paradoxically, the Vatican's involvement in that boom was initially the work of John's predecessor, the deeply spiritual and introverted Pius XII, who had great respect for the capitalistic system and the world of finance. He no doubt first became attracted to that world when his uncle, Ernesto Pacelli, was a key financial advisor to Pope Leo XIII. Young Eugenio Pacelli was something of a protégé of Uncle Ernesto and often went along when the uncle traveled on Vatican financial business. Three of Eugenio's nephews later were to rise to positions of eminence in the Italian financial world. When he became Pope Pius XII, Eugenio Pacelli was deeply receptive to the advice attributed by the Italian press to the American cardinal Francis Spellman, another Pacelli intimate: "Why give to charity one thousand lire today, when you can give ten thousand tomorrow if you invest it well?"

The advice was followed. By the time John became pope, the Holy See's financial tentacles had spread out into real estate, steel, cement, banking, milling, chemicals, pharmaceuticals, electric power, insurance, engineering, construction, and tourism.

With his characteristic aversion to administration or bureaucracy, Pope John preferred to keep his hands off the Vatican's money matters and to leave the whole thing very much as it had been set up by Pius. But he was too good to ignore the plight of the employees of the Vatican, most of whom worked for wages far below the prevailing levels in Italy. Salaries the equivalent of one hundred to three hundred dollars a month were common, even though inflation was taking a relentless toll on buying power. When John walked through the marble halls and richly decorated salons of the Vatican and read accounts in the press (often exaggerated, but still building a public image) of the Holy See as a financial power, he felt deeply distressed at what to him was nothing less than exploitation of workers.

When John broached the subject to his secretary of state, Tardini, the latter grunted that the Holy See could not possibly pay wages on a level with those in Italy generally. He pointed out that Vatican employees enjoyed very important fringe benefits that gave them an advantage over Italian workers. Many of them lived in Vatican apartment buildings at ridiculously low rents. They could buy duty-free groceries at the Vatican City supermarket, duty-free gasoline at the Vatican service station. Even more important, they were working for the glory of God.

This was not enough to satisfy the pope. John brooded about the problem, and one fine day he solved it with the same intuitive decisiveness he had displayed in summoning the council. Without consulting any of his top advisors, he simply raised wages of employees by nearly 50 percent.

The grouchy Cardinal Tardini was furious. The pope's action meant that Tardini must come up with an additional several million dollars that had not been budgeted. Other curial cardinals complained bitterly that their own budgets were being trimmed to accommodate John's "extravagance." The whole thing created such an uproar in the curia that John never meddled again with the Holy See's finances.

John's hands-off attitude left the Vatican to the media wolves so far as finances were concerned. As we have noted before, John did not alter the Holy See's official public relations structure and policies, and the practice of maintaining absolute secrecy on Vatican financial affairs contributed to vastly exaggerated estimates of Vatican wealth. The myth of the Holy See's riches grew till the Vatican developed the image of one of the world's financial powers. Books were written on the "Vatican Empire," and one author even estimated that the Holy See owned more than half of all the shares quoted on Italian stock exchanges (which would have amounted to nearly $6 billion at the time). A highly respected British publication estimated the Holy See's investment portfolio at around $2 billion. The Holy See kept silent, and so the public generally accepted these reports of Vatican wealth as true. This played into the hands of the Church's enemies, who didn't hesitate to denounce the Vatican as a greedy capitalist teamed up with reactionary forces to exploit the Italian working class.

During the height of the Cold War, Italy's Communist and Socialist parties were allied in all-out conflict with all those aligned with America and NATO, and in those days their targets naturally included the pro-NATO Christian Democratic party, which was backed by the Vatican. Marxists thus were ever on the lookout for any taint of corruption in the Holy See's financial activities. One of their favorite whipping-boys was Italy's biggest real estate firm, Società Generale Immobiliare, which was controlled by the Holy See.

Chairman of Immobiliare's board of directors was Count Enrico Galeazzi, that longtime intimate friend of Pius XII and of Pius's friend Cardinal Spellman. The intensely conservative Galeazzi was unhappy with the liberal, innovative John, and from his side the old pope kept the count outside his "Kitchen Cabinet." But John, preoccupied with preparations for the council and indifferent to administrative chores, left Galeazzi pretty much where he had found him, as perhaps the most powerful figure in the world of Vatican finance.

Galeazzi and his team guided Società Generale Immobiliare on a course that drew fire from leftist journalists and politicians.

Before the war, Immobiliare had bought up at ridiculously low prices vast amounts of rural land encircling Rome. After the war there was a massive expansion of the city's population, and Immobiliare reaped a golden harvest from constructing and selling luxury apartment buildings, office complexes, and hotels in the spreading Italian capital. The anticlerical press had a field day attacking this Vatican company for allegedly building for the upper classes while neglecting middle-income housing and ignoring the plight of immigrant workers, who lived in huts made of kerosene cans and mud on the city's periphery.

In late 1962, shortly after Pope John inaugurated the Vatican Council, the aggressive Immobiliare moved into the international real estate sphere and broke ground in Washington, D.C., to build a huge luxury apartment-hotel complex whose name, Watergate, eventually went into the world's political dictionary. The groundbreaking evoked an angry outcry from fundamentalist Protestants in the United States, who protested against this intrusion of papal financial power into the very capital of the nation. It was a serious setback for John's newly launched ecumenical movement, which aimed to bring all Christian communities closer together.

Immobiliare again caused John embarrassment when the company made an agreement with the American Hilton Hotel chain to build the Cavaliere Hilton on Monte Mario, a hill overlooking Rome. Leftists in parliament and the press denounced the "Fascist-clerical combine" which was putting an alleged eyesore on the hill and denying to strolling Romans a favorite view of the setting sun. Those devout Marxists loudly complained that the Hilton project violated a tradition that no building in Rome could be taller than the cross atop St. Peter's Basilica. The argument collapsed when someone took the trouble to measure and found that, even on top of a hill as high as Monte Mario, the roof of the Hilton would be lower than St. Peter's cross. The Hilton was eventually built and the controversy blew over, but it caused the Vatican a great deal of embarrassment and made it harder for John to promote dialogue with Italian Marxists.

Pope Paul Promotes a Policy of Christian Poverty

The Vatican's links with the world of capitalism continued to embarrass the Holy See under the liberal Paul VI. The pope who had been called the workers' archbishop when he was saying masses in the smoky factories of Milan suddenly found himself on the side of industrial corporations in labor disputes. A particularly nasty situation developed in 1971 when workers of the Vatican-owned flour-milling firm, Pantanella, occupied the plant and distributed leaflets attacking the Vatican for threatening to close down the company and leave its workers unemployed.

Another problem arose as Paul was preparing his encyclical "Humanae Vitae," banning artificial means of birth control. It became known that certain pharmaceutical firms in which the Vatican had a substantial interest were manufacturing contraceptive pills. To Paul, it became obvious that something had to be done to minimize the Vatican's presence in the financial-industrial world.

True to form, Paul sought to solve the problem by creating more bureaucracy. He set up a Prefecture for Economic Affairs, which was to supervise all the Holy See's finances (except for the Vatican Bank, which answered only to the pope). To head this new office, Paul named Cardinal Egidio Vagnozzi, a practical cleric who had served many years as apostolic delegate in Washington. Vagnozzi was to develop a new Vatican financial strategy with two basic elements: to diversify investments so that there would be much less concentration on the Italian scene; and to adopt a policy of never holding controlling interest (or management) in any company. Eventually the Pope's "finance minister," Cardinal Vagnozzi, could say proudly, "We no longer control a single company."

Instead of relying entirely on the old club of Black Nobles for making financial moves, the Holy See now began to channel investments through such international organizations as Credit Suisse of Zurich, Chase Manhattan, Bankers Trust, Hambros, the Rothschilds. The Holy See acquired shares in companies listed on the major stock exchanges of the West, including a heavy dose of holdings in the United States.

So far, so good. But in implementing the second part of the new strategy—divesting the Holy See of control of companies—the Vatican ran into problems that eventually mushroomed into nasty scandals.

The Holy See's ownership of Immobiliare had caused so much embarrassment that it was one of the first corporations that Vagnozzi sold off. He made the mistake of engaging the services of a brilliant financier, the Milan-based Sicilian Michele Sindona, to broker the sale. A devout Catholic, Sindona made contact with the Holy See through Cardinal Sergio Guerri, who then was pro-president of the Commission for Vatican City, in effect the governor of the State of Vatican City. (Sindona never met Pope Paul, though he once circulated the story that he had held nocturnal one-on-one meetings with the pope.)

At the time, Sindona was a rising star in the world of finance, not only in Italy but all over the West. He had come to Milan from his native Sicily at the time of the postwar "Miracolo Economico" and had set himself up as a tax lawyer. Eventually he was handling the tax problems of some of the country's most powerful corporations, and these relationships gave him a rare and almost exclusive inside knowledge of their finances. He used this inside information to buy and sell quietly and cleverly and slowly built his own financial empire. For tax advantages, he incorporated himself in Lichtenstein. Outside the most intimate banking and industrial circles of Milan, his name was still unknown in 1963 when the news burst on financial pages all over the West that an unknown Italian had bought control of the American firm Libby, McNeil and Libby. That "unknown Italian" was Michele Sindona, who bought and sold companies as easily as old-time Americans once traded horses and controlled as many as fifty or sixty at a time. His prime interest was in banking, and he eventually owned two of Italy's leading private banks and the Franklin Bank in New York.

Instead of simply brokering the Vatican's sale of Immobiliare, Sindona in the end bought the company from the Holy See himself. And that was about the extent of Sindona's dealings with the Vatican. In interviews in later years, he repeatedly said that he had never gone into financial ventures with the Vatican. The one link between him and the Holy See was that the Vatican Bank owned shares in Sindona's Italian banks, and Luigi Mennini, a layman who was number-two man in the Vatican Bank, sat on the board of directors of one of Sindona's banks. Even so, the press generally identified Sindona as "formerly the Vatican's top financial advisor" and continued to give him that label after he died of arsenic poisoning in his cell in Voghera prison near Milan in March 1986, after he had been sentenced to life imprisonment for alleged complicity in a murder.

Sindona expanded too fast and eventually went bankrupt on both sides of the Atlantic. When his Italian banks collapsed, the anticlerical press gleefully reported that the Vatican had lost heavily in the bankruptcy of its "partner" Sindona. Some newspaper accounts put the Vatican loss as high as $80 million. Like many others in the Italian financial world, the Vatican Bank did lose the value of the shares of Sindona's banks it had held. It was in fact a paper loss, and even then hardly a tenth of what the press was reporting. The shares had been amortized many times over by reinvesting the dividends received, and the loss easily was absorbed by the Vatican Bank. But the belief that Sindona had been a Vatican financial "partner" remains widespread and has tainted the Holy See's image enormously.

It was when he was trying to reform the Holy See's financial structure that Pope Paul introduced into the banking world a prelate destined to become one of the world's most controversial clergymen, the American Paul Marcinkus. Although Marcinkus had had absolutely no experience in banking or in any financial field, Pope Paul in 1969 named him head of the Vatican Bank and made him a bishop.

Paul Marcinkus in appearance and manner is the prototype of one ideal of the American Catholic priest: the man's man, the athlete, the down-to-earth prelate who cares little about the fine points of theology while tackling the practical problems of every-day life. Handsome and powerfully built (six feet three, 230 pounds) a cigar-chomper who likes a good drink, Marcinkus is living proof that "you don't have to be a patsy to be a priest." He enjoys good food (he also happens to be a good cook) and knows his wines, plays golf when time allows at exclusive Roman golf clubs, but invariably dresses in a somewhat shabby full-length black cassock and drives himself around in a compact Fiat.

Marcinkus was born into a devout Catholic family on January 15, 1922, in Cicero, Illinois, a town near Chicago whose chief claim to fame is that it produced Al Capone. His father and mother were Lithuanian immigrants, and things were tough back in Cicero during Paul's childhood. He once told me: "We were poor all right. My father worked first as a farmer, then as a steelworker, and wound up washing windows on downtown buildings."

After going to Catholic schools in Illinois, the newly ordained Marcinkus did a three-year term as assistant pastor in St. Christina Parish in Chicago, from 1947 to 1950, and that was the full extent of his pastoral activity. By 1950 he was in Rome working toward a degree in canon law and later joined the Secretariat of State and trained as a diplomat at the Pontifical Ecclesiastical Academy.

In his years at the Vatican's Secretariat of State Marcinkus caught the eye of Archbishop Giovanni Battista Montini, who was then undersecretary of state and in 1963 became Pope Paul VI. He sent Marcinkus to the field as a papal diplomat in Bolivia and Canada, but when Montini became pope he "borrowed" the big American from the Secretariat and included him in his personal entourage. Marcinkus became part of Paul's inner circle and often lunched at the papal table.

After his first international trip, to Jerusalem, ended in near-disastrous chaos, Pope Paul handed to Marcinkus the job of organizing his second trip, to Bombay. Marcinkus handled it so well that the pope gave him this task as a permanent assignment. He advanced and organized every one of Paul's trips after that and, until 1982, handled Pope John Paul's voyages as well. Television viewers following papal trips became familiar with the sight of the big man in the black cassock leaning against the crowds to protect and guide the pope through the mob. He sometimes used a bulldozer approach in organizing those voyages. A little Indian police guard once tried to keep Marcinkus from following Pope Paul up to the altar platform, stubbornly declaring that since Marcinkus was not wearing any credentials he could not proceed farther. The big American finally lifted the little policeman up bodily, set him to one side, and followed the pope onto the platform. In Manila in 1970, Marcinkus helped to subdue the Bolivian artist who tried to kill Pope Paul.

It was in advancing those papal trips that Marcinkus was at his most undiplomatic best. He knew how much was at stake in making all the arrangements, including security and logistics, and he was often blunt to the point of rudeness in refusing to compromise on the essentials. When planning Pope John Paul's trip to Britain in June 1982, Marcinkus had such a violent disagreement with Anglican officials that they threatened to ban him from Canterbury Cathedral.

Though he ruffled many a feather in host countries, Marcinkus did such a remarkable job of organizing papal trips that Pope Paul rewarded him with the post of heading up the Institute for Religious Works, better known as the Vatican Bank. It seemed a bit odd to name as head of the bank a priest with no banking experience, but Pope Paul had limitless confidence in the American's abilities. Marcinkus himself sees his talent not as an administrator but as an organizer. He once told me, "I have no banking experience, but I think I was chosen because of the organizational ability I showed during the papal trips."

Providing the technical banking expertise that Marcinkus lacked was the number-two man in the bank, Luigi Mennini, a veteran financier who had served on the boards of many of Italy's top financial corporations. Mennini was an associate of Sindona, and he also introduced to Marcinkus a rising Italian financier who headed the country's leading privately owned bank, Banco Ambrosiano. A practicing Catholic with a modest life-style, Roberto Calvi offered the dynamic Marcinkus channels for shifting the Vatican Bank's investments outside Italy to points overseas. Calvi's activism appealed to Marcinkus, who was eager to breathe new life into his bank. He once told me that his policy from the beginning was that the Vatican Bank "should be just as sharp as our competitors." That contact with Calvi was to lead Marcinkus and the bank into an international scandal, as we shall see later in this narrative.

The Institute for Religious Works certainly is a unique banking organization. Many Vatican officials argue that it should not be called a bank at all. Perhaps more properly it should be thought of as a massive trust fund set up to handle capital for religious orders, Catholic relief organizations, charitable enterprises, and Catholic schools. A typical client of the institute, for example, is Mother Teresa, whose religious order ministers to the dying in the slums of Calcutta. The institute acts as custodian for funds that Mother Teresa's order collects, and its job is to get the best possible return on those funds to promote the order's work. Contrary to what is often supposed, the institute has nothing to do with the operating budget of the Holy See. It would hardly be correct to use capital from Mother Teresa to pay Vatican employees or expenses for Holy See travel.

Though its terms of reference may be somewhat restricted, the institute on a day-to-day basis operates very much like a secular bank. It has the character of an offshore bank because it is located in the sovereign state of Vatican City, not in Italy, and so is completely free from Italian financial laws or controls. It has no board of directors, issues no public balance sheet, and is answerable in theory only to the pope himself. Its offices are a simple suite of rooms in the medieval Tower of Sisto VI, near the courtyard of San Damaso, which in turn leads to the Apostolic Palace, the pope's offices and residence. The main glass door has no security device and can be opened by anyone who passes.

Clients of the Vatican Bank are a restricted group. To open an account in the institute, you must be the head of a religious order, a clergyman in charge of a Church school, hospital, or similar institution, or a member of the Roman Curia. The privilege of banking at the institute is also extended to residents of Vatican City and to diplomats accredited to the Holy See. The pope has a personal account in the bank, number 16/16.

Anyone holding an account in the Vatican Bank obviously has tremendous special privileges, since he is not under the financial controls of the Italian government. And so over the years there have been repeated accusations in the Italian press that the institute was being used as a conduit for sending vast sums of money out of Italy to circumvent the country's currency regulations. There have been charges that Sindona used the bank on a massive scale for his wheeling and dealing (it has never been proven). And the Holy See's insistence on secrecy regarding its finances played into the hands of those ever ready to publish the most blatant accusations about the Vatican's "banking empire."

While Pope Paul was trying (with little success) to straighten out the Holy See's financial structures, he took some actions that in effect bequeathed to his successor an enormous budget deficit. The conscientious Paul tried to implement all the directives of the Vatican Council, and in his own bureaucratic fashion he did it by creating more bureaucracy. To the ten established congregations of the Roman Curia, Paul added seven new departments, which shot up the cost of running the Holy See. Among those departments were secretariats for Non-Christians (dialogue with Muslims, Buddhists, etc.) and for Nonbelievers (dialogue with Marxists and other atheists). To promote human rights he established the Commission for Justice and Peace. He also set up a Council for the Family and even a Commission for Migration and Tourism. In adding all these departments to the curia, Paul more than doubled the number of Vatican employees, from slightly more than one thousand when he became pope to around twenty-four hundred by the time he died.

It was not publicized at the time, but the Holy See's operating budget went into the red in the early years of Paul's reign. Those investments supervised by Cardinal Vagnozzi were not enough to meet the rising costs of the expanded curia nor to meet the increased expenses generated by inflation. Under Paul, however, the annual deficits were comfortably covered by the Peter's Pence, and so nothing was said or done about overspending. With all his attempts at reforming the structure, Pope Paul failed either to immunize the Vatican against financial scandals or to establish the Holy See on a sound budgetary footing.

John Paul II and the Great Bank Scandal

It was left to Pope John Paul II to bear the brunt of the budget deficits that were created by Paul's policies. When he was so hastily pulled out of Kraków to become bishop of Rome in the conclave of October 1978, John Paul of course had no idea that he faced financial problems inside the ornate halls of the Vatican. Given this pope's priorities, it is not surprising that it was a good six months after his election before he at last got around to taking his first look at the budget of the Holy See. It left John Paul in a state of shock. After all that had been written and reported about the financial power of the Vatican, the new pope learned that the Holy See faced a budget deficit for 1979 of more than $20 million, a frightening sum in a total budget of about $60 million.

The deficit was growing steadily not only because of the expansion of the curia but also because of a problem familiar to governments all over the world at that time—inflation. Living costs in Italy were rising at a rate of 22 percent a year, and the Holy See was obliged to increase salaries and pensions of its employees and retirees. Those costs alone were eating up around 60 percent of the total budget. Other costly items were Vatican Radio, a massive utilities bill for all of Vatican City, and expenses of the diocese of Rome. The new departments set up by Paul were spending heavily on publications, travel, seminars, and conferences.

It was the Vatican's "minister of finance," Cardinal Vagnozzi, who first showed that disastrous budget to Pope John Paul. Not a very cheerful soul at best, the old cardinal added little comfort when he said, "Holy Father, if things continue in this way, the Holy See will be bankrupt in five years."

With all its alleged wealth, how can the Vatican be in the red? We have already noted that reports of vast Holy See riches were greatly exaggerated. To cover its annual operating budget, the Holy See has income from its real estate, profits from its supermarket and gasoline station in Vatican City, sale of postage stamps, museum fees. But the prime source of budgetary funds is from investments generated by the capital that Mussolini agreed to pay in the settlement with the Vatican in 1929, the Special Fund administered by APSA under the overall supervision of the Prefecture for Economic Affairs. Honoring the Holy See's policy of secrecy, Cardinal Vagnozzi never told me exactly how much that fund amounted to, but in a conversation in 1980 he let me know that the "order of magnitude" was $200 million. Late in 1987, Vatican officials reported that the Holy See's investments in stocks and bonds amounted to $175 million. This did not include the Holy See's gold and monetary reserves—to be used only in emergency—nor its real estate. And, as we have explained, the resources of the Vatican Bank were not to be used for the Holy See's annual budget.

Quite clearly, returns from the investment portfolio no longer could cover the Vatican's budget. The Peter's Pence— collected in Catholic churches around the world every June 29— was increased after John Paul's election, and for his first years it covered the deficit. But the relentless march of inflation pushed the shortfall ever higher. By 1986 the deficit had soared to a staggering $55 million. For 1987, it was around $60 million, far beyond the Holy See's resources.

The deficit problem was a bitter blow for Pope John Paul II, above all because it meant that he would have to divert an excessive amount of his time to the dreary area of finance. In desperation, he took the highly unusual step of summoning the entire College of Cardinals to Rome, the first time in four hundred years the college had been called together to do anything except elect a pope. At this critical point, it was John Paul's newly appointed secretary of state, Casaroli, who stepped into the breach. Although his strong point was diplomacy and he was totally inexperienced in financial matters, Casaroli skillfully maneuvered to have a fifteen-member commission of cardinals appointed to find the money to cover the Vatican deficit. The commission was headed by two very practical cardinals—John Krol of Philadelphia and Joseph Hoefner of Cologne—both of whom managed rich dioceses and knew how to raise money.

The commission of cardinals helped increase the Peter's Pence and elicited other special contributions from wealthy dioceses to help bail out the Vatican. But a great deal more has to be done. The cardinals have put heavy pressure on the pope to reduce spending. More than that, Krol and Hoefner have warned the pope bluntly that it is hard to persuade the Catholic faithful around the world to continue giving on such a scale when the Holy See refuses to publish a balance sheet. Responding to such pressure, the Vatican at last has made public its budget—in very broad outline—but old habits are hard to break and around the curia it still is widely assumed that the Vatican's finances are nobody's business but its own.

That budget problem proved to be a minor issue compared with the great financial scandal that broke over the Holy See in the summer of 1982. On June 17 of that year, Roberto Calvi, the president of Banco Ambrosiano, was found hanging from Blackfriars Bridge in London. British police initially called it suicide but later conceded that it might have been murder. Whatever the cause of the man's death, the gruesome incident gave the world's media a rare opportunity to blacken the name of the Vatican. Fleet Street newspapers instantly christened Calvi "God's banker" and called him one of the pope's top financial advisors. His bank had collapsed, and he had left a shortage of $1.3 billion. The press immediately speculated that Archbishop Paul Marcinkus was deeply involved in this shady affair.

Even after his dear friend and patron Paul VI died, Marcinkus had continued to rise in the Vatican. Pope John Paul not only confirmed him as head of the Vatican Bank but also made him "pro-president" of Vatican City, in effect governor of that tiny state. The new appointment meant that he was raised from bishop to archbishop. But the Ambrosiano bankruptcy put him under a cloud and seriously interrupted his career.

Marcinkus's name immediately was linked to the Calvi affair when an Italian magistrate sent to the archbishop a "judicial communication," advising him that he was under investigation in connection with the Ambrosiano case. It was revealed that Marcinkus had imprudently issued "letters of patronage" to Calvi on behalf of two shadowy holding companies in Panama, which in turn owned six other companies of doubtful status. It appeared that Calvi had "lent" much of the $1.3 billion to those eight companies, and what happened to the money after that no one seemed to know.

Even more embarrassing, the Vatican (including Marcinkus) had learned roughly a year earlier that it might even own those shady companies. Some one had listed the companies in the records of the Banca del Gottarda in Switzerland and attributed their ownership to the Vatican. If the Vatican Bank in fact owned the companies, it would be liable for the $1.3 billion. To pay off that kind of a debt, said a Rome banker at the time, "the pope would have to sell St. Peter's." Marcinkus flatly denies that the Vatican owns those companies, or ever owned them, and once said, "If we owned them, there must be some piece of paper somewhere proving it. Nobody can show me such a piece of paper."

The Vatican Bank officially owned less than 2 percent of Banco Ambrosiano shares, but suspicion arose that it might own a much larger percentage indirectly. Those shadowy Panamanian companies apparently spent much of the missing money buying Ambrosiano shares. If the Vatican owned those companies, it might then own a big share of Ambrosiano and thus be considered a partner with Calvi in fraudulent bankruptcy. Marcinkus made no secret of the fact that the Vatican Bank owned 8 percent of Calvi's Nassau-based subsidiary, Banco Ambrosiano Overseas, Ltd. (and Marcinkus for a time served on the Nassau bank's board of directors). The Nassau bank allegedly had brokered the loans to the shadowy Panamanian companies. The Vatican Bank also owned 4 percent of Calvi's Banco Ambrosiano Holding, his European financial outlet.

With all these links to Calvi, Marcinkus became Topic A in much of the world press. He appeared on the cover of *Time*'s European edition, over a heading "The Great Vatican Bank Scandal." The anticlerical Italian media got special delight out of attacking Marcinkus. The radical Rome daily *La Repubblica* carried two pages of cartoons on the American archbishop, including a comic strip entitled "The Adventures of Paul Marcinkus." One of the cartoons showed a lawyer asking, "Honorable judges, I have a bishop client who wishes to know if it is possible to commute a sentence of ten years in prison to ten years in purgatory."

According to top banking sources in Rome, what apparently happened was that Calvi miscalculated the value of the dollar, got himself deeply into debt, and tried to maintain solvency by listing the missing $1.3 billion as assets in the form of loans to those Panamanian companies. Calvi had borrowed about $400 million on the European money market, which he invested mostly in Banco Ambrosiano shares. Unluckily for him, the shares were quoted in Italian lire while his debts were in dollars. When the dollar suddenly soared to a record value and the lira slumped, Calvi found himself hopelessly indebted.

Marcinkus's big mistake was issuing those letters of patronage to Calvi. When this bit of information first became public, many assumed that this was the "smoking gun" that would convict the archbishop-banker. But it turned out that the letters were not guarantees; they were nothing that would back up a loan, only kind words for Calvi's companies. Also, they had been issued on September 1, 1981, which was after all Calvi's indebtedness had been incurred. Not a single loan was secured, or even influenced, on the basis of those letters. Furthermore, Marcinkus had a note from Calvi canceling the letters and promising they would never be used in any way to cause "any damage, present or future," to the Vatican Bank. Marcinkus had issued the letters under pressure from friends of Calvi and to give the banker time to set his house in order. The letters expired in June 1982, and after that Marcin-kus refused flatly to give Calvi any further help.

Events of Calvi's last desperate days showed that he was not "God's banker" and indicated that the Vatican did not owe him money. When Marcinkus stonewalled against giving Calvi any more help, the banker frantically searched all over Italy for some contact with the Holy See who might be able to pressure the American to help him.

In late spring of 1982, when the Bank of Italy had reported the $1.3 billion shortage in the accounts of the Banco Am-brosiano, Calvi looked for help to a Sardinian "fixer" named Flavio Carboni (later arrested by Italian police), who pretended to be well connected at the Vatican. Carboni eventually made contact with Monsignor Hilary Franco, an American middle-level functionary in the Holy See's Congregation for the Clergy. Franco is an interesting and energetic person who once served as aide to Bishop Fulton Sheen in Rochester and at one time was assigned to the apostolic delegation in Washington. He has been at the Vatican for many years and knows his way around the place. But the fact that Calvi had to work through Carboni and Hilary Franco in itself showed clearly that he had no influential contacts in the Vatican.

Hilary Franco told me he himself was surprised when Car-boni came to him and asked if he would receive Calvi. Perhaps Carboni approached Franco because, like Marcinkus, the monsi-gnor was an American and lived at Villa Stritch, a hostel for American clergy who work at the Holy See, where Marcinkus also lived for many years. In any case, Franco says he agreed to see Calvi, and the banker called on him three times. When the monsignor gently inquired as to how he might be of assistance, Calvi replied, "I am undergoing an emotional and spiritual crisis. I desperately need your religious guidance."

They talked at great length about Calvi's state of emotional distress before the banker finally got to the point. He begged Franco to arrange a meeting for him with Marcinkus. The monsi-gnor noted that this was an odd request, because he was aware that

Calvi had known Marcinkus for at least eight years. Why did he need an introduction from someone like Franco?

"Because I want to be sure to be received positively at the Vatican Bank," answered Calvi.

Monsignor Franco agreed to try. He telephoned Marcinkus, but the American archbishop at that moment was accompanying the pope on his trip to Britain. He arranged, instead, a meeting with Marcinkus's deputy and Calvi's one-time friend, Luigi Mennini. The meeting was set for May 31, 1982. To Calvi's plea for an extension on loans reported to amount to about $300 million, Mennini replied with a blunt no.

Ten days later Calvi slipped out of Italy. From his places of refuge, first in Austria and later in London, he continued to telephone his aides to urge them to put pressure on the Vatican. The final plea was made by a Calvi confidant in Rome on June 16. Another refusal. The next morning Calvi was found hanging from Blackfriars Bridge.

Calvi's reaching out to Hilary Franco as the last straw is cited by Marcinkus's friends as a clear indication that, in fact, Calvi had not lent that missing money to Vatican-owned companies. If the Vatican had owed him $1.3 billion, he could easily have avoided bankruptcy by listing that loan as an asset on the Banco Ambrosiano books. Instead he was begging for an extension on money he owed the Vatican to help him cover that shortage of funds. Marcinkus's supporters say this is proof that Calvi was a debtor to the Vatican, not a creditor.

Details of Calvi's last-ditch pleas were not generally known at the time, and in the wake of the Ambrosiano failure there were loud outcries from creditor banks, demanding repayment of their money and claiming that the Vatican Bank was responsible. It was time for the Holy See to act. But who would act?

Marcinkus, under investigation by Italian magistrates and widely accused by press and public, was hardly one to serve as an impartial arbiter in the case. As he was president of the Vatican Bank, his only superior was Pope John Paul himself, and the pope was deeply involved in that late spring and summer with trips to

Britain, Argentina (because of the Falklands war), Portugal, Switzerland, and Spain. At this point the gentle figure of Cardinal Casaroli moved into the lead role in this tense drama. Although the pope already depended heavily for administration on "Don Agostino," the Vatican Bank until then had eluded the cardinal's control. He and Marcinkus had never gotten on well, and to avoid troubling the waters, the pope had left the big American fully in charge. But with around 120 foreign banks clamoring for their money, the pope was obliged to hand the problem to his subtle secretary of state.

A consortium of Italian banks had been formed to settle the claims against the Banco Ambrosiano by creditors inside Italy. That left around $600 million in unpaid claims by foreign creditor banks. In late 1983, things became particularly acute when those foreign banks drew up a writ against the Vatican Bank. It was never served, but it conjured up visions of endless litigation.

Marcinkus insisted that his bank had no obligation to pay that money and saw no reason to come up with a penny of it. In long discussions inside the Vatican, he repeatedly put his case in the simplest and bluntest of terms: "We admit no responsibility. We pay nothing. Period."

For the subtle "Don Agostino," nothing is ever that simple. He favored the diplomatic way: negotiation and compromise rather than confrontation. And so began a lengthy struggle between Casaroli and Marcinkus. Their conflict was a remarkable study in contrasts between the Anglo-Saxon and Mediterranean mentalities. On one side was the blunt American, tough and handsome as John Wayne, ever ready to call a spade a spade, dead against giving an inch. On the other side was the gentle, soft-spoken, smiling Italian, rubbing his hands together and nodding as if in assent but never saying a flat yes or no, always probing for some point of compromise.

Casaroli proposed to the Italian government the appointment of a six-man mixed commission to make an exhaustive investigation of the affair; three members of the commission would be named by the Vatican and three by the Italian Ministry of the

Treasury. The commission's eighty-six-page report was inconclusive, however, with the commissioners split three ways. The three
appointed by the Holy See cleared the Vatican Bank of any
responsibility. Although the Vatican Bank held shares of the two
Panamanian holding companies, the Vatican-appointed commissioners insisted that this did not constitute proof that the Holy See
owned those companies. (Marcinkus said that the shares were held
only as collateral against loans.) These three commissioners further pointed out that if the Vatican Bank had owned those companies, it would have regularly received their balance sheets, which
was not the case. They added further that the Vatican Bank
clearly had never managed the companies and until July 1981 was
not even aware of their existence and so could not have been
responsible for their activities.

On the other side, two of the commissioners appointed by the
Italian Ministry of the Treasury found the Vatican Bank guilty,
arguing that documents supporting the bank's ownership of the
Panamanian companies had more legal status than those denying
that ownership. They also reported that "all the functionaries of
the Banco Ambrosiano" who had anything to do with its foreign
operations assumed that those Panamanian companies were
owned by the Vatican.

The third ministry-appointed commissioner found the Vatican Bank not guilty, but only for lack of evidence. While conced-
ing that absolute proof that the bank owned the companies in
question did not exist, he noted that "at least since 1974, without
any possibility of doubt, there was a very close relationship between Roberto Calvi and the Vatican Bank, having the aim, or at
least the result, of covering activities and positions that were not
exactly orthodox by Roberto Calvi."

This did not prove that Marcinkus and his bank were guilty,
but, in Casaroli's eyes, neither did it remove all the doubts. To him
the case was not clear enough to allow the Vatican to adopt a
high-and-mighty posture and refuse to pay anything. There was
that writ drawn up by the foreign banks, and Casaroli felt it would
be infinitely damaging to the prestige and image of the Vatican

to be drawn into court. He foresaw as much as ten years of litigation—always covered in great detail by the press—if the Holy See refused to make any concession. There already was heavy pressure on the pope himself to intervene and settle the question, most notably from groups of Catholic laymen in and around Milan who had been shareholders in the Banco Ambrosiano. And the campaign in the press continued.

Marcinkus saw the threat of lawsuits and the press campaigns as a kind of blackmail to force the Vatican to pay up. He argued that articles were being planted in the press and lawsuits threatened because other banks had gotten burned, and they knew that the Vatican was an easy target. He insisted that these banks would have fought to the bitter end if they had been in the Vatican's situation, but they knew the Holy See preferred to settle things quietly, even at a heavy cost.

Marcinkus complained, "If we keep sweeping things under the carpet, after a while it will pile up so high we'll stumble on it." He argued that giving in would only be paying off pressure groups, paying off to stay out of court.

In the end it was the subtle Italian diplomat who won out over the outraged American banker. Pope John Paul opted for Casaroli's proposal to make a settlement and wind up the nasty affair once and for all. The pope had no desire to have the Vatican dragged through the courts while he was touring the world propagating the Christian message. He gave Casaroli the green light to negotiate a settlement with the creditor banks.

After some intense and extremely complicated negotiations, Casaroli concluded an agreement with the 120 creditor banks in early 1984. The pope then summoned to Rome his fifteen-man financial advisory commission of cardinals, and Casaroli explained the proposed deal to them in detail. The Vatican Bank was to pay heavily, but this was not to be an admission of either legal or moral responsibility, only a "voluntary contribution" as a means of bringing the case to an end. On March 1, 1984, the commission of cardinals gave the agreement its approval. On May 25 the agreement was formally signed with representatives of the 120 creditor banks in the headquarters of the European Free Trade Association in Geneva.

The foreign creditor banks agreed to settle for $406 million of the $600 million owed to them. Of this amount, the Vatican Bank agreed to pay about 60 percent, which came to around $240 million. Part of the remaining 40 percent was raised by selling off Banco Ambrosiano assets outside Italy. In the end, the creditor banks got about seventy cents on the dollar of what was owed them, which was considered an exceptionally good settlement under the circumstances. The Vatican Bank made its payment of nearly a quarter of a billion dollars in cash, without having to touch its reserves. Marcinkus at the time told a friend, "It's taking a big bite out of us, but it won't ruin us."

There was a bit of champagne-popping in Geneva as the Ambrosiano agreement was signed with those foreign creditors, but conspicuously absent were any Vatican officials. The embittered Marcinkus signed the agreement in his office back at the Vatican, had his signature authenticated, and sent it to Geneva. To the last, he believed that the Holy See could have come clear without paying if it only had stood its ground.

The Geneva settlement averted a damaging civil court trial for the Holy See, but Casaroli's payoff did not close the case. A criminal investigation regarding possible fraudulent bankruptcy was still going on. As often happens in Italy, the investigation ground on quietly for years and dropped out of the public eye until the shattering news came on February 26, 1987: Arrest warrants had been issued for Marcinkus, Mennini, and the number-three man in the Vatican Bank, Pellegrino de Strobel. Investigating magistrates had concluded that the Vatican Bank had acted as an umbrella for Calvi's illicit operations abroad, that it owned a substantial share of Banco Ambrosiano, and that it therefore shared responsibility for the bankruptcy. Marcinkus and his men insisted that they were innocent.

It had been five years since the Ambrosiano collapse and three years since the financial settlement. The three Vatican bankers remained inside the sovereign state of Vatican City (with which the Italian state has no treaty of extradition), and so it was impossible to serve the warrants on them. To protect its men, the Vatican pointed to Article Eleven of the Lateran Treaty of 1929 regulating relations between the Holy See and Italy, which stipulates that there can be no interference by the Italian state in "the central institutions of the Catholic Church." Italy's highest court later accepted the Vatican's interpretation and ruled that Marcinkus and his two colleagues could not be arrested or brought to trial in Italy. But however much the Holy See may protect its men, this case is bound to drag on for many years, always besmirching the Vatican's image.

Though the pope gave Marcinkus his loyal backing through the entire incident and refused to dismiss him in the face of massive pressures from outside to do so, there is no doubt that the scandal interrupted what had been a meteoric rise in the Vatican ranks by the big archbishop. At least for the time being, the situation blocked his becoming a cardinal. When John Paul made Marcinkus pro-president of the Commission for the State of Vatican City in 1981, it was taken for granted that he would get a cardinal's hat at the next consistory. He could become president of the commission only if he were a cardinal, and so the pro-president title was given him presumably till a consistory was held. But in February 1983 the pope created eighteen new cardinals—and Marcinkus was not among them. The biggest blow came in April 1984, when the pope named yet another set of cardinals and reshuffled the curia. Instead of making Marcinkus president of the Vatican City commission, the pope put Cardinal Sebastiano Baggio into that post, directly above Marcinkus and blocking his way to further advancement.

The Ambrosiano scandal convinced the pope more than ever that he must try to keep his distance from temporal affairs of the Holy See. Yet as sovereign of the independent State of Vatican City, John Paul could not avoid getting involved in earthly matters. During his pontificate, Vatican City employees had formed their own labor union and sometimes agitated for higher pay and better working conditions from a pope who was defending workers' rights all over the world. Nasty problems with the Italian government arise when Italian courts try to arrest Vatican City citizens.

And so the Polish pope simply gave up his role as head of the State of Vatican City. In early April 1984, John Paul took the unprecedented step of handing over the exercise of sovereignty of the little state to none other than old reliable "Don Agostino" Casaroli. He sent a *chirografo papale* (literally a letter written in the pope's own hand) to "Our Venerated Brother Agostino Casaroli," informing him "we have decided to confer on you in your capacity as secretary of state a high and special mandate to represent us in the civil government of the State of Vatican City and to exercise in our name and in our place—always referring to us, especially in cases of particular importance—the power and the responsibility inherent in our temporal sovereignty over that state. . . ."

Pope John Paul then felt freer to take off for Papua New Guinea or El Salvador or Gabon, concentrating on purely Catholic and spiritual matters, while "Don Agostino" dealt with the labor union and the state budget—and bank scandals. And as he passed on the power and responsibility to Casaroli, the pope no doubt recalled Christ's warning "Ye cannot serve God and Mammon."

7

POPES AND INTERNATIONAL DIPLOMACY

"When the Pope Speaks, the World Listens . . ."

The Cuban missile crisis of October 1962 put the two superpowers on a collision course, the closest they yet have come to World War III. The Soviets were installing missiles in Castro's Cuba, and Kennedy told Khrushchev bluntly, "They must be removed" . . . or else. While the world teetered on the brink of destruction, old Pope John XXIII moved into the breach. On October 25, John broadcast a moving appeal over Vatican Radio, urging leaders of both sides to settle the crisis through negotiation instead of war, "to promote, to favor, and to accept negotiations at every level and at all times, a prudent and wise principle that attracts the blessings of heaven and earth." On the following day, October 26, the leading newspaper of the atheistic Soviet Union, *Pravda*, published John's appeal on its front page. Within hours Khrushchev announced he was withdrawing the missiles. The crisis had ended.

The papal appeal alone had not resolved that crisis, but it made a great contribution. The speech had not been delivered out of the blue. John made it in response to unofficial appeals from both American and Soviet intellectuals, and it had been approved in advance by both Kennedy and Khrushchev. It was a tremendous help for the Soviet leader in finding a face-saving exit from the danger into which he had fallen.

Christmas, 1967, was a gloomy day for Americans. The Vietnam War had reached its lowest depths in frustration and near-despair. President Lyndon Johnson personally flew to Saigon for a Yule-season visit, and on his return flight to Washington he made one stop—Vatican City. To avoid having to spend time in ceremonial meetings with Italian government leaders, Johnson flew by helicopter from the Rome airport to the Vatican. In those days there was no proper heliport on papal territory, and the presidential chopper had to land on a tennis court behind the Apostolic Palace with U.S. embassy staffers using flashlights to illuminate the landing site. The president had a lengthy and intense talk with Pope Paul VI about the search for peace in Vietnam. He then helicoptered back to the airport and took off, leaving a highly irritated group of Italian politicians, who felt snubbed by Johnson. It was significant that in that critical moment, the president of the United States did not have time for the leaders of a NATO government but did have time to see the pope.

The armies of Chile and Argentina were mobilizing in December 1978, ready to fight over their Beagle Channel dispute. They were closer to war than was generally known at the time. American diplomats involved in the case have told me that the two countries were within forty-eight hours of all-out military conflict. It was then that President Jimmy Carter's personal representative to the pope, Robert F. Wagner, made an urgent visit to Archbishop Casaroli, "foreign minister" of the Holy See. Wagner's message: The American president wondered if the newly elected Pope John Paul II would be willing to intervene in a last-ditch attempt to keep those two Catholic countries from going to war. The reply was an unequivocal yes. The pope immediately contacted the two governments and persuaded them to renounce use of force in favor of a negotiated settlement. With the Holy See acting as mediator, the two sides entered diplomatic talks, which ended happily when their foreign ministers came to the Vatican to sign an agreement settling the dispute. Because of papal action, another war had been averted.

These three incidents demonstrate the truth of what John XXIII once said: "When the pope speaks of peace, men listen."

It is one of the greatest measures of the international stature of the See of Peter that men do listen to what the pope says. And not only do Catholics listen, but also Protestants and Communists and Muslims. The Holy See has no military divisions and only 108.7 acres of sovereign territory, but it functions on the world scene with the backing of tremendous prestige and respect.

A measure of the Vatican's influence is the fact that well over one hundred governments have full diplomatic relations with the Holy See, and they are governments that represent a broad spectrum of religions, races, and ideologies. Queen Elizabeth is head of the Church of England and yet she maintains an embassy to the Holy See. The secular United States has its ambassador to the Vatican. So does Fidel Castro's Cuba, Marxist Yugoslavia, Shinto Japan, and a bloc of Muslim countries including Egypt, the Sudan, Syria, Turkey, Kuwait, and even Khomeini's Iran. The only remaining ambassador of Taiwan in Europe is accredited to the Holy See. The Lithuanian government-in-exile keeps a legation at the Vatican. The Soviet Union does not have formal relations with Rome, but top Soviet leaders always call on the pope when they visit the Eternal City.

Popes consider international diplomacy part of their function, along with their general pastoral activity. Vatican diplomacy has a dual aim: On the one hand, it seeks maximum freedom for the Church everywhere, so that it can carry on its work of evangelization; on the other hand, it aims at promoting the Christian values of peace and justice all over the world. In a speech to the Vatican's school of diplomacy in 1951 (when he was still Archbishop Montini), Pope Paul defined the goals of Vatican diplomacy: "Diplomacy of the Holy See has this characteristic: It sends its representatives into various countries not only to defend the rights of the Holy See, of the Church, but sends them also to defend the rights, to serve the needs of the people in those countries."

On another occasion, Paul said: "If pontifical diplomacy were to disappear from the world, the diplomatic corps would find itself deprived of a kind of model which points out the aims, controls the methods, and perhaps unconsciously lives diplomacy. . . . it is the art of peace."

Both John XXIII and Paul VI reached the papacy through diplomatic careers. The present pope, John Paul II, had no diplomatic experience, but in many ways he is the most political of modern pontiffs, ever ready to lend the influence of the Vatican to solving international problems. All three have been activists on the international scene, each dealing with governments of the world in his own style. John relied heavily on personal contacts and informal arrangements. Paul sought to put negotiated understandings into written contracts. John Paul never hesitated to exploit a position of strength but was pragmatic enough to accept half a loaf when necessary.

Not only do popes have moral prestige and spiritual influence but the Holy See also has a highly professional diplomatic corps with four hundred years of experience (the oldest continuously existing diplomatic corps in the world) to help in promoting peace and justice internationally. The practice of sending papal representatives abroad goes back to the early centuries of Christianity, but it was not until the year America was discovered that a full-fledged papal diplomatic corps was established, with nuncios appointed on a permanent basis to function as ambassadors fully accredited to kings or heads of states. The Spanish pope Alexander VI in 1492 sent Francisco des Prats to Spain as his nuncio. In short order, nuncios were dispatched to other major capitals of Europe—in 1500 to Venice, in 1513 to Paris, in 1513 to Vienna, in the same year to Lisbon, in 1560 to Florence, in 1577 to Brussels, in 1582 to Cologne.

To train its diplomats, the Vatican has a school of diplomacy in Rome where well-chosen priests with degrees in canon law come to take a two-year course. Founded in 1701 by Pope Clement XI, the school is called the Pontifical Ecclesiastical Academy and is housed in a 250-year-old palazzo just behind the Pantheon and facing the building where Galileo was tried. It was originally called the Academy of Ecclesiastical Nobles because all its members had to come from noble families. Today, those future diplomats are chosen from among the best and the brightest young priests in the Church, with papal nuncios abroad ever on the lookout for promising young candidates. Among the graduates of the academy are Popes Clement XIII, Leo XII, Leo XIII, Benedict XV, and Paul VI. The roll of alumni also includes Cardinal Casaroli and Archbishop Marcinkus. When he was still Monsignor Eugenio Pacelli, Pope Pius XII taught diplomacy there, from 1909 to 1914.

Strange protocol problems may arise when a papal representative is accredited to a non-Catholic country. Papal nuncios are clergymen, and this caused a problem in Paris in 1796 when the French Revolution put into power an atheistic, anticlerical regime. The French Directory refused to deal with an ecclesiastic, and so the nuncio had to call himself "Count" Pieracchi instead of "Archbishop," and had to address his secretary as "Monsieur" instead of "Father" François Evangelisti.

When the Holy See and Egypt began negotiations to establish diplomatic relations a cultural problem arose. In the West, it is a sign of respect for men to uncover the head; in the Middle East, it is a sign of respect to cover the head. And so for many months the Vatican's undersecretary of state, Giovanni Battista Montini, wrangled with his opposite number in the Egyptian foreign office, Adly Andrawes, about whether the Egyptian ambassador should wear his tarboosh (fez) when he called on the pope. Montini insisted the tarboosh be removed; Andrawes was adamant in insisting that it be worn. As Andrawes related the story to me many years later, he finally settled the problem by shouting at Montini: "You must understand that the tarboosh is a part of the ambassador's uniform! Asking him to remove his tarboosh is like asking him to remove his trousers!"

Montini gave in. The ambassador called on Pope Pius XII with tarboosh on head.

The Vatican tends to be modest and self-deprecating about the quality of its diplomatic corps (Cardinal Tardini, when secretary of state, once huffed, "If the Vatican diplomatic corps is the best in the world, I would hate to see the second-best!"). But no one can deny that the Holy See's diplomats have left a remarkable trail of successes in their history. One of their more notable victories was at the Congress of Vienna, which was convened in 1814 to redraw the map of Europe after the final defeat of Napoleon.

The French army under Napoleon had carried the pope off to exile in France and had established its own regime in what had been the Papal States. And so when the secretary of state, Cardinal Ercole Consalvi, went to Vienna, he had few bargaining chips to play in that intense game of European diplomacy. He negotiated so skillfully that he got the Papal States restored to the pontiff.

The Holy See's diplomatic skill was demonstrated in France after the fall of the Second Empire, when Pope Leo XIII, a graduate of the Vatican's school of diplomacy, rallied to the French republican cause. This horrified Catholic conservatives, but by doing so Leo took the curse off Catholicism in the new France.

Pope John's Personalized Diplomacy

Pope John XXIII was not among those trained for a diplomatic career at the Pontifical Ecclesiastical Academy, and this might even have helped him to score dramatic successes on the international scene through the use of pragmatic, intensely human gestures without regard for diplomatic protocol. He achieved important diplomatic breakthroughs without signing a single treaty. It was all done through unofficial personal contacts.

Elected at a moment of great promise for international peace, John set out to ease the tensions of the Cold War by bringing the superpowers closer together. He was deeply impressed by the possibilities offered in the happy coincidence of having in power at the same time the two "K's"—Kennedy and Khrushchev—two progressive spirits who gave humanity so much hope. John's problem was that the Holy See did not have direct diplomatic channels to either Moscow or Washington. Conspicuously absent from the more than a hundred countries that had diplomatic relations with the Holy See were the two superpowers, the governments that had their fingers on the nuclear trigger. In his characteristic style, Pope John sought to make up for the absence of formal relations by appealing to the two leaders on a personal basis, relying on his personal charisma. Though he made some progress with both, in the end he had far more impact on the "K" in Moscow than on the "K" in Washington.

John failed to understand the depth of Kennedy's political problem as the first Catholic to become president of the United States. The old pope naïvely assumed that Kennedy, as a good Catholic, certainly would want to establish diplomatic relations with the Holy See. John did not realize that precisely because he was a Catholic, Kennedy had to lean over backwards to avoid giving the impression that he was unduly influenced by the papacy.

Kennedy's caution was rooted in a history of church-state relations that goes all the way back to the Founding Fathers, who strongly opposed any formal dealing with the papacy. In 1779, John Adams warned the Continental Congress not to send an envoy to the Papal States because he feared the pope in turn "would send to Washington a Catholic legate or nuncio; in other words, an ecclesiastical tyrant, which, it is to be hoped, the United States will be too wise ever to admit into their territories."

Even so, America's relations with the papacy began surprisingly early. The United States had a consulate in the Papal States in 1797, and diplomatic relations at the ministerial level were established by President James K. Polk in 1848—relations with the pope as ruler of a sovereign state, not as head of a religious organization. United States envoys from the beginning were instructed to distinguish carefully between the pope's roles as temporal head of the Papal States and as spiritual leader of the

Catholic Church. American trade in those days was very much Europe-oriented, and President Polk said at the time, "The interesting political developments in those [Papal] States, in my opinion, make such a step useful for our commercial interests."

Both the House and Senate gave overwhelming approval for funds to establish the new American legation in Rome, and it remained there till 1867. That year a false rumor spread that the pope was shutting down an American Protestant church in Rome. The rumor reawakened old American suspicions of the papacy, bringing back the cry of "Rum, Romanism, and Rebellion" as the great trio of evils, and an outraged U.S. Congress cut off funds for the legation. The American minister, Rufus King, hung on until his money ran out, then hauled down the Stars and Stripes, locked up the legation, and went home. The 1867 law banning funds for an American diplomatic mission to the pope remained on the books until 1983.

After the pope lost his temporal sovereignty in 1870, the question of diplomatic relations became far more complicated. It now was a question of relations not with a state that covered a strategic geographic territory but with the head of a church, which seemed to contradict the American principle of separation of church and state and gave a strong argument to anti-Catholic forces in the country determined to block any papal foothold in the United States. And so from 1867 until 1984 there were no formal diplomatic relations between Washington and the Holy See.

A substitute was worked out between Franklin D. Roosevelt and Pius XII. In 1936, Cardinal Eugenio Pacelli, then Vatican secretary of state, accepted the invitation of some close American friends to spend his October vacation in their Long Island home, instead of in Switzerland, as was his usual habit. Accompanied by his intimate friend Count Enrico Galeazzi and shepherded in the United States by Archbishop Francis Spellman, Pacelli soon learned that his vacation could not be as private as he had expected. Somewhat to his surprise, he was invited to visit Roosevelt in the president's Hyde Park home. (He later commented to a friend that he was relieved that Eleanor Roosevelt was not present, "because she is a very difficult person.")

That meeting laid the groundwork for close cooperation between FDR and Pacelli during the war years. Galeazzi discreetly made four more trips to Washington, quietly exploring the possibilities for better relations, while Cardinal Spellman gave him all assistance. In March 1939, Pacelli became Pope Pius XII. In September World War II broke out. And on Christmas Eve, 1939, Roosevelt announced to a stunned American public that he was sending Myron C. Taylor to Rome as his "personal representative" to the pope.

The master politician FDR had worked out a remarkable new system for relations with the Vatican over a White House lunch with Spellman on October 24, 1939. To avoid having to ask approval of the Senate for Taylor's appointment (which would have stirred up a political hornets' nest), he would not formally establish diplomatic relations but would send a personal representative to the pope, an appointment that would not require Senate approval. He also eased the way by announcing the appointment while senators and congressmen were away from Washington on Christmas vacation. At the time FDR wrote to Pope Pius, "To you, whom I have the privilege of calling a good friend, better an old friend, my most respectful regards at this Christmas time."

Roosevelt was unaware that addressing a pope as "an old friend" was a shocking violation of Holy See etiquette. But Pius gladly overlooked this little gaffe. He was delighted that at long last there would be an American representative at the Vatican. The following day in the Consistorial Hall of the Apostolic Palace he told his curial cardinals the news and added, "This is a Christmas announcement which could not be more welcome."

Meanwhile, the Holy See had for decades kept a papal representative in Washington, though without diplomatic status. In 1893 pope-diplomat Leo XIII sent Archbishop Francesco Satolli to Washington as "apostolic delegate." He was not accredited to the U.S. government and had no diplomatic status. His official function was to represent the pope to the American Catholic episcopate. But he was on hand just in case there was need of a papal channel to the American government. Ever since then, there has been a papal representative in the American capital.

After Myron Taylor gave up his post in 1950, there was no "president's man at the Vatican" for many years. In 1951, President Harry Truman tried to go all the way to establish full diplomatic relations with the Holy See and asked the Senate for approval of General Mark Clark as ambassador. To help things along, Pope Pius sent his undersecretary of state, Montini, to Washington to discuss the nomination. The appointment of Clark provoked such an uproar from anti-Catholic elements that Truman withdrew the nomination and dropped the idea completely. He never opened the subject again.

President Eisenhower in 1953 appointed Clare Boothe Luce ambassador to Italy, and she at first hoped to double as representative to the Holy See as well. A convert to Catholicism, she was deeply interested in the Church and understandably hoped to develop close relations with the Vatican during her Roman stay. She soon was to learn that the Holy See did not do things that way.

Ever fearful of losing some of its prerogatives to the Italian state, the Vatican on principle does not accept the "doubling up" of ambassadors in Rome. It is common practice for ambassadors of smaller states to be accredited to several countries at once, and the Holy See does not object to a diplomat resident, for example, in Madrid, serving as ambassador to the Vatican as well as to Spain. But the pope will not hear of an ambassador to Italy doubling as envoy to the Vatican. The Vatican will not even agree that missions to the Holy See and Italy be housed in the same building. The British once tried to put their legation to the Vatican in the same building as their embassy to Italy, going so far as to propose separate doors for their ambassador to Italy and their minister to the Vatican. The Holy See would not accept even that arrangement.

Just to be sure Clare Luce understood the situation clearly,

the Vatican daily, *L'Osservatore Romano,* carried an editorial explaining that for an ambassador to double as envoy to both Italy
and the Holy See "would be contrary to the traditions" of the
Vatican. Given the extremely formal and protocol-conscious
mood of the curia under Pius XII, this meant that contacts between the United States and the Vatican would be minimal without the presence of an American representative to the Holy See.
Even so, devout Catholic Clare Luce could not bear being in
Rome and not having contact with the pope. And so she prevailed
upon Count Galeazzi to arrange for an audience.

Because of the delicacy of the situation, Galeazzi explained
to Mrs. Luce that the meeting must be held in secret and kept
secret. She was driven to the Apostolic Palace in a Vatican limousine, lest her embassy automobile attract attention. Galeazzi took
her to a private elevator, which rose directly to the papal library.
Not even the top protocol officials in the Vatican knew that the
meeting was taking place.

When the interview ended, Count Galeazzi took Mrs. Luce
back to her home in the same anonymous limousine. He breathed
a sigh of relief when he at last escorted her into the embassy
residence, silently congratulating himself that the whole thing
had been brought off without publicity. But awaiting Mrs. Luce
was an Italian journalist, and the moment she saw him the lady
exclaimed jubilantly, "Guess where I have been! I have just had
a private audience with the pope!"

So much for secrecy.

When Pope John was elected, he broke through the protocol
barrier inherited from Pius to set up an unofficial channel to the
Americans. As usual, he simply circumvented his stiffly formal
curia and handled things on a personal basis. A member of his
trusted Kitchen Cabinet, a young diplomat named Igino Cardinale, had grown up in Brooklyn and easily established informal
contacts with friends in the U.S. embassy in Rome. Eventually a
junior political officer at the embassy was given the task of maintaining liaison with Monsignor Cardinale on a purely informal,
unofficial basis.

In addition to this day-to-day unofficial channel, John used a vast array of informal contacts in trying to establish a rapport with Kennedy. To deal with the touchy Cuban missile crisis, John relied on Norman Cousins, editor of the *Saturday Review of Literature,* who had good relations with intellectuals around Kennedy, such as Ted Sorenson and Arthur Schlesinger. In his eagerness to break through to Washington, John even violated the longstanding rule that the Holy See never takes the initiative in establishing diplomatic relations with any government. He sought the help of a leading Catholic politician, Amintore Fanfani, for a time prime minister of Italy, in sounding out Washington on the possibility of setting up relations.

Fanfani's envoys were politely rebuffed. With his eye on the next election and eager to win a second term, Kennedy was determined to maintain his distance from the papacy. He kept official contacts with the Holy See to an absolute minimum, only permitting his ambassador to Italy, Frederick Reinhardt, to attend the opening session of the Vatican Council after the Holy See used all its influence to persuade him to do so.

Wily old Pope John still had an ace to play. He firmly believed that if he could meet John Kennedy personally, he would be able to make progress in establishing some kind of rapport, even informal and unofficial. A great opportunity dropped into his lap when the American First Lady, Jacqueline Kennedy, scheduled a trip to Rome and requested a private audience with the pope. The request was granted with enthusiasm.

A Vatican protocol officer reported later that as the moment of the audience approached, John sat in his private library going over in his mind the protocol of this momentous occasion. How should he address the lady? As an American she might be called simply Mrs. Kennedy, but the pope would be speaking to her in French and wondered if he should address her as Madame. While waiting for the visitor to enter the Library, John was mumbling to himself "Mrs. Kennedy, Madame, Madame, Mrs. Kennedy." When the door opened and the lady walked in, he simply broke into a broad smile, extended both hands, and exclaimed warmly, "Jacqueline!"

The meeting with "Jackie" went so well that John had high hopes of making the same kind of contact with her husband. Things began looking up in early 1963, when the Holy See learned that President Kennedy planned to visit Europe that summer. His itinerary included Italy, and no president can visit Italy without calling on the pope. It looked as if, at long last, the two Johns would meet face to face. Sadly, the meeting never took place. Pope John died on June 3 that year. One month later, Kennedy came to Rome and called on John's successor, Paul VI, in the same Library where the old pope had received Jacqueline.

In contrast with his limited success with Washington, Pope John scored dramatic diplomatic victories in dealing with the other "K," the charismatic Khrushchev. His breakthrough to Moscow was even more remarkable when set against the bitterness between Catholicism and Communism that prevailed when Pius XII died.

The 1917 Bolshevik Revolution had brought to power in "Holy Russia" an atheistic regime with an avowed antireligious ideology, but the patient men then at the helm of the Catholic Church were not totally discouraged. After all, the Holy See had negotiated a concordat and had diplomatic relations even with the French revolutionary regime, which also was totally anticlerical and atheistic. And so in the early years of Communist rule, Pope Pius XI conducted long and painstaking negotiations with the Lenin government aimed at some kind of agreement that would give Catholics in the Soviet Union at least minimum rights and protection.

The pope made a major mistake, which had a great deal to do with the failure of those negotiations. To hedge his bets in case the talks failed, Pius XI tried to set up a secret hierarchy inside the Soviet Union, in the hope that it would retain the structure of the Church there even if the regime refused contacts with the Vatican. At one point the pope's representatives had established an underground hierarchy of four bishops and seven apostolic administrators. The Soviet regime, of course, knew all about it, and when Stalin came to power his police arrested all those clandestine bishops and administrators, along with hundreds of priests, and wiped out the underground Catholic Church. At the same time, negotiations for a church-state agreement collapsed completely. There followed decades of unremitting hostility between the Holy See and Moscow.

When Pius XII became pope in 1939, he adopted a totally hostile line toward the Soviets. His hatred of Communism perhaps dated back to his days as nuncio in Munich, when, in 1919, Bavaria was temporarily proclaimed a "Soviet republic." A gang of Red Guards charged into the nunciature and called for Pacelli. The archbishop met them with calm and dignity, but there was a frightening moment when an officer of the Red Guards shoved his pistol into Pacelli's chest and demanded the keys of his automobile.

Pius's fears of Communism appeared justified after World War II, when a new wave of persecution of the Church swept over Eastern Europe. Backed by the Red Army, Communist regimes consolidated their power in country after country behind the Iron Curtain, which had fallen across Europe "from Stettin on the Baltic to Trieste on the Adriatic." Imposition of Communist power involved suppressing the Church in a persecution that some compared with that of the era of the martyrs under the Caesars. Bishops, priests, and nuns were arrested and humiliated on a massive scale, Church schools were closed, Church property confiscated. In one Eastern European state after another, the great leaders of the national Catholic communities were arrested— Wyszynski in Poland, Mindszenty in Hungary, Stepinac in Yugoslavia.

It was during that period that Pius XII became known as the Chaplain of NATO because of his uncompromising attacks on Communism. His hostility reached its peak on July 1, 1949, when his Holy Office issued a decree excommunicating those who voted Communist or joined the Communist party. It now seemed that the breach was irreparable, that there no longer was any hope of bridging the gap between the Marxist and Catholic worlds, no further possibility for compromise.

That was indeed a dark period, but as the years passed events proved that the gap could be bridged, at least partially—not by classical diplomatic negotiations or the drafting of written agreements, but through contact between two remarkable personalities. Both came from peasant backgrounds (and sometimes displayed the manners of peasants). On the one side was Nikita Khrushchev, whose "de-Stalinization" policy had stirred hopes everywhere that freedom might yet come to the people in Communist lands. On the other side was Pope John XXIII, the "interim pope" who had vowed to open the windows of the Church to the winds of change. In changing the Vatican's policy toward Communists, John gave a supreme demonstration of how personality can alter the course of the papacy. These two charismatic leaders stretched out their hands to each other not with abstract proposals or documents but with folksy personal gestures.

It was Khrushchev who broke the ice by wishing Pope John a happy birthday. Out of the blue, on November 25, 1961, a letter arrived from the Soviet ambassador in Rome, addressed to the pope. On behalf of "Mr. Nikita Khrushchev," the ambassador expressed his "congratulations to His Holiness John XXIII on the occasion of his eightieth birthday, with the sincere wish for his good health and success in his noble efforts toward strengthening and consolidating peace in the world by solving international problems through frank negotiations."

This was the kind of breakthrough John sought, but it horrified the Old Guard in his curia, who were still waging the Cold War. Against the advice of many conservatives in his entourage, Pope John hastened to respond in warmest terms, thanking Khrushchev for the greetings and promising to pray for peace and for the people of the Soviet Union.

Now began a series of events that brought the two sides ever closer together. True to form, John once again circumvented his curia in pushing these new developments and depended instead on his loyal Kitchen Cabinet and his personal charisma. This was especially evident early in March 1963, when two Soviet "tourists" arrived in Rome. They were Khrushchev's daughter, Rada, and her husband, Alexei Adzhubei, editor of *Izvestia*.

Like so many other visitors to the Eternal City, Alexei and Rada asked for an audience with the pope. Adzhubei sent word that he was bringing a special message from his father-in-law for Pope John. Cardinal Ottaviani in the Holy Office and many top officials in the Secretariat of State were absolutely against granting the audience, lest it appear to be a betrayal of millions of Catholics suffering under Communist regimes.

The pope himself officially said neither yes nor no to the request for an audience. Through his secretary, Loris Capovilla, he subtly arranged for the Soviet couple to be present in the Throne Room along with nearly fifty other persons, including many journalists, who had gathered for a special occasion. The son-in-law and daughter of Khrushchev were driven beneath medieval archways into Vatican City, he wearing a dark suit, she with her head covered by a heavy veil, just like good Catholic pilgrims.

At the reception, John made a speech but made no mention of the presence of the Soviet pair. As the reception ended, the pope moved around in the crowd a bit, shaking hands and expressing warm greetings yet still paying no heed to the Adzhubeis. As the crowd left through the main entrance, Alexei and Rada quietly were directed into the papal library. There the highest-ranking Soviet personality ever to visit a pope up to that time spent eighteen emotion-filled minutes with the supreme pontiff of the Catholic Church.

The message Adzhubei brought from Khrushchev was a stunning surprise for John. The Soviet leader suggested establishment of diplomatic relations between Moscow and the Holy See. It was a somewhat awkward moment for the pope, because he knew such a step was premature. But he parried the thrust deftly, murmuring something about how even God had to take six days to create heaven and earth and therefore men should be patient in their endeavors. He then shifted the conversation to a purely personal level. Turning to Rada, John asked how many children she had and what were their names. She told the pope that she had three sons, and when he learned that one of them was named Ivan (the Russian equivalent of John), he told her with warmth that his father also was named John. He sent very special greetings to Ivan, adding "I am sure the other two will not be jealous." Turning back to Alexei, the pope observed that even though Alexei was an atheist, he would not object to receiving "the blessing of an old man" for his children. He presented a rosary to Rada and papal medals to Alexei. Khrushchev's daughter's eyes filled with tears and even Alexei appeared deeply moved. That folksy meeting inaugurated a dialogue between the Holy See and the Kremlin that has continued down to the present.

An indication of how far out of step John had gotten with his own curial team was the editorial carried by the Vatican's *L'Osservatore Romano* on the same day the pope met Adzhubei. The newspaper, which is controlled by the Vatican's Secretariat of State, sharply attacked Marxism, complaining that "Communism is just what it always has been, atheist, materialist, in theory and in practice. Pope John XXIII feels compelled to attack it." Significantly, *L'Osservatore* never reported the meeting with Adzhubei. Soviet bureaucrats also were caught off guard. When rumors spread over Rome that the pope had met the Adzhubeis, the Soviet embassy put out a denial, insisting that "Mr. Adzhubei did not meet the pope, although he did enter the papal library."

By now things were moving quickly toward a totally new relationship between Vatican and Kremlin. Following contacts by Monsignor Jan Willebrands, then number-two man under Cardinal Augustin Bea at the Secretariat for Christian Unity, Khrushchev on October 10, 1962, gave permission for Russian Orthodox observers to attend John's Vatican Council. The surprise permission came too late for the observers to be present at the opening ceremony, but four days later they were there; it was the most dramatic contact between Russian Orthodox and Catholics in many decades.

Forever bypassing his curia, John scored another breakthrough with Khrushchev through the mediation of Norman Cousins, who called on the Soviet leader on December 13, 1962. Cousins was not even a Catholic and stated clearly to Khrushchev, "I am not an official messenger and do not represent anyone." But during his visit he made an appeal on behalf of Pope John for the release of the Ukrainian Catholic Metropolitan of Lvov, Jozef Slipjy, who had been in prison for eighteen years and was believed to be the last survivor of eleven Ukrainian bishops arrested by the Soviet regime. Khrushchev agreed. In February of the following year, Monsignor Willebrands went to Moscow to meet Slipjy, told him he was free, and startled the world by bringing the bewildered old prelate to Rome. It was a spectacular development, and John had pulled it off without even consulting his official team in the curia.

In addition to dealing directly with Khrushchev, the old pope made a successful probe into Moscow's satellite, Hungary. As usual, John made the first move through a channel outside the Vatican bureaucracy. One day in 1962, the pope whispered to the archbishop of Vienna, Cardinal Koenig, "Why don't you go to see Cardinal Mindszenty? Maybe we should invite him to the council."

Koenig was stunned. Mindszenty, the primate of Hungary, had lived in the American embassy in Budapest since 1956, when he had sought refuge there to escape arrest and possible death after the failure of the anti-Moscow uprising. In Vienna, Koenig was nearer to Eastern Europe than any other top Catholic churchman, but until then he had not thought of going into the Communist area. When he expressed doubts that the Hungarians would allow him into the country, Pope John chuckled and answered, "Leave it to us to open the frontier for you. Go buy yourself a ticket."

The frontier indeed was open to Koenig, and he called on Mindszenty, in the first high-level Church contact with the old cardinal since 1956. That meeting started a process which eventually led to Mindszenty's release and set the stage for John's successor, Pope Paul, to conclude an agreement with the Hungarians regularizing the status of the Church in that country.

The stunning pace of improvement in relations was not entirely due to the goodness of Khrushchev's heart, of course. The two shrewd old peasants clearly saw great mutual advantages for both sides in better understanding. For the Vatican, there was the prospect of improved (though certainly not perfect) conditions for the Church in Communist lands. For Khrushchev, there was the prospect of a muting of the Vatican's anti-Soviet propaganda and of cooperation in the international field (as had happened during the Cuban missile crisis of 1962). Khrushchev had given permission for the Russian Orthodox observers to attend the council on the understanding that the council would not condemn Communism. Both John and Paul VI stuck by this understanding.

It took courage and determination for the popes to keep John's commitment not to attack Communism during the council. By the time of the last session, in 1965, heavy pressure had built up among the council fathers to condemn Marxism. Many bishops feared that history would judge the Church harshly for not speaking out courageously against oppression in the Soviet bloc, just as Pope Pius XII had been savagely attacked for his failure to come out loud and clear in defense of Jews during the Nazi Holocaust. Nearly three hundred bishops banded together in demanding that the council's document "The Church in the Modern World" include a section on Communism. There were more than two hundred amendments proposed from the floor calling for condemnation of Marxist regimes. Because of John's commitment, Pope Paul intervened personally to see that all these proposals were rejected. The council did not condemn Communism.

This was a striking Khrushchev success. The council's silence on Marxism contrasted with the agenda proposed for the council that had been tentatively planned by Pius XII. A suggested item on that agenda was "Against those who support Communist doctrine, against those who propagate the class struggle . . ."

John's dealing with the Marxists predictably enraged Catholic conservatives. The right-wing Italian magazine *Il Borghese* fumed: "The Holy See has in reality renounced its crusade against Marxism and is seeking every possible accord with the Communists. . . . The council has buried Pius XII for the second time."

In reply, the supporters of Pope John could point to benefits reaped by the Church from this warming of Marxist-Vatican relations. As the council opened, it was not clear whether bishops from the "Church of Silence" in Eastern Europe would be able to come to Rome. By the time the council ended in 1965, no less than eighty-nine bishops from Communist countries in Eastern Europe had been allowed to come to Rome and to return to their dioceses unmolested. John's highly personalized Ostpolitik was paying dividends.

When he died in 1963, Pope John had not signed any agreement with a Communist government, nor had he gotten anything in writing from the Soviets guaranteeing even minimal rights for the Church. But the impact of his personality had opened the door wide to a new era for Catholics in Eastern Europe, and his successor gladly walked through that door to formalize the new era.

Pope Paul's Formal Diplomacy

Whereas John had circumvented official structures to make his breakthrough by means of personal contact and expressions of good will, Pope Paul VI, the superbureaucrat, characteristically tried to put everything in writing, to formalize it all officially. It was providential that such a pope should follow the charismatic but disorganized John, to pull together and make permanent the openings the "interim pope" had bequeathed to him. Paul could not have succeeded without the legacy of John's good will, but without Paul, all John's efforts might have been wasted.

With his penchant for neatly organizing everything, Pope Paul VI felt very much the need for a systematic arrangement in Vatican-American relations. The desirability of having a regular channel between the two was dramatically demonstrated during the Vietnam War, which created a serious misunderstanding between the Holy See and Washington. When President Lyndon Johnson stopped off to see the pope on his return from Vietnam the day before Christmas Eve in 1967, he was shaken by the intensity of Paul's feelings about the American bombing of Vietnamese cities. At one point, in demanding to know why the United States didn't stop the bombing, the pope slapped his desk and raised his voice to a shout. It was a shout of sorrow rather than anger, but it stunned the American president.

What Johnson did not know was that the American bombing of Hanoi had wrecked a papal scheme to mediate a peaceful settlement in Vietnam. In late November 1966, after an unlikely sequence of events, Pope Paul used an Italian Communist delegation to send a peace message to Ho Chi Minh. A Communist party official, Antonello Trombadori, had sent word discreetly to the pope that the delegation (headed by Enrico Berlinguer, later to become head of the party) would be happy to deliver any message the Holy See wanted to send to North Vietnam. Paul's aging secretary of state, Cardinal Cicognani, had spent many years as apostolic delegate in Washington and knew that such a move, if it ever became public, would provoke a strongly negative reaction in the United States. He and most other curial cardinals urged the pope to ignore the Communist message. The agonizing Paul went through hell deciding what to do. It was only at the last minute, as the delegation was mounting the Alitalia charter plane on the early morning of November 29, that Paul's private secretary, Monsignor Macchi, arrived breathlessly at the airport to put a packet into Trombadori's hands.

The papal message asked the North Vietnamese to allow Catholic relief teams and supplies into their area. More important, the pope urged Ho to accept a peaceful settlement and offered the Holy See's good offices in seeking such a settlement. The Italian Communists delivered the message, and the initial response from the North Vietnamese was cautiously positive. But on December 13 and 14 there was a massive, indiscriminate bombing of Hanoi by American planes, and any hope for a peaceful settlement was lost, at least for many years. The papal gesture went for naught.

It was no wonder that the frustrated Paul slapped his desk when he met Johnson.

Pope Paul continued to try, without success, to steer the Vietnam conflict toward a peaceful settlement. At one time he even offered the Vatican's Lateran Palace in Rome as a venue for peace talks (they took place in Paris instead). And all through that period of tension there was no American representative in Rome to explain Washington's point of view. Obviously there was a crying need for direct, formal relations between president and pope.

Just as John had secretly violated the principle that the Holy See does not request diplomatic relations, so also Pope Paul took the initiative, broaching the subject with Nixon when the president called at the Vatican in 1969. Paul showed a better understanding of the American scene than John had. He told Nixon, "We don't want another Mark Clark case," nor did the pope want another "Myron Taylor arrangement." The solution, he hoped, would lie somewhere in between.

The pope pursued the subject by sending his "chief of staff," Archbishop Benelli, to Washington in January 1970 for talks with Nixon, Secretary of State William Rogers, and National Security Council chief Henry Kissinger. In the end, an arrangement was worked out which, in the words of a Vatican official of the time, "neither side wanted but which both sides accepted." It was in fact another "Myron Taylor arrangement," with the difference that this time it lasted through four presidents—Nixon, Ford, Carter, Reagan.

Nixon appointed Henry Cabot Lodge as the man who would visit the Vatican on his behalf whenever there was need for the two sides to confer. Like Taylor, Lodge had no diplomatic status and so his nomination did not have to be approved by the Senate. The fact that Lodge had such towering personal prestige made the whole thing more palatable to the Holy See than it might have been, but even so, around the Vatican's Secretariat of State there were grumblings that the arrangement set a bad precedent and was not fair to countries who went to the trouble and expense of having full diplomatic relations. One day Paul's "foreign minister," Casaroli, was talking with a journalist in his office when an aide came in to announce that Henry Cabot Lodge was waiting to see him outside. The journalist shuffled his feet to show his willingness to get out of the way, but Casaroli motioned him to stay. With a broad grin, he told the newsman, "If they are not willing to have proper diplomatic relations with us, let him wait!"

Though the arrangement was not perfect, it was a big improvement over what had gone before. One of the great advantages was that it provided Paul with a direct channel for explaining to Washington his energetic efforts to improve the Vatican's relations with Eastern Europe.

On the Eastern front, Paul moved beyond John's personal diplomacy to dialogue, to negotiations, to agreements that were signed and sealed. A realist with a fine touch for formal diplomacy, Paul had no illusions about Communist governments. He knew that during his lifetime the Church could not expect to achieve full freedom under such regimes. But he set out "to save that which can be saved" ("salvare il salvabile"), on the assumption that the half loaf is better than no loaf at all. Paul's top diplomat Casaroli explained the policy: "It is not so much a 'modus vivendi' [a way of living] as a 'modus non morendi' [a way of not dying]."

Casaroli characterized Paul's policy this way in a lecture in Milan: "Not everywhere, not everywhere in the same form or with the same constancy, not always crowned with success. Nowhere easily. But rather decisively and with—one could say—a movement hard to reverse."

The hope was to keep the Church in Eastern Europe from dying until the distant day when full freedom would return. And the man whom Paul entrusted with the highly delicate task of negotiating this hope was the self-effacing Casaroli, the greatest diplomat in the Church and one of the greatest in the world.

Casaroli never has held a diplomatic post abroad, but he has handled some of the most delicate Vatican diplomatic assignments. His style is characterized by patience, good humor, and tolerance. He has an infallible memory, often recalling something that a person has told him years before and using it to effect in negotiations.

Casaroli began his own opening to Marxists at home in Italy. He shocked some conservative Vatican colleagues by developing an easy and relaxed friendship with top Italian Communist party leaders. On the international level, he has lunched with Fidel Castro and talked with Soviet leaders inside the Kremlin. Casaroli first contacted diplomats from Communist states when he attended an innocuous conference on consular rights in Vienna in 1961, and he came to know them well in the following decades. Because of this, enraged right-wing Catholics once put up, within sight of St. Peter's, posters demanding, "Excommunicate Casaroli, the Red Excellency of Compromise!"

Pope Paul made full use of the "Red Excellency" in his drive to penetrate Eastern Europe. The pope had scored points with the Soviets by honoring the commitment not to attack Communism at the council and by his policy on Vietnam. The way was clear to continue negotiations for Soviet-bloc concessions to the Church in Eastern Europe, in exchange for cooperation on international issues.

One of the successes Paul achieved, with Casaroli as his chief negotiator, was in Hungary. The year Paul was elected, the Hungarian Church was in a wretched state. Five of the fifteen Hungarian bishops were in jail, and seven of the others were not allowed to function. Six of the eleven dioceses had no head at all, and the others were in the charge of very old and feeble bishops.

Pope John had broken the ice by sending Koenig in to see Mindszenty, and Paul followed up on this opening by sending Casaroli in on a series of visits. By 1964 Casaroli had realized the impossible—he signed an agreement with the Hungarians. Things moved slowly, but by 1976 all Hungarian dioceses were headed by bishops acceptable to Rome. Casaroli himself is quick to concede that things are far from perfect for the Church in that Communist state. He once told me, "In Hungary, our bishops have enough freedom to perform perhaps only fifty percent of their functions." He then added with a chuckle: "But that is better than thirty percent."

Another success of the Paul-Casaroli team was the establishment of diplomatic relations with Yugoslavia—the first time the Holy See had reached such an agreement with an Eastern European Marxist state. On March 25, 1971, Marshal Tito himself, along with his wife, was received in audience by Pope Paul in the Vatican's Apostolic Palace. By this time it had become commonplace for top Communist officials to follow the pattern set by Adzhubei and to call on the pope. In April 1966, Soviet Foreign Minister Andrei Gromyko visited Pope Paul, in the first of a long series of papal audiences that Gromyko had with both Paul and John Paul II. A new peak was reached on January 30, 1967, when none other than the president of the Soviet Union, Nikolai Podgorny, met Pope Paul in a private audience at the Vatican. Over the years since then, popes have received such Eastern European leaders as Hungary's Kádár, Rumania's Ceauşescu, Bulgaria's Zhivkov. During Paul's reign, the Vatican eventually had bishops whom it approved functioning in all Eastern European countries except Albania.

The papal opening to the East paid an additional dividend in 1972, when the Soviet Union actively supported an invitation to the Holy See to attend the Helsinki conference on European security as a participating delegate, not simply as an observer. It seemed odd for the Vatican, which had no military power, to attend such a conference, but Casaroli explained to the group why the Holy See was there: "Admittedly, there are many areas in which the Holy See cannot participate in these deliberations, but there is one area in which an interest and specific competency arise and which is universally recognized: It is the area of moral values."

Paul's successes certainly did not mean that all was well in Eastern Europe. The long dialogue often took the form of steps backward after steps forward. In Czechoslovakia, for example, things were going well for the Church until the Soviet invasion after the "spring of 1968," which brought in its wake a new wave of oppression. Overall, however, the Ostpolitik launched with an exchange of birthday greetings has given the Vatican at least half the loaf and, as Casaroli said, perhaps has set in motion a process that cannot be reversed. The same Casaroli on another occasion explained that "a Church deprived of liberty and forced to continual compromise is always better than no Church at all." This was the situation in 1978 when a pope was elected who came from the heart of Eastern Europe itself.

John Paul Forgives the KGB

The election of a Slavic pope created a new situation in the Vatican's international relations, for both the East and the West. John Paul II believes in dialogue and would not go back to the Cold War approach of Pius XII, but he is far less accommodating than Paul VI. He wants the Church to demand its rights, making such a moral impact that it cannot be ignored even by the most hostile of regimes. His willingness to speak out against Communist oppression—even while maintaining contacts with Marxist states—made a deep impression on certain powerful anti-Catholic groups in the United States and lessened their resistance to diplomatic relations between Washington and the Holy See. Obviously, things had changed a great deal since the Mark Clark case. This was made clear when John Paul visited the United States in October 1979 and was received at the White House by a Southern Baptist president, Jimmy Carter.

The visit was a major step toward breaking through the barrier of bigotry, but things were not always so rosy in Vatican-American relations in John Paul's early days. After Reagan became president, he once irritated the pope by claiming that John Paul supported him in invoking economic sanctions against Poland. In fact, the pope had written a confidential letter to Reagan, thanking him in a general way for his support of the Polish people but not mentioning sanctions at all.

The Reagan "revelation" made it look as if the pope were playing a double game. Only a short time before, the bishops of

Poland had issued a declaration opposing sanctions—and that declaration had been approved by John Paul. One of the pontiff's best friends told me at the time that "the pope was put in the position of either calling Reagan a liar or admitting that he himself had lied to the Polish bishops." The same person said the pope was "stunned" that Reagan had apparently used the papal confidential letter for political purposes.

The Holy See put out a communiqué clarifying the situation, and the Italian press carried headlines saying "Pope Denies Supporting Reagan's Sanctions." That closed the subject, but the pope's good friend summed up the papal response to it all: "Diplomacy is not one of the strong points of the administration now in Washington."

Ironically, this incident was a major factor in encouraging Pope John Paul to press for diplomatic relations with Washington, since it seemed very clear that improved contacts were necessary to avoid such problems in the future. When President Reagan visited the pope in 1982, John Paul subtly brought up the subject. In November of the same year, Cardinal Casaroli saw Reagan in Washington just at the time that the first NATO nuclear missiles were deployed in West Germany, Britain, and Italy, a move that had prompted the Soviet Union to break off nuclear arms talks.

The Vatican had offered its mediation in an effort to get the two sides back to the conference table, and Reagan told Casaroli he would be happy if the Holy See would go ahead. The shrewd Casaroli adroitly exploited this opening. Moving his right hand back and forth as if he were writing in the air, Casaroli told Reagan: "Of course, we will do our best to mediate. But, Mr. President, you should understand that we could do this much better if we had diplomatic relations with the United States."

Reagan got the message.

In late 1983, Congress repealed the law of 1867 banning funding for a diplomatic mission to the pope. In January 1984, at the pope's annual reception for the diplomatic corps, a jubilant John Paul singled out American ambassador William Wilson (a wealthy California friend of Reagan's who until then had been the president's special representative to the pope) with special greetings and announced that the Holy See and the United States had established full diplomatic relations. For the first time in history, the United States had full diplomatic relations with the head of a religious organization. John Adams must have turned over in his grave.

One cynical journalist wrote at the time that the new arrangement would have no importance except "to give Wilson a better seat at diplomatic functions." In fact, it did mean a better seat for him, since until that time Wilson had to sit out with the crowd instead of among the accredited diplomats—complete with top hats and wives—at papal functions. But the move had far deeper significance. In a talk with me about his new status, Wilson said, "This is not the kind of post where I will be negotiating sales of Phantoms," but he saw the Holy See as "a great listening post, and having full diplomatic relations opens up to us channels of communications that we never had before."

In that listening post an American ambassador can get a unique view of the Middle East through close contact with patriarchs of Oriental-rite Catholic churches in that region. He can keep up-to-date on Latin America and often will have access to information not available to U.S. embassies on the scene. He can better coordinate United States–Vatican refugee assistance and relief programs.

Even before Wilson became ambassador, the value of close contacts with the Vatican had been demonstrated. When the American hostages were being held in Khomeini's Iran, the Holy See, through its pro-nuncio in Tehran, was able to make useful contacts on behalf of the United States. In March 1983, President Alvaro Magana of El Salvador dramatically announced that an early presidential election would be held, viewed at the time as a major step toward political liberalization in that country. Significantly, he made the announcement in his speech welcoming John Paul II when the pope arrived at the Ilopango–San Salvador airport. The announcement and its timing had been worked out in triangular negotiations between Washington, the Vatican, and the El Salvador regime.

Having solid diplomatic relations with Washington obviously strengthened John Paul's hand in dealing with the Soviet bloc, since the Soviets were eager to have influence in the Vatican comparable to that of the West. Things had gone well for them with Popes John and Paul, but the election of a Slavic pope created a certain nervousness among the regimes of Eastern Europe, and with good reason. In the early months of his reign, John Paul II showed that he intended to give Eastern Europe a high priority. He elevated to the post of secretary of state—the highest position in the curia below the pope himself—that veteran specialist on Eastern European affairs Agostino Casaroli. To replace Casaroli as "foreign minister" (in fact head of the Vatican's Council for Public Affairs) John Paul appointed another specialist on the area, Archbishop Achille Silvestrini, who had been nuncio in Belgrade and Helsinki and was Casaroli's trusted deputy in many delicate negotiations with Eastern European governments. Next in line, as undersecretary of the Council for Public Affairs, John Paul named Monsignor Audrys Backis, a naturalized American born in Lithuania whose specialty was Eastern Europe. He also appointed a "roving nuncio" for Eastern Europe, who traveled regularly to Poland, Czechoslovakia, Bulgaria, and Hungary.

John Paul's tougher stance toward Communism drew considerable flack from Marxist regimes, but it also scored successes. One such success was the Polish regime's agreeing to a papal visit to Poland in 1979. Pope Paul had tried for more than a decade to visit Poland but was always kept out. John Paul made two visits to Poland in the first four years of his papacy.

The Czech press regularly attacks John Paul as "anti-Socialist," and the regime there has toughened its oppression of the Church since the Slavic pope was elected. But in December 1983, the Czech foreign minister, Bohuslav Chnoupek, called on the pope in the Vatican. The Communist regimes don't like this pope, but they cannot ignore him or his Church.

John Paul's policy has its dangers, as was tragically demonstrated in St. Peter's Square on May 13, 1981, when the pope was gunned down and very nearly killed by a Turkish terrorist, Mehmet Ali Agca. Though it will never be proven juridically, a good case can be made that the shooting was plotted on orders of the Soviet Union. Agca himself confessed that he had been paid to do the shooting by the Bulgarian secret service on behalf of the Soviets. Italian courts until now have failed to come up with enough evidence to convict a group of Bulgarians named by Agca as organizers of the plot. But as a crusty old American ambassador told me at the time: "Did anyone ever prove that Stalin ordered the assassination of Trotsky? No. But does anyone, I repeat, anyone, doubt it? When the Russians organize such a plot, it is so well tiered that no one can ever find the fingerprints that would convict them in court. The same thing happened in the case of the shooting of the pope. Through many intermediaries, the Soviets found a known killer, technically and psychologically capable of carrying out the job, a right-winger who did not come from a Communist country, and hired him to do the dirty work."

Did the pope have a premonition that he would be an assassin's target? It may be that he did. Inside Vatican City on the morning of May 6, 1981, John Paul stood before the image of the Madonna of Lourdes to greet a new contingent of Swiss Guards. In his welcoming speech, the pope told them, "We pray to the Lord that violence and fanaticism may be kept far from the walls of the Vatican." Exactly one week later there was violence and fanaticism inside Vatican City, when the Turk shot the pope.

At the highest level in the Vatican they believe that the Soviet regime plotted that assassination attempt. This conclusion was reached soon after the shooting, and one of the first to reach it was the gentle Casaroli. He even publicly hinted at the likelihood of a conspiracy six weeks after the shooting when he told an ecumenical gathering in St. Peter's, "A heart, or perhaps hearts, a hostile heart has armed an enemy hand to strike the pope."

Immediately after the shooting, top Vatican officials examined the possibility that it might have been the work of some Latin

American terrorist group. This theory was discarded for lack of clear motivation and absence of circumstantial evidence. The conclusion was that only the Soviet Union had a clear motive for eliminating the Polish pope.

"We don't know who organized the plot in detail," a curial cardinal who is extremely close to John Paul told me. "But we certainly know whose interest it served—that of the Soviet Union."

The Soviets may have felt they had to get rid of John Paul because of the role he was playing in Poland. Although he lived in Rome, the pope by 1981 had become the national leader of the Polish people. Since they could not form opposition political parties, Poles had to look to the Church as their vehicle of national identity. (This often happens under oppressive regimes. The Orthodox Church served the same purpose during the centuries of Ottoman Turkish control of Christian countries like Greece and Bulgaria.) The aged primate of Poland, Cardinal Stefan Wyszynski, had led the Polish people from the time of the Communist takeover, but by 1981 the tough old cardinal was in the throes of a terminal illness, and his mantle clearly had fallen on John Paul II.

The Polish pope had demonstrated his control over his people in June of 1979 during his first return visit to his homeland after being elected pontiff. Here was the Great Communicator at his best, among his own people, speaking his own language, making them laugh or weep or cheer with the turn of a phrase or a meaningful gesture. He sometimes would lift up his manuscript before the crowd and toss it away dramatically and then speak extemporaneously with deep personal feeling. Sometimes, during a pause for applause, someone far, far away on the edge of the crowd would begin singing an old patriotic Polish hymn. Slowly the song would sweep over the crowd till a million people were singing in unison, while the pope sang along with them, tears running down his cheeks. It was the same all over Poland, from Warsaw to Kraków to Gniezno to Częstochowa: massive crowds turned out in perfect discipline, thousands of them having walked for miles to see and hear their leader, keeping order among themselves so that the police would not have the least excuse to interfere. When local Communist authorities told a crowd of teenagers there was no transport available to take them to a papal rally, they simply walked forty miles to be there.

Those millions who turned out to welcome their pope knew they were challenging the power of the Communist regime. And it was obvious they were impressed anew with their own power to stand up to the Russian-imposed government, a power they had forgotten they possessed. The pope awakened in them a sense of national identity that had long lain dormant. A leading Polish bishop told me that during John Paul's visit the Polish people "broke through the barrier of fear." I recall watching the pope stirring the crowds at Jasna Gora and thinking that he had the same kind of control of the Polish people that Ayatollah Khomeini had demonstrated earlier that year in rallying the Iranian people to overthrow the shah. A Vatican bishop traveling with the pope watched that crowd and remarked that "by wiggling a little finger" John Paul could have detonated a revolution that would have overthrown the regime in twenty-four hours.

The pope did not call for open rebellion, but the impact of his visit produced near-revolution in the months following. In the summer of 1980, Polish workers went on strike all over the country, and at the gates of the shipyards of Gdansk workers lifted up massive photos of Pope John Paul II as their symbolic leader. Out of that wave of strikes emerged the trade union Solidarity, created in defiance of the regime and representing the greatest challenge to Communist authority in Poland since the beginning of the Soviet occupation.

The Soviets knew as well as did those of us who traveled to Poland with John Paul that it was the pope who had evoked this upsurge of national feeling. The Soviet news agency Tass blamed the pope for the rise of Solidarity and accused the Vatican of "training and sending 'specialists' in Catholic propaganda to other Socialist countries of Eastern Europe." In Poland's neighbor Czechoslovakia the regime showed great concern about the political impact of the Slavic pope. Before he made his 1979 visit to Poland, the Czech government did its best to persuade the Polish regime not to allow him to come. The Czech rulers were very much afraid that there would be a spillover of nationalism from Poland into Czechoslovakia.

In the opinion of top Vatican sources, it was the events in Poland that moved the Soviets to try to eliminate John Paul. A Holy See official who is a former diplomat explained to me Moscow's attitude in those pre-Gorbachev years:

"The Soviets still consider Germany a great potential threat to their security, and, whatever else, they are determined to maintain direct geographical contact with East Germany. Poland lies across the railway and road links to Germany, and so, at all costs, it must be kept under Soviet control, like Czechoslovakia and Hungary. Other Eastern European countries, like Finland, Albania, Yugoslavia, and even Rumania, can follow independent policies. But the three that lie between the Soviets and Germany cannot be allowed to go.

"There are those who say the Soviets would never plot the shooting of the pope, for fear of exposure in the eyes of the world public. But they have shown they care little about public opinion when their security is endangered in one of those three vital states. They invaded Hungary in 1956 and Czechoslovakia in 1968 in the face of worldwide condemnation. They were ready to take similar drastic action in Poland. There the Soviet intention was to cut off the head of Polish nationalism. That head was the pope."

Though they may blame the Soviets privately for that dastardly deed in May 1981, the pope and his team have decided simply to forget it. Just as the pope went to Rebibbia prison to forgive Mehmet Ali Agca, so he forgives the Russians for plotting to kill him. What else could be done? It does not serve Catholic interests to break with the entire Communist bloc, which would be the consequence of a public denunciation of the KGB. John Paul knows how important it is to maintain contact with Moscow's leaders and to keep open every possible channel of communication in Eastern Europe. There are hopes for eventual papal visits to Czechoslovakia and Yugoslavia. And the crowning voyage of all just might be a visit someday to the Soviet Union itself.

And so the pope continues the Ostpolitik begun by John and Paul, but with his own special style. He continues to welcome to the Vatican top Communist officials—Foreign Minister Andrei Gromyko twice visited John Paul in Rome. The pope continues to send his roving nuncio around Eastern Europe, constantly probing to see what may be done to improve the status of the Church. The Vatican does not yet have diplomatic relations with Poland, but the Holy See and Warsaw have set up representative offices, similar to the Holy See's earlier arrangement with the United States.

While keeping these links with the Soviet Union and its allies, the pope has his eye on another great power—China. One of the shortcomings in the Vatican's global strategy is the lack of a major base in the Far East, where the Philippines is the only country with a Catholic majority. Christian missionaries have worked actively in Japan with full freedom for more than a century, yet the total Christian population is barely half a million out of more than one hundred million in that country. Christianity—Catholicism as well as Protestantism—is growing in South Korea at a breathtaking pace, but Christians there are still a minority, and in any case, South Korea's influence in the Orient is limited. In the eyes of the Vatican, the great potential is in China, where the Catholic community, numbering somewhere between three and five million souls, is cut off from Rome. The Communist regime permits Catholic activity, but mainly by the "Patriotic Church," which has no links with the Holy See. The Vatican has been separated almost completely from the Catholics of China since 1951, when the regime of Mao Tse-tung expelled the papal nuncio.

Here is clearly a case where successful Vatican diplomacy could pave the way for a vast expansion of the Catholic Church in the Far East. So far, there has been no success, but the Holy See continues to try. Popes Paul and John Paul II have sent signal after signal to Beijing in the hope of reestablishing contacts in that country, but to no avail. The Chinese opening to the United States and Western Europe did not include an opening to the Holy See.

For many years now, the only official contact between the Holy See and Beijing has been an exchange of bulletins between the astronomical observatories of China and the Vatican. Jesuits in China trained many of that country's astronomers, and even after the Communist takeover, scientific exchanges continued. Twice a month the Vatican's observatory at Castel Gandolfo receives a packet from Beijing, and twice a month the Holy See's astronomers send one back containing their scientific findings. (The packet from Beijing often contains a bit of political propaganda along with its scientific information.)

The famous Casaroli patience has been well demonstrated in his efforts, so far unsuccessful, to make some kind of breakthrough to Communist China. One of the biggest problems that eventually would have to be solved is that of bishops who have been ordained by the "Patriotic Church" without papal approval. When a newsman once asked Casaroli if these bishops have not been ordained illicitly, he answered, "Some things are not legitimate but are valid. That which is valid but not legitimate can be legitimized." When asked if those bishops, because of their illicit ordination, were not automatically excommunicated, Casaroli answered, "They would be excommunicated only if fully aware of what they were doing. This could be determined only by examining case by case. It has been impossible to examine a single case, and so no one has been excommunicated."

Asked if he detected any Chinese response to the many overtures sent by the Vatican, Casaroli answered with a grin, "I have not yet learned to read the Chinese alphabet."

In any case, the lack of response so far has not discouraged Casaroli, who looks at things in the perspective of history and does not expect to get everything at once. A person who knows him extremely well said, "If the patience of the Chinese is infinite, that of Casaroli is eternal."

Pope John Paul also continues to hope that the Holy See

eventually will exchange something more than data on the stars with the Chinese people. On the return trip from his voyage to the Far East in 1984, the pope was asked when he expected to visit China. He replied in one word: "Patience."

That word effectively sums up the basic style of papal diplomacy.

8

PAPAL IMPACT ON EVOLVING CHURCH TEACHING

Saint Paul said nothing for or against artificial insemination. Thomas Aquinas did not discuss the morality of trade unions or political democracy. Saint Augustine could not foresee the threat of nuclear conflict when he drew up the guidelines for a "just war."

It is obvious that with the evolution of scientific knowledge and social concepts, the teaching of the Church has to evolve and adapt. The supreme teachers of the Church, the popes, are custodians of a body of dogma that is unchangeable, but it is their duty to proclaim updated Church teaching on moral problems when new questions are raised by scientific progress. Their name is Peter in the sense that they cannot alter matters of faith, but their name is John or Paul or John Paul in dealing with new moral issues or social ethics in a rapidly changing world. Each pope has ample space to make his individual impact on Church teaching. He may issue completely new doctrine on totally new moral questions. Or he may come up with a social message that differs radically from what his precursors have taught.

The trio of popes with whom this book is concerned were activists who made an indelible imprint on Catholic teaching and thinking, in adapting traditional doctrine to modern situations, in changing the teaching on social questions, and in fashioning original concepts to respond to moral problems posed by modern science.

John on Anti-Semitism, Labor Unions, and Democracy

Good Pope John pioneered in the realm of social ideas, but he steered clear of most of the new issues involved in what is called moral theology, the rules of personal morality. He was a traditionalist in theology and shrank from taking a hard stand on either dogmatic or moral matters. In general, he left it to the council to deal with those weighty issues. After all, at the council were all the bishops and leading theologians of the Catholic world. But the advance of science could not be ignored completely by any modern pope, not even John, and in his encyclical "Mater et Magistra" he wagged a warning finger at adventurous applications of discoveries in the field of genetics: "The transmission of human life is entrusted by nature to a personal and conscious act and as such is subject to the all-holy laws of God: immutable and inviolable laws which must be recognized and observed. For this reason one cannot use means and follow methods which could be licit in the transmission of the life of plants and animals."

One of John's great contributions was putting the Church clearly on record against anti-Semitism. Today this may sound like an obvious stand, but it must be remembered that the papacy had a black record on this subject; popes kept Roman Jews in the ghetto as long as they had power to do so. Only eighty-eight years before John's election, Jews at last were allowed to move out of the Roman ghetto—and only because popes no longer held secular power in the Eternal City.

For centuries, anti-Semitism in Catholic teaching was accepted as a fact of life. In 1555 Pope Paul IV, who set up the Inquisition in Rome, issued an edict imposing humiliating restrictions on Jews, because "it is absurd and improper that the Jews, who have fallen into eternal servitude by their own guilt, should presume . . . to make so bold as to live intermingled with Christians, to wear no distinguishing mark, to employ Christian servants, even to purchase houses." The fanatical Paul IV installed torture chambers mainly to be used against Jews and sent many of them to burn at the stake in Rome's Campo dei Fiori.

The laws and rules imposed by Paul IV and his successors at various times required Roman Jews to wear yellow hats (yellow veils for women) to distinguish them from Christians; restricted their economic activity to dealing in old rags; enclosed them within the walls of a congested ghetto; forced them to amuse carnival crowds by racing down Via del Corso after being stuffed with a heavy meal; forbade their living anywhere in the Papal States except Rome and Ancona; and required them once a week to listen to a Christian sermon in a designated church (to be awakened with whips if they dozed off during the service).

As the papal tombola turned, there frequently were humane popes who rescinded the anti-Jewish restrictions and often employed Jews as their personal physicians and financiers. Children in the Roman ghetto used to chant "Good pope, bad pope, bad pope, good pope," a reflection of the uncertainties the oldest Jewish community in Europe faced when a new pope was elected. But even the kindness of "good popes" was offered in patronizing fashion, reflecting the rulers' benevolent nature rather than their recognition of human rights.

The capriciousness of papal behavior toward Jews was shown within the lifetime of one pope, Pius IX. "Pio Nono," as the Romans called him, began his long reign in 1846 as one of history's most liberal and humane pontiffs. One of his first acts was to tear down the walls of the Roman ghetto and give Jews permission to circulate freely in the city. He rescinded all restrictive regulations against them. But during the republican revolution in Rome in 1848, Pius barely escaped with his life, fled to exile in Gaeta, and on his return to Rome after the defeat of the rebellion was transformed into an arch-reactionary. Convinced that the Jews had supported the revolutionaries, Pius took his revenge by putting them back into the ghetto, with all that implied.

The ghetto finally was destroyed in 1870, when papal rule over Rome ended, but Jewish relations with popes remained uncertain. The attitude of Pope Pius XII toward the Jews was ambiguous, to say the least. Pius was a great diplomat, but in his determination to maintain good relations with the German Third Reich he seemed to have developed moral myopia regarding Nazi atrocities. A Vatican historian once boasted to me of how Pius's shrewd diplomacy enabled the Church to "come out of World War II with very strong relations even with such disparate people as the Allies and the Germans, the Vichy French and the French Resistance. Any one of them would have denounced the pope had he made strong statements favoring one or another, but he remained aloof. He was so aloof that some even accused him of virtual responsibility for the Holocaust."

Pius's "aloofness" regarding the massacres of Jews has been savagely criticized since the war. In Berlin in 1963 there was the first staging of the play *The Deputy* by the German playwright Rolf Hochhuth, who put heavy blame on Pius for not speaking out against the Holocaust. In 1972 the American Sam Waagenaar, in his book *Ghetto on the Tiber*, accused Pius of remaining silent while the Germans deported thousands of Jews from the pope's own diocese of Rome. In 1980 an American priest, John Morley, complained that whatever help Pius gave to persecuted Jews was mainly to those who had converted to Catholicism.

The Vatican's reply to all this is that Pius in fact did all he could to help the Jewish community but felt he could be more effective if he did it in a quiet, diplomatic fashion. In 1980 the Holy See issued a 685-page report full of documents from the secret archives of the Vatican, painting a picture of Catholic churchmen sheltering Jews on orders of Pope Pius. There are messages of gratitude to the pope from organizations like the American Jewish Committee and the Committee to Save the Jews of Europe. There is a message from Pius to the Nazi-backed regent of Hungary, Nicolas Horthy, urging him to help persecuted Jews. A Catholic historian, Father Derek Holmes, in a 1981 book claims that at least half the Jewish population of Rome was sheltered from the Nazis inside Vatican City and in other Vatican properties.

This argument will go on forever, but the fact remains that Pope Pius, a pontiff ever eager to speak his mind on any public issue, never during the war denounced Nazi atrocities in clear and unequivocal terms. I have heard many explanations for this from the Vatican, none of them very convincing. Pius's longtime private secretary, the German Jesuit Robert Leiber, once told me, "If Pope Pius did not speak out more loudly, it was because he did not know how Hitler would react."

Another explanation was that the pope was not aware of all the massacres of Jews; one very well informed Vatican source says Allied troops occupying Rome kept papal diplomatic couriers from getting through to the pope with details of the Auschwitz gas chambers. Writing in the Vatican's own daily, *L'Osservatore Romano*, Monsignor Alberto Giovanetti claimed that Pius did not discriminate against Jews, because "the silence of Pius XII—if there was a silence—held not only for the Jews but for all victims of Hitler's furor." Monsignor Giovanetti's most revealing apology was that if Pius had strongly condemned Nazi actions "it might even have ended diplomatic relations between the Third Reich and the Holy See."

Thus the papal tombola brought a major change in Christian-Jewish relations with the election of Good Pope John in 1958. The old pope communicated his basic kindness toward the community the first time he received a Jewish delegation. Instead of delivering a complicated allocution, he simply walked to them with arms outstretched and said with warmth and obvious sincerity, "I am Joseph, your brother."

As Archbishop Roncalli in Istanbul during World War II, John had worked hard to give all possible help and relief to Jewish refugees from Nazi-occupied lands in the Balkans. He felt the full impact of the Holocaust while nuncio in Paris, when he was shown films of Jewish bodies piled high in Buchenwald and Auschwitz. He wept at the ghastly sight and screamed, "Come mai? Il corpo mistico di Cristo! Come mai? Il corpo mistico di Cristo!" ("How could this be? The mystical body of Christ!")

On Good Friday in March 1959, only a few months after his election, John startled traditionalists when, without warning, he interrupted a prayer in the Good Friday liturgy and ordered, then and there, that the phrase "the perfidious Jews" be deleted. Thereafter he made it a rule that the adjective "perfidious" be permanently removed from the prayer, since it implied that Jews were a people without faith.

The old pope was aware that a simple show of friendliness to Jews was not nearly enough. The Church must take an official, decisive stand against the crime of anti-Semitism. And so he encouraged his close friend and counselor Cardinal Augustin Bea to draft a document on the subject which the council would approve. Bea was just the man to entrust with the task; nearly forty years before he had published in a German theological journal an article tearing to bits the alleged "dogmatic" basis for Christian prejudice against Jews.

The vicious resistance that John and Bea ran into was in itself a measure of the need for a document condemning anti-Semitism. As recently as the year 1962, a powerful minority of the world's bishops still insisted on condemning the Jewish people for "deicide," the killing of God. When Bea's document was first circulated, the bishops returned it with their secret comments appended. Among them were comments like "It is right and true to speak of deicide on the part of the Jews," "The doctrine rejecting deicide is not certain," and "We cannot wholly free the Jewish people from the offense of deicide." Italian Bishop Luigi Carli wrote at the time, "The Jewish people of the time of Jesus ... were responsible as a group for the crime of deicide. Even Judaism after the time of our Lord shares objectively in the responsibility for deicide."

More important, powerful members of the Roman Curia that John had inherited opposed the Bea document, and they made no secret of it. They publicly insisted that Bea's draft contradicted the biblical account of the crucifixion and refused to admit that the Jews as a people were not guilty of deicide.

The most telling blow by the curial reactionaries was an appeal to Arab governments. They sought to undermine the Bea initiative by quietly calling in ambassadors of Arab states and warning them that the Church was about to take "a pro-Jewish position." Till that time, the Vatican had tended to support the Arabs on the Palestine issue, especially on the question of internationalizing Jerusalem. The Holy See had diplomatic relations with several Muslim states but had never established such relations with Israel. To Arabs, the Bea doctrine looked like a change to a more sympathetic Vatican feeling toward Israel, and the Old Guard in the curia encouraged that view.

The strategy worked—at least for a while. There was an outcry from the Arab world against the Bea document. Arab Christian communities warned that they would be subjected to pogroms if the document was approved. The diplomatic old pope advised Bea to withdraw the document "until things cool down a bit." It was shelved, but not canceled, to await a more propitious moment.

John died before the next session of the council began, but the document defending the Jewish people lived on. It was approved by an overwhelming majority (1,763 votes to 250) in the last session of the council, in October 1965. The council fathers solemnly declared that the Church "deplores the hatred, persecutions, and displays of anti-Semitism directed against the Jews at any time and from any source"—in effect, a condemnation of the behavior of many popes down the centuries. The declaration was seen by many as a monument to the memory of Good Pope John.

The word aggiornamento ("renewal," or "bringing up to date") was the keynote of John's council, and the pope made his own special contribution to bringing the Church up to date on social issues. Most of his social message was contained in his two major encyclicals, "Mater et Magistra" and "Pacem in Terris."

Even dictators today usually pay lip service to democracy,

and it is somewhat startling to realize that Pope John was the first pontiff in Catholic history to endorse it. John's immediate predecessor, Pius XII, did not favor parliamentary democracy unless those sitting in the parliament were a Catholic elite, "a select body of men of firm Christian convictions." For many centuries, right up until 1870, popes had set a most undemocratic example when they ruled the Papal States as absolute monarchs. The "pope-kings" maintained their absolute monarchy long after the French Revolution and nearly a century after democracy had taken root in the United States and Britain. The Church had some catching-up to do in its teaching on political science, and John provided that updating. In his encyclical "Pacem in Terris" only a few months before he died, he declared: "It must not be concluded, however, that because authority comes from God, therefore men have no right to choose those who are to rule the state, to decide the form of government, and to determine both the way in which authority is to be exercised and its limits. It is thus clear that the doctrine which we have set forth is fully consonant with any truly democratic regime."

Pope John's predecessors advocated giving relief and all assistance to the poor and needy, but they rejected the idea that this task was the duty of the state. Since the sixth century, when Gregory the Great took over from Roman emperors the practice of distributing grain to the people, popes have justified the wealth of the Church as "the patrimony of the poor," the source of help for the weak. In 1891, Pope Leo XIII, considered a shining light as defender of human rights, denounced those who would replace Christian charity with state relief. Pope John instead argued for the welfare state, insisting that a human being should have as a right, not as a matter of charity, "security in cases of sickness, inability to work, widowhood, old age, unemployment, or in any other case in which he is deprived of the means of subsistence through no fault of his own." And he declared it the duty of governments to ensure that these rights are fully granted.

The old pope also broke with his predecessors in endorsing free trade unions. Until he spoke out, modern popes generally advocated a paternalistic form of worker organization, very much on the lines of the "corporations" of Mussolini's Fascist regime and somewhat similar to those in Franco Spain. In his encyclical "Quadragesimo Anno" in 1931, Pope Pius XI spelled out his idea of a model trade union: A corporation, comprising owners and workers in each industry, would act as an entity of the state in regulating all individual unions in that industry. If a dispute could not be resolved through negotiation within this framework, a magistrate of the state would make the decision. Strikes would be forbidden absolutely.

Pope John, in "Pacem in Terris," strongly defended the "right of assembly and association." He also proclaimed the right of workers to freedom within their organizations, to "act within such societies on their own initiative and on their own responsibility in order to achieve their desired objectives."

This may sound like a cliché today, but John was speaking only eighteen years after the fall of Fascism, at a time when there still was a powerful pro-Fascist minority in Italy and when Franco still ruled Spain. And most of those Fascists and Francoists were at least nominally Catholic.

Paul VI: Encouraging Liberation Theology

Unlike his predecessor John, Pope Paul VI accepted the challenge of answering questions on modern developments in the field of moral theology, although he often found it an onerous task. His conscience would not allow him to take the easy way out and entrust all these problems to the council or to special commissions. As we have noted in an earlier chapter, he was forced to issue a major encyclical on birth control because science had posed a new moral question by producing an effective contraceptive pill.

Among the other moral questions Paul faced was that raised by modern medical progress in developing techniques for keeping a human body functioning even when the person is totally unconscious, has no hope ever of achieving any kind of awareness again, and, sometimes, has been declared clinically dead. In such cases, is it licit to "pull out the plug" and permit such a body to die? Paul's opinion: "In such cases would it not be a torture to impose the restoration of a vegetable existence in the last phase of an incurable illness? Doctors should seek to alleviate suffering instead of prolonging as long as possible with every means, and at all costs, a life which is not fully human."

This was not an endorsement of "mercy killing." Paul was not saying that doctors should take a life. He advised only that it is licit to refrain from using the most advanced medical techniques simply to keep an unconscious body functioning in a hopeless, terminal illness.

Like Pope John, however, Paul made his most positive contribution to Church teaching in the realm of social problems. In early 1967 Pope Paul expressed his advanced social thinking in his encyclical "Populorum Progressio," a document that was revolutionary not only for the Church but also for the secular world.

A social activist from his youth, Paul sought to inject the same activism into his pontificate. In January 1967, he set up the Pontifical Commission for Justice and Peace, whose members were so activist that the commission came to be called the Roman Curia's left wing. Its first president was a liberal Canadian, Cardinal Maurice Roy. Its secretary (number-two man) was an American, Monsignor Joseph Gremillion, a Louisianian who had developed a sharp social consciousness from contact with Mexican migrant workers in the American Southwest. He brought onto his team a group who were deeply aware of social ferment all over Latin America. This team found Pope Paul most sympathetic to their ideas, and in a few months this "mix" of liberal pontiff and activist commission produced "Populorum Progressio."

Paul created a sensation in breaking with his papal predecessors in approving violent revolution in the most extreme cases. Even the liberal Pope John could not go that far. In "Pacem in Terris" he had warned:

"There are some souls . . . who, on finding situations where the requirements of justice are not satisfied or not satisfied in full, feel enkindled with the desire to change the state of things, as if they wished to have recourse to something like a revolution.

"It must be borne in mind that to proceed gradually is the law of life in all its expressions; therefore in human institutions, too, it is not possible to renovate for the better except by working from within them gradually."

To buttress his case against revolution, John quoted his predecessor Pius XII, who had said, "Salvation and justice are not to be found in revolution, but in evolution through concord."

Pope Paul moved ahead of both John and Pius when he left the door open for revolution. In "Populorum Progressio" he said parenthetically, "Revolutionary insurrection—except in the case of an evident and prolonged tyranny which gravely threatens the fundamental rights of the person and damages in a dangerous fashion the common welfare of the country—is a source of new injustices."

The liberal pope qualified this by warning strongly against trying to correct one wrong with a greater wrong, but his qualifying phrases were drowned out by the phrase permitting revolution in certain circumstances. This phrase went a long way toward making "Populorum Progressio" almost a charter for liberation theology, the movement of leftist Catholics who take what sometimes resembles a Marxist stance in calling for revolution, especially in Latin America.

Even more than John, Paul called for state intervention on behalf of the welfare of people. He went so far in this direction that many critics accused him of advocating socialism, an ideology that had been bitterly fought by most popes from the late nineteenth century onward. Old Pius XI had fulminated: "Religious socialism and Christian socialism are contradictory terms; no one can be a good Catholic and at the same time a true Socialist."

Pope Leo XIII had approved state intervention in cases of blatant exploitation of workers by employers, but in general he warned that the state should minimize its interference. He agreed, however, that the state should act to suppress strikes or uprisings by workers, and should intervene if "among the proletariat there is a substantial disturbance in relations with the family."

It would have outraged many of his predecessors to hear Paul declare that it is "the duty of public powers to choose, or even to impose, the objectives to follow, the goals to reach, the methods to achieve them, to stimulate all organized forces in common action" and that the function of such planning is "to reduce inequality, to combat discrimination, to free man from servitude."

Another bit of pioneering by Paul was his denial that ownership of private property is an absolute right, a stance that contradicted the views of his modern predecessors, including the liberal John. Modern popes had sanctified private property, even though the primitive Christian community presided over by the Apostle Peter shared its worldly goods in a simple form of communism. The biblical book The Acts of the Apostles says that "all that believed were together, and had all things common; and sold their possessions and goods, and parted them to all men, as every man had need."

The primitive community, of course, believed that the return of Christ was imminent, that they lived in a temporary society where there was "no abiding city," and therefore there was no need to develop a productive economy. Things were different by the end of the nineteenth century, when most of the Christian West was being buoyed upward toward unparalleled prosperity on the wave of free-enterprise capitalism. In 1891, Pope Leo XIII responded to the needs of the time by declaring that "the first and most fundamental principle, therefore, if one would undertake to alleviate the condition of the masses, must be the inviolability of private property." Pope John agreed with Leo. In "Mater et Magistra" he wrote that "private property, even of the means of production, is a right which the state cannot suppress."

By the time Paul VI became pope, the world's masses had undergone so many abuses at the hands of unfettered free enterprise that he was deeply aware of the need to put a brake on capitalism. And so he wrote in "Populorum Progressio" that "private property does not constitute an unconditional and absolute right for anyone. No one is authorized to reserve to his exclusive use that which goes beyond his needs when others lack the necessities of life." He even approved expropriation of private property by the state "when required for the common welfare."

John Paul II and Body Language

Pope John Paul II is fired with the same zeal for human rights and social justice as were John and Paul, but probably his strongest impact on Church teaching has been in the field of moral problems related to sex and the family. The Polish pope's approach to these problems is strikingly different from those of his predecessors, although in fundamental teaching he does not disagree with them.

Something new in John Paul's style is his emphasis on culture as a vehicle for evangelization. He wants to place Christian teachings within the context of real human experience instead of relying entirely on theoretical analysis. For example, during his several trips to black Africa he heard a great deal about polygamy. Catholicism is growing at a breathtaking pace in black Africa, and the Church faces the challenge of inculturation, adapting Catholicism to the indigenous cultures. In this case, what should the Church do about polygamy, a basic marital institution in much of Africa? Many black African bishops and even some cardinals were sons of polygamous marriages.

John Paul had no intention of approving polygamy, but his African travels convinced him he should know more about that custom. On his return to Rome after his third African trip, he discussed with some scientists the possibility of making an analysis of polygamy, based on observation of practical human experience in a controllable situation. He talked about setting up such a study in Jerusalem, where he hoped that a scientific comparison could be made between Muslim polygamous families and Jewish and Christian monogamous families in the same cultural and economic environment. The results certainly would not change Christian teaching on marriage, but the pope hoped it would buttress and clarify that teaching. The study has not been set up as yet, but the pope's interest in it was indicative of his approach.

In his examination of sex and related problems, John Paul adopted a similar down-to-earth approach, an approach that Paul VI never could have used. Paul studied sex by meditating over biblical and theological works and interviewing moral theologians and Catholic experts. John Paul talked directly with men and women who have married and had children and know what sex is all about.

A leading moral theologian of the sixties described Paul's attitude toward sex as a "conviction formed by traditional training that sex is sacred but supremely dangerous." John Paul teaches that sex should be enjoyed.

Why the vast difference in two popes who were practically contemporaries in time? Perhaps it was because Wojtyla's priestly vocation came only after he had considerable experience in secular life—as factory worker, miner, actor, playwright—while Montini from boyhood lived in a sheltered Catholic environment. Perhaps it was because Wojtyla's priestly career until his election to the papacy was pastoral, dealing with human beings and their problems every day, while Montini spent the greater part of his career inside the Roman Curia. In any case, says a curial cardinal, "John Paul is far more practical, more down-to-earth than was Paul. The latter was interested in lay men and women but more in terms of organizations. John Paul is interested in them as flesh-and-blood human beings. Paul never could have delivered the speeches on sex that John Paul has given."

While Paul was agonizing over the birth control problem in the sixties, he often worked in the relative peace and quiet of the summer residence at Castel Gandolfo, the cool papal retreat fifteen miles from Rome. John Paul also uses that retreat as a place to mull over moral issues. Pope Paul would invite theologians, cardinals, bishops, technicians—all theoretical people and all men. When John Paul wanted to probe into certain sex-related problems, he invited a husband and wife to spend a few weeks with him.

John Paul's "consultants" during the summer of 1984 were old friends of his from Kraków. The husband, Andrzej Poltawski, is a professor of philosophy in Poland, and his wife, Wanda, is a psychiatrist specializing in family problems. Not only had the couple experienced marriage and parenthood themselves but they also had experience in dealing with the problems of hundreds of other couples and were mature enough personally and profession-ally—and well enough acquainted with John Paul—to speak with total frankness.

The Polish pope is a superb questioner and a good listener, and day after day he spent hours with the couple in the privacy of the wooded Castel Gandolfo gardens. Through such contacts John Paul went a long way toward making up for the fact that his vows of celibacy had denied him the personal experience of marriage.

One subject explored during those long and intimate talks was the subject of the infertile period, those days in the month when a woman cannot conceive. What about the sex act during the infertile period? Did not the couple feel a sense of incomplete-ness then, asked the pope, when they knew that children would not be conceived? The Polish couple disagreed emphatically. On the contrary, sex during that period allowed for a more intimate acquaintance with each other, a total absorption in mutual love, unalloyed by any other intention or responsibility.

For John Paul this opened up a new concept. He now saw that sex during the infertile period could have positive effects. Instead of being a purely contraceptive practice (approved by the Church), it should be used primarily to help a couple enrich their understanding of each other.

It is on the basis of this kind of examination of real human experience that he has made a unique contribution to moral theol-ogy, which he calls the theology of the body. A moral theologian in Rome says that John Paul's teaching on the theology of the body is "an intellectual construction which is John Paul's major achievement as a religious thinker."

After he became pope, John Paul developed his ideas in a

series of lectures at his weekly public audiences. In one talk he explained his innovative theory of "body language": "The human body is not merely an organism of sexual reactions, but it is, at the same time, the means of expressing the entire man, the person, which reveals itself by means of the 'language of the body.' . . . As ministers of a sacrament which is constituted by consent and perfected by conjugal union, man and woman are called to express that mysterious 'language' of their bodies in all the truth which is proper to it. By means of gestures and reactions, by means of the whole dynamism, reciprocally conditioned, of tension and enjoyment—whose direct source is the body in its masculinity and its femininity, the body in its action and interaction—by means of all this man, the person, 'speaks.' "

In pursuing this line of thinking, John Paul has spoken more explicitly about sex than any other pope in history (at least in public). When his 1969 book, *Love and Responsibility*, was published in Italian, several conservative cardinals in the Roman Curia were shocked that a priest should so freely speak of things like sexual pleasure and orgasm. His healthy view contradicts an old Church attitude that all sex, in marriage and otherwise, is deeply suspect, and that women are agents of the devil in the flesh. He also shocked many a Catholic prude when he publicly spoke of the pleasure of sex.

John Paul once reminded a general audience that according to the Book of Genesis there is a "pure value of the body and of sex" in the eyes of God. In *Love and Responsibility* he wrote more precisely: "To enjoy sexual pleasure, yet without treating the other person like an object, that is the core of the problem of sexual morality. . . . The Creator foresaw this joy and joined it to the love of men and women, on condition that their love develop normally from the sexual impulse, in other words, in a way worthy of people."

The fundamental condition for enjoying sex, in John Paul's teaching, is that neither partner be used as a "sex object." He created a sensation when he tried to explain this to a general audience and stated his view that a man could commit adultery with his own lawfully married wife. He told the audience: "Let us dwell on a situation described by the Master, a situation in which one who 'commits adultery in his heart' by means of an interior act of lust (expressed by the look), is the man. . . . Adultery 'in the heart' is committed not only because man looks in this way at a woman who is not his wife, but precisely because he looks at a woman in this way. Even if he looked in this way at the woman who may be his wife, he could likewise commit adultery 'in his heart.' . . . Man can commit this adultery 'in his heart' even with regard to his own wife, if he treats her only as an object to satisfy instinct."

The press had a good time with this speech. Turin's leading daily, *La Stampa,* reported that "now Pope John Paul tells us that we cannot even desire our own wives." Writer Giorgio Manganelli in the Milan daily *Corriere della Sera* opined that the pope's teaching made things easier for philanderers, who "no longer need that endless round of cover-ups, tricks, juggling of the daily calendar, and the buying of useless and expensive presents for two women at once. Now the pope says, 'You can have infidelity in your own house.' "

Some militant women initially were outraged at the papal speech. An American nun in Rome at the time complained that the pope was being "sexist" because he seemed to view the case from the point of view of the lustful man. She remarked with bitterness, "We can do without his advice on such matters, thank you."

In fact, the pope was defending the rights of women. He did present the idea from the viewpoint of the man "looking with lust" in his heart, but he also used the phrase "in this case" the woman is the object, indicating that it could work the other way as well. Most important, he was denouncing any view of the woman as a sex object, an issue dear to the hearts of American women's liberation. In this pope's view, marital sex must be a mutual act; conjugal love is communication, two persons speaking to each other through the language of the body.

In the context of old-fashioned Catholicism, this was a major advance in moral teaching. In some conservative Catholic societies, including Italy, it had long been assumed that when a woman married she relinquished the right ever to resist her husband's demands, no matter what the circumstances.

Pope John Paul has applied his teaching on the "language of the body" in dealing with some of the most controversial moral questions that he has faced, those relating to artificial procreation. The issue of "test-tube babies" (fertilization in the laboratory instead of in the womb) did not exist when Karol Wojtyla was a theological student. Not until a few months before he became pope was the first baby born who had been conceived in this way—a British girl named Louise Brown. The practice caught on quickly. Moral theologians in Rome warned the pope that in the West around 15 percent of married couples were unable to produce children by the natural process and an estimated one-fifth of those would opt for test-tube fertilization. Only a few years later came the phenomenon of the "womb for rent," the surrogate mother who would carry a child in her body and deliver it for another woman in exchange for money.

The situation was further complicated for John Paul II because the patriarch of Venice had made an ambiguous statement regarding the first test-tube baby. He wrote of Louise Brown in a Venetian daily: "I extend my warmest good wishes to the English girl whose conception was produced artificially. As for the parents, I have no right to condemn them. If they acted in good faith and with good intentions, they could even gain great merit before God for what they had desired and what they had asked doctors to accomplish." The patriarch added reservations about the dangers of artificial fertilization, warning that science might become "like the sorcerer's apprentice," who unleashed mighty forces without being able to control them. Even so, his comments blurred the Church position, and adding impact to the article was the fact that the patriarch happened to be Cardinal Albino Luciani, who very shortly thereafter became Pope John Paul I.

Other popes, going back to Pius XII, had spoken out on this question even before it became a practical reality, but none had spelled out the Church view in a formal declaration. Bishops and theologians around the world were confused on this extremely vital moral issue. It became obvious that the Church needed an official and precise document from the Vatican clearly outlining Catholic teaching on the subject.

With his usual passion for clarity in presenting Christian doctrine, Pope John Paul II provided the document that was demanded. Instead of issuing an encyclical, he did it in the form of an "instruction" from the Congregation for the Doctrine of the Faith in February of 1987. The document was signed by Cardinal Ratzinger, but, in the irreverent words of a seasoned Vatican observer, "It had John Paul's footprints all over it."

The document rejected all forms of artificial procreation, including artificial insemination, fertilization "in vitro," and surrogate motherhood. It raised a storm of controversy, recalling that which followed Pope Paul's "Humanae Vitae." Among liberal Catholics, the hardest idea to swallow was the ruling against artificial insemination and test-tube fertilization even when the donors of sperm and egg are husband and wife. It was easy enough to see that involvement of a third party (a man who was not the husband, for example, as donor of the sperm) would violate traditional Church teaching on matrimony and parenthood. But what could be wrong with artificial procreation when sperm and egg are from a married couple?

Here John Paul's teaching on body language entered into the argument. The document referred to the pope's earlier utterances in explaining: "Spouses mutually express their personal love in the 'language of the body,' which clearly involves both 'spousal meanings' and parental ones. The conjugal act by which the couple mutually express their self-gift at the same time expresses openness to the gift of life. It is an act that is inseparably corporal and spiritual. It is in their bodies and through their bodies that the spouses consummate their marriage and are able to become father and mother. In order to respect the language of their bodies and their natural generosity, the conjugal union must take place with respect for its openness to procreation; and the procreation of a person must be the fruit and the result of married love. . . . Fertilization achieved outside the bodies of the couple remains by this very fact deprived of the meanings and the values which are expressed in the language of the body and in the union of human persons."

With a suggestion of understatement, the document was subtitled "Replies to Certain Questions of the Day." I once asked Pope John Paul how he could so categorically formulate Christian doctrine on all these "Questions of the Day" when the traditional rulebooks had nothing to say on them. He answered without hesitation: "We emphasize the transcendental worth of the human person. Some modern scientific and medical developments are apt to make of the human person a product, an object. We insist that the human person must never be treated as an object; he must always be considered the subject. That is the basis for our teaching, the absolute standard."

This is the rule the pope applies whether he is talking about nuclear war or terrorism or political oppression or racism—or about a man looking on his wife as a sex object.

9

POPES AND THE WINDS OF CHANGE

Pope John Ventilates Those Stuffy Rooms

A cartoon in *Time* magazine showed Pope John XXIII pulling back the curtains and opening the windows of the Church. The next panel showed Pope John Paul II slamming shut the windows and closing the curtains.

The cartoon was both an exaggeration and an oversimplification, and yet none can deny that the history of the Vatican for the past thirty years has been that of popes coping with the revolution touched off by old Pope John. Nor can it be denied that he opened the windows of the Holy See to allow the winds of change to blow through—and then left it to his successors to receive the full force of the gale. The conscientious Pope Paul dutifully kept the windows open but often complained of the draft. John Paul II slammed shut the windows to doubt and speculation and experimentation, but he carried on the reforms of his immediate predecessors.

Admittedly, the Vatican was a stuffy place badly in need of

fresh air when John was elected in 1958. Though the papacy's temporal domain had been reduced to the tiny State of Vatican City, the pontiff was still surrounded by the pomp and ceremony of a medieval court. It seemed just plain silly to that dumpy old peasant Angelo Roncalli to find himself carried on the shoulders of his subjects in a *sedia gestatoria*, shielded from the heat and sun by fans of ostrich plumes, wearing garments shot through with golden thread and decorated with the most precious of jewels, and ceremonially "protected" by a guard of aristocrats possessing "a gallant nobility of at least a century," richly attired in red-and-white livery and high black riding boots with silver spurs—descendants of the Papal Light Cavalry who had fought to the last man in defense of the pope against Emperor Charles V in 1527.

In the court of the peasant pope was the "majordomo of His Holiness" and the "master of the chamber," offices whose history went all the way back to the Roman Empire. There were private stewards, who for more than seven hundred years had kept strangers out of the papal kitchens and tasted the papal food to guard against poison. There was the "sacristan to His Holiness," whose original duty was to taste the bread and wine before the pope consecrated it during the mass. There were the *foriere maggiore*, whose job was to go ahead of a traveling pope to make sure he had lodgings at each stop, and the "superintendent of the posts," who originally saw to it that carriages and fresh horses were available. These and many other offices in the papal court were held on a hereditary basis by men from the old noble families of the Papal States, many of whom hung portraits of popes in the galleries of their forebears.

The same year that the pope lost his temporal power the Church had sought to increase his ecclesiastical power enormously by proclaiming the pontiff infallible in matters of faith and morals. The council fathers at the First Vatican Council did not declare that the pope was always right, but they did proclaim him infallible when "he speaks 'ex cathedra' (from the chair of Peter) . . . regarding faith and morals." This proclamation was pushed through by the Roman clique as a way of shoring up papal power to cope with the challenges of such heretical or subversive movements as modernism and socialism.

Along with this cloak of infallibility, Pope John inherited another weapon of papal power aimed at controlling the minds, if not the bodies, of men. This was the Holy Office, which at the time of Pius IX was still called the Inquisition. The Holy Office no longer could "reduce heretics to ashes" nor could it prescribe tearing off their genitals with red-hot irons, as it once did. But during the time of Pope John, the head of the Holy Office, Cardinal Ottaviani, continually tried to take action against some of the greatest Catholic thinkers of the twentieth century, including Teilhard de Chardin and Yves Congar.

During his reign—much of it under Pope John—Ottaviani came to be known as the Holy Terror of the Holy Office and Big Brother in a Cassock. When progressive bishops at the council called for modernization of the Holy Office, a joke went round Rome that Ottaviani agreed fully, that he had given orders to "get rid of the old-fashioned custom of burning heretics at the stake. From now on we will use the electric chair!"

In Pope John's day Ottaviani's Holy Office still maintained the Index of Forbidden Books, a list of writings that devout Catholics must never see. The very existence of the Index showed how far removed the Church was from Milton's call to "let Truth and Falsehood grapple" in the open marketplace of ideas. Ottaviani and company were determined to make no concessions to what they considered Falsehood. The minds of Catholics were not to be contaminated with error. Freedom of thought and education had no place in the Vatican that Pope John inherited.

The Index dated back to 1559, during the reign of that old inquisitor Pope Paul IV. Printers at the time were running into difficulty because often books they had printed at considerable expense were condemned by the Church and could not be sold. To avoid this kind of financial loss, the printers petitioned the pope to issue a list of forbidden books.

Looking through the old *Index Librorum Prohibitorum* makes

you wonder how a good Catholic could have been a fully educated person when the Index was in force. The list included some of the great thinkers and literary figures of recent centuries—John Locke, Thomas Hobbes, John Stuart Mill, Rousseau, Voltaire, Kant, Descartes, John Milton, Victor Hugo, Ugo Foscolo, Gustave Flaubert, Alexandre Dumas (and his son), Daniel Defoe, Balzac, the poet Alphonse de Lamartine, along with that great Jewish philosopher who lived in the Muslim world during the Golden Age of Islam, Moses Maimonides. For some unfathomable reason, the *Grand Dictionnaire Universel* of Pierre Larousse also was on the list. (For some equally unfathomable reason, Karl Marx never made it!)

It is also a bit shocking to find proscribed by the Index "The Holy Bible, with notes drawn from diverse English authors," "The Book of Common Prayer," and eight versions of the New Testament in various languages. The Index even listed such devotional works as "Sermons on the Epistle of St. Paul to the Romans," by the great medieval preacher John Chrysostom, and "The Works of St. Cyprian, translated into French."

Since the Vatican no longer had police power, men like Ottaviani and his predecessors needed some other authority for imposing their edicts ruling out competition for Christian doctrine. This authority in many Catholic countries took the form of concordats, special treaties between the Holy See and secular states which gave the Church a privileged position with guarantees as binding as constitutions. Though they differed in detail from one country to another, concordats normally established Catholicism as the state religion and gave the Church sweeping power over a nation's moral, religious, and educational life. Through the concordat, the Church usually controlled such matters as marriage and divorce (and so managed to outlaw divorce in most cases). Catholic teaching usually was made obligatory in public schools, with teachers paid by the state but appointed by the Church.

The concordat system was directly opposed to ecumenicism, since it gave the Catholic Church a privileged position and was used to discriminate against non-Catholic churches. Even after World War II, during the reign of Pius XII, a preacher of the evangelical Church of God near Naples was arrested for putting on his church bulletin board statements denying that the pope was vicar of God; he was charged with violating Article 8 of the concordat, which forbade insults against the pope, in speeches, writings, or deeds. Only a few years ago, an Italian priest named Ernesto Buonaiuti was excommunicated for his modernist theories and the University of Rome was forced to fire him from his teaching post; the concordat ruled that apostate priests could not hold any position that brought them into contact with the public.

The stifling atmosphere of the old Church of pomp and special privilege was given a good airing by Pope John. He changed almost nothing structurally, but through his style, his spirit, and his deeds he opened the windows to winds of change that blew through the Church long after his death.

Pope John did not dismantle the imperial papal court, but his democratic style and obvious contempt for protocol showed how out-of-date it was and pointed the way toward its end. He did get rid of those ostrich plumes, and he scandalized the old aristocrats by often walking instead of bobbing along in the *sedia gestatoria*. His style so irritated the Black Nobility that one Roman count told me, "It looks as if this pope is trying to introduce into the Church some of that democracy which has been such a disaster everywhere else."

The old pope did not turn the Church into a complete democracy, of course, but he did whittle away at papal powers. At one time as he was preparing for the council some of the Old Guard suggested he simply reconvene the First Vatican Council, which had never formally concluded its work because of the occupation of Rome by the Italian army. Recalling that the council had proclaimed papal infallibility, John answered this one with his usual wit, "No. We are infallible enough already."

Without issuing any new laws on the subject, John broadened the base of participation in Church decisions by appealing to bishops all over the world to speak their minds on what the council should do, and to speak up freely during council debates. This was a radical departure from the habit, so well established at the time, of Rome telling the bishops what to think. When bishops began arriving at the council in the autumn of 1962, most of them assumed it would be an "Ottaviani council," with the Old Guard of the curia running the show. They were stunned when they began getting discreet phone calls from John's secretary, Monsignor Capovilla, dissociating the pope from his own curia and urging the bishops to speak their minds freely. Progressive prelates began to understand that, without explicitly saying so, Pope John wanted reform. An astonished American bishop very shortly afterwards remarked, "We are hearing men dare to say things publicly that we had privately been thinking a long time ourselves."

Instead of approving with docility a set of traditionalist propositions drawn up by the curial group, the council turned into a full-scale debate on burning issues facing the Church at the time, with totally free expression of a wide range of viewpoints. Ottaviani was appalled at what he called "this dissent" in the Church, and he went to the pope to complain vehemently about it. John answered with a chuckle, "You shouldn't be surprised. At the Council of Trent, the debate once got so hot that one bishop pulled another's beard off!"

Without actually getting into debates during the council, John created situations in which liberal voices could at least be heard against the conservatives who dominated the assembly at the beginning. At one point the council reached what looked like a hopeless deadlock on a document on biblical revelation drafted by a commission chaired by Ottaviani and reflecting the old cardinal's sentiments. John broke the logjam by calling back the document and appointing to draft a revised version a new commission on which Ottaviani was neatly balanced by a powerful liberal, Cardinal Bea. As usual, John had not taken a position directly supporting the liberals; he had just made it possible for the liberals to have equal time.

A typical case of John's protecting the innovators of the

Church was his getting around Ottaviani when the old reactionary expressed outrage that the liberal Jesuit theologian Karl
Rahner had come to Rome for the council. The progressive Cardinal Koenig of Vienna had brought Rahner along as his special
theological advisor. Ottaviani had tried at least three times to have
Rahner's work condemned, and an Ottaviani ally, Monsignor
Francesco Spadafora of the Pontifical Lateran University, only
shortly before had called Rahner a "formal heretic." To Ottaviani
it was unthinkable that such a "heretical" personality should be
a theological advisor at the council. The Holy Office head went
directly to the pope and demanded that he order Rahner to leave
Rome and stay away from the council. John blandly feigned
surprise that Rahner might have slipped into error, and he
"solved" the problem with a seemingly naïve suggestion: "Why
don't you discuss the matter with Cardinal Koenig?"

After that conversation, Ottaviani gave up. Rahner stayed on
at the council.

Pope John did not abolish the Index of Forbidden Books, but
his public stand in favor of intellectual freedom was in itself the
death knell of the Index. In his encyclical "Pacem in Terris," the
pope declared that natural law gives every human being "the right
to freedom in searching for truth and in expressing and communicating his opinions."

Perhaps John's hardest battle with the conservatives was over
his openings to non-Catholics and non-Christians. In setting up
the Secretariat for Christian Unity under Cardinal Bea, John went
a long way toward getting rid of the Catholic Church's claim to
exclusivity in truth. As usual, he had to do battle with Ottaviani
in this field. Only a short time before the secretariat was set up,
Ottaviani ordered that an ecumenical prayer service planned in
Rome be canceled. Pope John moved in and overruled him. The
prayer service involving Protestants and Catholics took place, a
truly revolutionary act in the Rome of that time.

The very salutation of John's "Pacem in Terris" opened
windows to the world and again outraged curial conservatives. In
the past, encyclicals normally were addressed to Catholics, but

Pope John set a precedent by addressing this one also to "All Men of Good Will." Just to make sure the point was understood, John had an advance copy sent to Nikita Khrushchev in the Kremlin. It was a clear signal that the head of the Catholic Church considered the atheist who headed the Communist world a "man of good will."

This gesture could not have come at a worse moment for Cardinal Ottaviani. At that very time, Ottaviani was working with a group of conservative Catholic politicians to form a new political party in Italy whose reason for existing would be to fight Marxism without compromise. The existing Italian Catholic party, the Christian Democrats, had "betrayed" the Church (in Ottaviani's eyes) by opting for an *apertura a sinistra* (opening to the Left), which meant bringing the Socialist party into the government. Cardinal Ottaviani and his friends sought to set up a new bulwark against the Left by building a completely new, totally conservative Catholic party which, they hoped, would be led by Senator Giuseppe Pella, a highly respected one-time prime minister whose anti-Marxist credentials were impeccable.

Under the circumstances, it is not surprising that Ottaviani, in his capacity as head of the Holy Office and guardian of orthodoxy in the Church, went to see the pope and argued intensely and passionately that the draft encyclical should be revised to avoid "misleading" the faithful regarding Marxists. The normally diplomatic John bluntly refused to move an inch this time. He went ahead with his encyclical, and in so doing pulled the rug out from under the Ottaviani project for a new party. It was impossible to attract respected Catholic politicians to a party that ran counter to the pope's teachings. (Added to the impact of "Pacem in Terris" was the widely held suspicion that the pope's own private secretary, Monsignor Capovilla, was the author of the *apertura a sinistra*.)

Rising above the purely Italian scene, "Pacem in Terris" in effect called for an *apertura a sinistra* on a global scale. John's document was truly ecumenical, with respect to Christians of other denominations, those of other religions, and those of no religion at all. The dictates of natural law, said the pope, "provide Catholics with a vast field in which they can meet and come to an understanding both with Christians separated from this Apostolic See, and also with human beings who are not enlightened by faith in Jesus Christ, but who are endowed with the light of reason and with a natural and operative honesty. . . . One must never confuse error and the person who errs. . . . Meetings and agreements, in the various sectors of daily life, between believers and those who do not believe or believe insufficiently because they adhere to error, can be occasions for discovering truth and paying homage to it."

John did not specifically name Marxism but his reference to it was clear when he wrote: "Who can deny that those movements, insofar as they conform to the dictates of right reason and are interpreters of the lawful aspirations of the human person, contain elements that are positive and deserving of approval?"

Such utterances foreshadowed the end of the stifling atmosphere of the Ottaviani era, the end of trying to control men's minds with censorship, the end of discrimination against and persecution of those of other faiths.

As we have written earlier, the great act of Pope John was summoning the council. And in his speech in St. Peter's Basilica opening that council, John sounded the keynote of his revolution: "The substance of the ancient doctrine is one thing, the way in which it is presented is another."

Paul Feels the Chilling Drafts

Following the familiar pattern of the relationship between these two popes, Paul VI, the bureaucrat, put into writing the spirit of John. He did it with his deep sense of responsibility, his conscientiousness and sincerity, but he did it often in agony, always with caution and concern.

Paul was not obliged to carry on the council that John had summoned; when a pope dies, a council over which he is presiding comes to an end unless his successor chooses to reconvene it.

Paul chose to reconvene it, though he never would have had the decisiveness to summon a council on his own. He even had considerable worry about reconvening this one. As he signed the document reopening the council, Paul sadly told a friend, "I must drive a train on a track that I have not chosen."

Whatever reservations he might have felt privately, this cautious and reluctant revolutionary presided over more changes in the Church than had any pope in many centuries. Paul translated into concrete reforms those broad lines traced by his predecessor's style and utterances. He abolished the Index of Forbidden Books; made Holy Office investigations more modern and humane; got away from use of the word "heretic" in investigations of alleged doctrinal error; put the liturgy into modern languages ranging from English to Pidgin; internationalized the Roman Curia; instituted more than fifty national bishops' conferences around the world to give the Church a more local character than it had known in centuries; created the World Synod of Bishops as an advanced form of "collegiality" between pope and bishops; appointed a whole generation of liberal bishops in the United States, Latin America, and elsewhere, bishops whose voices now are being felt strongly on issues of human rights and nuclear war; made a sweeping revision of the mass; pushed the ecumenical movement to frontiers undreamed-of a decade before; pioneered in "inculturation," the process of adapting Christianity to non-European cultures; and introduced sweeping changes in religious orders and Catholic schools to make them more open, more modern, and more democratic.

Under Paul, the wish expressed by John to grant other faiths the same civil rights as those enjoyed by Catholics became a reality. Paul promulgated a document issued by the council declaring that the Church "does not put its hope in the privileges offered it by the civil authority." Paul followed up by initiating dialogue with the Italian state and many other governments to modernize their concordats and eliminate the special privileges that had been claimed by the Catholic Church. Today in Italy Catholicism is no longer the state religion, and the Italian state has given equal rights to numerically small communities like Methodists and Jews.

Paul followed the model of Pope John's simplicity in abolishing the papal court. He broke the news to a gathering of three hundred Vatican nobles who had called to offer New Year's greetings to their "monarch" in January 1964. Paul explained that the pope of the late twentieth century was "no longer the temporal ruler about which clustered in past centuries the social categories to which you belong." He eventually issued a *motu proprio* dismantling the papal court and transforming it into the "papal household," in which there were no more hereditary posts and in which all offices were open to commoners.

This was a bitter pill for the Black Nobility, who felt that their proven loyalty to the papacy deserved reward. Indeed, they had served the popes with dedication. After Napoleon's armies had wiped out the Papal States and left the Holy See treasury empty, it was the nobles who from their own pockets financed the pontiff's Light Cavalry to ensure his defense. A member of the princely Rospigliosi family (from which came Pope Clement IX, elected in 1667) told me that after Rome fell to the Italian army in 1870 his grandfather refused to enter Rome, often spending five days to travel between his estates north and south of the city rather than enter the capital ruled by an "illicit" king, even though he could have made the trip in half a day if he had passed through Rome. The new sovereign of unified Italy, King Victor Emmanuel II, made the gesture of recognizing the titles of the Black Nobility, but they refused to recognize him as monarch and boycotted his court. Even after World War II, some leading families of the Black Nobility refused to accept invitations to dine with the president of Italy, whom they considered a usurper. After Paul's announcement that the papal court would be abolished, an old patrician Roman lady warned that "the strength of a monarch lies in the loyalty of his nobles!"

The old patrician had not realized that, as Pope Paul explained, "history marches on. . . . The religious mission of the Roman Pontificate has taken on new forms." Not only did he abolish the papal court but he also got rid of other imperial trappings. Paul was the last pope to be crowned. (He gave his jeweled tiara to be sold; the money was to be donated to charity.) His successor, John Paul I, began his reign with a high mass on the threshold of St. Peter's, in place of the elaborate coronation ceremony of the past.

Getting rid of the "imperial papacy" was a major change in style inside the Vatican, but any Catholic worshiper attending Sunday mass will be deeply affected by another of Paul's great reforms—the modernization of the liturgy and introduction of modern languages in place of Latin. Paul's liturgical reform, following a recommendation by the council John had summoned, emphasized the Church as "the People of God" (in contrast to the old concept of the Church as the hierarchy); such innovations as having the priest face the congregation instead of the altar and using vernacular languages instead of Latin allowed for vastly greater participation by the people.

Liturgical reform presented problems to the long-suffering Pope Paul. A conservative French bishop, Marcel Lefebvre, came near to causing a schism in the Church because of Paul's reforms, and in particular because of the liturgical changes.*

There were some less serious difficulties in making the liturgical changes. In Tuscany, there was an awkwardness in having the priest say in Italian, at the end of the mass, "Andate in pace" ("Go in peace"). That sounded innocuous enough, except that in Tuscan dialect the phrase "Andate in pace" is used brusquely, as when chasing away a beggar who is making a nuisance of himself. It was as if the priest were telling the congregation something like "The mass is finished. Now, get lost!"

That was not as bad as a problem posed by using Pidgin as a liturgical language. In describing the introduction of Pidgin in religious ceremonies, two missionaries who work in Papua New Guinea told me they dreaded to see Ash Wednesday arrive. The

---

*Paul eventually suspended Lefebvre from his episcopal functions, but he has continued to ordain priests on his own. He has threatened to consecrate bishops without Vatican approval, which would create a schism in the Church.

problem: "Ash" in Pidgin is something slightly more obscene than "Dung-belong-fire."

These minor wrinkles were eventually ironed out, and today Paul's reformed mass is a lasting reality. Since the changes were introduced, a whole generation of Catholics has grown up who do not even remember the old Latin mass. Surveys of bishops around the world conducted by the Vatican in recent years indicated that an overwhelming majority of them believe the new mass has taken root firmly and is here to stay.

Adapting the liturgy to modern languages and cultures fit into the concept of inculturation of the gospel, especially in the Third World. Pope John had pioneered in creating the first black African cardinal, and Paul VI followed through energetically, creating more black cardinals and many more black bishops. He was the first pope to visit black Africa, and he canonized black African saints and authorized the use of African music as well as African language in the liturgy.

Helping Africans to recognize that Christianity belonged to them as well as to the whites was a monumental task. On one occasion after Paul had consecrated a new black African bishop, a group of friends in the bishop's native village called on his father to express congratulations that "George has been made a bishop." The old father was an animist and a polygamist who had countless wives and innumerable children. His response to the congratulations: "Let me ask you two things: First, what is a bishop? Second, who is George?"

On a papal trip to Zaire, I got an idea of how fast inculturation had moved in one generation in black Africa. At an evening mass in a massive parish church in Kinshasa, I found the place packed to capacity, with standing room only and very little of that. I was told that vast numbers of the people there regularly walked as far as ten or fifteen miles to attend mass. Choir leaders were situated at points all over the church and led the people in singing joyful African hymns set to African rhythms while they swayed from side to side, their bodies pressing against each other—a far cry from Gregorian chant! On the walls were paint-

ings and sculptures, African style, of a black Christ and a black
Madonna and black saints. The priest who walked down the
center aisle wore as a "mitre" a monkey-skin cap, the monkey tail
hanging down his back. He was flanked by two spear-carriers
who escorted him to the altar.

The Church in Africa indeed has become an African
Church—a great change from the white man's Church brought
in by the colonial powers and imposed on the population. It was
obvious that the people I saw in that Kinshasa service now believe
this is their own, indigenous religion, and they will never go back
to a Church of Latin masses and European music and an all-white
canon of saints. It is no wonder that the Catholic Church is
growing faster in Africa than in any other area in the world.

One of Paul's greatest reforms was in "humanizing" and
modernizing the Holy Office. In the council that John summoned, there was a powerful campaign for reforming the Holy
Office, and in the end the council fathers voted to reform the
entire curia, including the onetime Inquisition. It was left to Paul
VI to carry out this reform, following the spirit of the council.

A longtime and passionate advocate of freedom of thought
and conscience, Pope Paul in December 1965 issued an apostolic
letter that revolutionized the Holy Office. With this document
Paul abolished the Index of Forbidden Books and changed the
name of the Holy Office to the Congregation for the Doctrine of
the Faith and modernized its procedures.

Under the new guidelines, the terms "heresy" and "heretic"
are not used. The word "error" is employed instead, and error is
not considered a crime. Monsignor Jozef Tomko, then an official
of the congregation (now a cardinal), in introducing the changes,
told a news conference: "Today, we proceed in these matters
pastorally, aimed at convincing rather than coercing. The torture
chambers and burning at the stake are no more."

Inquiries into reported error are not considered trials (like
that of Galileo, for example) but investigations. The one being
investigated is fully informed of the complaints against him and
is given a chance to respond fully. He is also provided with a

"defender" to point to the positive aspects of any writing being investigated, as well as to stress the merits of the author. Before the reform, a theologian could be accused, tried, and convicted without even being told what the charges were or given a chance to defend himself.

Once the doctrinal congregation concludes that error is "likely or possible," it must appoint two experts to prepare, independently of each other, a report on the case. If the congregation eventually concludes that doctrinal error exists, it will so report to the pope himself. If the pontiff approves the decision, a direct dialogue with the "erring" author begins, after which the congregation sends its final decision to the pope for approval. The author will be asked to correct his writings if error is established. Some sanctions are permitted if the author refuses to correct his errors. The congregation may simply issue a public declaration calling the man "an author in error," but in extreme cases he may be fired from his teaching job, if he is employed in a Catholic university or holds a Catholic professorship. As we shall see, Paul VI was reluctant to employ these sanctions; his tougher successor, John Paul II, did not hesitate to use them when he ran into problems with theologians.

Many Church conservatives complained that Paul was "pulling the teeth of the watchdog of the Faith" at the very moment when a healthy watchdog was needed most. Indeed, those winds of change now were blowing almost at hurricane force. Rarely in history have Catholics so blatantly disobeyed papal orders as in the period after the Vatican Council. What was historically new in this rebellion was that the rebels did not leave the Church; they remained Catholic and insisted that they were good Catholics. They were what the articulate Father Andrew Greeley called do-it-yourself Catholics who made their own rules.

The do-it-yourself approach was applied most openly to Pope Paul's famous birth-control encyclical, "Humanae Vitae." Immediately after the document was released, forty-one Catholic priests in Washington signed a statement denouncing it. The highly respected Catholic theologian Father Charles Curran declared that couples had a right to practice artificial contraception if their consciences so dictated; immediately six hundred priests, theologians, and Catholic laymen went on record in support of Curran's view. In West Germany five thousand laymen at the Church's annual "Catholic Day" voted a resolution warning Pope Paul that they simply could not accept "Humanae Vitae." French bishops put out a statement that in effect left the issue to the conscience of the married couple. By this time, hundreds of millions of Catholics already were using the pill and continued to do so in defiance of the papal ban. A Roman theologian sadly summed it all up with the phrase "Birth control is Pope Paul's Vietnam."

Birth control may have been Paul's Vietnam, but it was not his only problem. It seemed that the traditional teaching of the Church had suddenly come under fire, and from some of its most noted theologians. One after another, Catholic theologians took positions that so modified Church doctrine as to leave it almost unrecognizable. Some saw the Virginity of Mary as only symbolic. Others stressed the humanity over the divinity of Jesus. There was widespread pressure for Church approval of divorce and remarriage, of abortion, of premarital sex in the context of true love. Sacraments were being viewed as symbols of commitment only. Polls showed that a majority of American seminarians wanted to be allowed to marry. Tens of thousands of priests and nuns asked to be released from their vows and returned to the life of laymen and laywomen.

In the midst of all this, the pope's "chief of staff," Archbishop Benelli, rang the alarm bells daily, rushing in to report to the already worried Paul the latest cases of disobedience. Paul feebly tried to restore papal authority, but he never was resolute enough to do so. At one point he replied to criticism by telling the council fathers, "I am your servant—and I am your chief."

The "suffering pope" projected the image of servant more than chief. He did try to stem the tide of dissidence by speaking out in increasingly pessimistic and alarmed style, but his inability to communicate effectively doomed his effort to failure. He in-

voked the new rules of his own reform of the doctrinal congregation in a vain attempt to bring to order some leading "erring"
theologians. During Paul's reign investigations were begun of the
noted Belgian Edward Schillebeeckx, the Swiss Hans Kung, and
the American Charles Curran. But the basically liberal Paul could
not bring himself to close the windows that John had opened. Not
one of the investigations of those theologians reached a conclusion
during Paul's long reign.

Paul tried to hold the line on priestly celibacy, but even there
he could not be completely rigid. In the face of widespread demands to allow priests to marry (and alarming reports that many
priests in fact were marrying), the pope issued his encyclical
"Sacerdotalis Caelibatus," reaffirming the traditional rule requir-
ing celibacy for priests. In the document, Paul called celibacy a
"precious jewel in the crown of the Church." But he was lenient
toward priests too weak to obey the law. During Paul's fifteen-
year reign, 32,357 priests asked to be released from their vows.
Though he suffered each time he handled one of those cases, the
kindly pope granted all except 1,033 of these requests. Meanwhile,
during Paul's term in the papacy there was also the greatest decline in vocations in the history of the Church.

At one point Paul briefly looked decisive when he reaffirmed
the Church's traditional teaching on the Eucharist, but again, his
subsequent actions left matters confused. He issued an encyclical
on the Eucharist entitled "Mysterium Fidei," which was widely
assumed to be aimed at a group of Dutch and Belgian theologians
who were teaching that the essential change in the bread and wine
in the mass is in the significance of the elements rather than in
their substance. Paul's document took an unabashedly traditional
line and even warned against changing the usual terminology in
reference to the sacrament. But the pope privately assured a curial
official that he had not intended to condemn those theologians
with the encyclical. Shortly afterwards, one of them, Father Schillebeeckx, and the primate of Holland, Cardinal Bernard Jan Alfrink, told a news conference that they had been assured by Rome
that the new theories did not contradict the encyclical. It now

appeared that "Mysterium Fidei" had been issued mainly to placate certain Roman conservatives, while to the liberals Paul was
saying that theological speculation on the subject could continue.

Paul had put into Church law and practice the reforms John
wanted and the council willed, but at his death the time had come
for consolidation and a return to certainty. Paul's successor provided that consolidation.

John Paul: Closing the Windows to Winds of Dissent

When John Paul II took over in the Vatican, he began immediately to turn back the tide of dissent and doubt, speculation and
experimentation. This did not mean that he turned back the calendar to the pre-1960 era. He has not canceled the reforms of the
council and of his immediate predecessors in the papacy. In fact,
he has enthusiastically maintained innovations like the modernized liturgy, the use of vernacular languages in the mass, the
concept of the Church as the People of God, which opened up
new roles for the laity; and he followed Pope John's lead in
treating social action as an essential element of the gospel message,
in contrast with the "otherworldly" view of much of the Church
before the council. It sounded like something right out of "Pacem
in Terris" when John Paul told newsmen on the plane flying to
Chile, where an oppressive dictatorship held power, "To the
gospel belong all the problems of human rights, and if democracy
means human rights, it also belongs to the message of the
Church."

In the field of ecumenism, he did not, like Paul, make great
strides toward structural unity with other faiths, but he advanced
the "dialogue of charity" with those of other religions. He promoted ecumenicism in actions more than in words or documents.
He was the first pope to enter Canterbury Cathedral, the first to
preach in a Lutheran church, the first to enter a synagogue. On
a chilly October day in 1986, he set a spectacular precedent in
interfaith cooperation when, at his suggestion, representatives of
religions from around the world gathered with him to fast and

pray for peace in Assisi. Along with the pope and Orthodox and Anglican bishops were Buddhist monks and turbaned Muslim sheikhs and Sikhs and even American Indians puffing on their pipes of peace.

Supporting the reforms of the council, however, did not mean that the Polish pope would allow any tampering with Church doctrine or discipline. The widespread disobedience that Paul had tolerated was intolerable for a pope who had come out of the Communist world, where Catholic dissent was unthinkable. As a Vatican official put it shortly after Wojtyla's election, "The only way to keep the faith in Communist countries like Poland is to have no doubts, no pluralism, absolute faith. If you are thrown into a Communist prison you don't want any possible speculation on the living presence of Christ. You want to believe totally and absolutely."

Karol Wojtyla took the same attitude toward the entire world when he became head of the Universal Church. He could not force individual Catholics to obey, of course, and so in place of coercion he emphasized clarity. A close friend of the pope who often lunches at the papal table explained to me: "John Paul II believes that people today—and especially the youth of today— demand a crystal-clear presentation of the Christian message and resent it when their bishops try to 'accommodate' them by watering down that message. This pope believes that people have the right to know without any doubt what the message is so that they can decide for themselves whether to take it or leave it, without confusion."

If the message is to be presented with such clarity, the teachers of that message must perform their task with diligence and strictness. For John Paul, this has meant that Catholic bishops and theologians, priests and nuns, must fall into line with the pope and speak in a united voice. Bringing them all into line in the confused post-conciliar period was a formidable task, but the Polish pope took it on with energy and determination.

As was Pope Paul, the new pontiff was deluged with requests from priests for dispensation from their vows. In the first two years of his reign, around six thousand priests asked to be released, most of them wanting to marry. The Polish pope proved far less accommodating than his predecessor. He did not approve a single request in those first two years. He later began granting some, but imposed such strict conditions as to keep the figure to a minimum. It can be argued that this toughness has produced results. While priestly vocations plummeted under Pope Paul, they have been on the rise every year since 1979, John Paul's first full year in office. (The decline has continued in the United States and Western Europe, but in the world as a whole there has been an annual increase under the present tough pope.)

The Polish pope has been equally decisive in dealing with errant nuns. In December 1984, twenty-seven American nuns signed an advertisement in *The New York Times* that disagreed with official Catholic teaching on abortion. The pope reacted with a speed that stunned even those accustomed to his decisiveness. He ordered the superiors of those nuns to get a public retraction from each of them or dismiss them from their orders.

His drive for clarity and unity inevitably put the tough Polish pope onto a collision course with some of the Church's leading theologians, including Schillebeeckx, Kung, and Curran. Predictably, the pope's stern actions provoked cries of anguish from the liberals, who loudly complained that John Paul had restored the Inquisition and turned the calendar back to pre-council days.

In fact, the pope rigorously conformed to the procedures laid down in Pope Paul's reform of the doctrinal congregation. The difference between him and Paul was that he used the rules maximally while Paul used them minimally. John Paul was careful that his actions against theologians would not deteriorate into the witch-hunts of the past, but at the same time he was determined to establish clearly what was authentic Catholic teaching and what was not.

The Schillebeeckx case was the best example of the application of the new rules by John Paul. In December 1979, only a little more than a year after John Paul's election, the Belgian Dominican Father Schillebeeckx was inside the old Holy Office Palace, answering questions put by the doctrinal congregation on some of his writings, in particular those which cast doubt on the divinity of Christ and the nature of the priesthood.

To the gleeful Western media, the Schillebeeckx case looked like another Galileo inquisition or a replay of the Scopes Monkey Trial, Roman style. Journalists poured into Rome, networks demanded the right to film the proceedings live, special press arrangements were demanded.

The plot thickened on the eve of the hearing when, in an interview on Vatican Radio, a French theologian who was to participate in the examination of Schillebeeckx compared the Belgian's theories with the Arian heresies of the early Christian era. This made it look as if the theologian indeed was being accused of heresy and might be condemned as a heretic.

It was not to be. A few hours after the interview was broadcast, the telephone rang in the office of Father Roberto Tucci, head of Vatican Radio. The voice on the phone was that of the pope himself, and an angry pope he was. He gave Tucci a dressing-down for broadcasting such an interview and ordered him to apologize personally to Schillebeeckx.

The "trial" itself turned into a rather friendly hearing. No dunce cap was placed on the theologian's head (as had been done during the Inquisition to indicate that the defendant already was assumed to be guilty before the trial began), nor was he required to kneel and recant, as was Galileo. The pope himself had passed down the word that Schillebeeckx must be treated with special courtesy out of respect for his standing as a scholar. The word "heresy" never was used in the discussion.

The Belgian sat at a round table along with three theologians and Archbishop Alberto Bovone, who, as secretary of the doctrinal congregation, presided over the hearing. In an adjoining room and available at any time to enter into the discussion was Schillebeeckx's "defense counsel," Father Bas Van Iersel, dean of the theological faculty of Nijmegen University, where Schillebeeckx taught. In an amiable atmosphere (coffee was served while they talked), the three theologians questioned Schillebeeckx. Matters went so smoothly that they were able to cancel a tentative after-noon session and wind up everything on the second morning.

The congregation then asked Schillebeeckx to clarify pub-licly certain passages in his writings. He did so, but the Vatican was not satisfied. After lengthy correspondence, the Holy See finally issued a public statement declaring that some of the Belgian theologian's views on the priesthood were "at variance with the teaching of the Church." There was no charge of heresy, no punishment. The Vatican was simply following the new rules laid down in Paul's reform and putting the record straight as to what was authentic Church teaching.

The Swiss Hans Kung was next. The blow fell with dramatic abruptness. Only a few days after the Schillebeeckx hearing had ended, Cardinal Bernardin Gantin of the Commission for Justice and Peace held a rather unexciting news conference in the Vati-can press office on the pope's upcoming "Day of Peace." When the conference ended, Father Romeo Pancirolli, then head of the press office, rose to read what was expected to be a routine an-nouncement. In fact, he announced another spectacular papal crackdown:

"This sacred congregation [the doctrinal congregation] by reason of its duty is constrained to declare that Professor Hans Kung, in his writings, has departed from the integral truth of Catholic faith, and therefore he can no longer be considered a Catholic theologian nor function as such in a teaching role."

It was yet another example of John Paul's toughness, in such strong contrast with Paul's delicacy. Kung had been under inves-tigation ever since 1967 and had been given repeated warnings right through the end of the reign of Paul VI, all of which he ignored. He had been invited to Rome for discussion but some-what arrogantly refused. The doctrinal congregation had found problems with Kung's challenging the dogma of papal infallibility and denying the Magisterium's exclusive right to interpret the deposit of revealed truth. And he had blurred the line between the ordained priesthood and "the priesthood of all baptized peoples."

Hans Kung was neither excommunicated nor "defrocked."

His books are still sold in Catholic bookshops. The Vatican announcement merely indicated that when Kung speaks or writes, he is expressing his personal opinion, not Catholic doctrine. Kung continues to teach at the University of Tübingen in Germany, but not as a Catholic theologian. In short, the pope was saying: "This man is free as an individual to say or teach or write whatever he likes, but the public must understand that what he teaches is not Catholic doctrine."

On the American scene, the most spectacular case involving an action by John Paul against a theologian was that of the influential moral theologian Father Charles Curran of Catholic University in Washington, D.C. Just at the time he was trying to maintain traditional Catholic morality against the sexual revolution of the sixties, John Paul felt that Curran's teaching on sex-related matters was contributing to a scandalous permissiveness among Catholic lay persons and even inside the priesthood. Alarming reports poured into Rome from the United States of priests having affairs with nuns, of priests entering into homosexual marriages, of students at Catholic universities sleeping together at night and then going hand in hand to the communion rail the next morning. Something had to be done about Curran because, as a Catholic professor in Rome said, "He has became a symbol of a whole school of new sexual ethics."

After years of correspondence between the doctrinal congregation and Curran, the Vatican on August 19, 1986, made public a letter to the theologian telling him that "in the light of your repeated refusal to accept what the Church teaches . . . you will no longer be considered suitable nor eligible to exercise the function of a professor of Catholic theology."

The Vatican action provoked a tidal wave of protest from liberal American Catholics. Supported by many other leading theologians, Curran insisted that he had the right to dissent from Church teachings that had not been proclaimed infallible by a pope or a council, and he pointed out that most moral teachings never have been proclaimed infallible. There also were loud complaints that the Vatican action violated academic freedom, and that the reputation of Catholic universities was being threatened. Pope John Paul flatly rejected all these complaints.

Only three days after the announcement of the action on Curran, I had the privilege of dining with the pope and discussing the Curran case with him in his summer residence in Castel Gandolfo in the Alban hills. Accompanied by Joaquín Navarro-Valls, the layman who heads the Vatican press office, I was ushered through the arched gateway of the palace by the Swiss Guard on duty and welcomed by the papal secretary, Monsignor Stanislao Dziwisz.

The pope spends two months every summer at Castel Gandolfo, the nearest thing to a vacation that he ever gets. He continues to work while there, but his load is lightened by eliminating all private audiences. He still has his weekly general audience, he still meets the public for the "angelus" at noon on Sunday, and he continues to work on important documents and pronouncements.

Monsignor Dziwisz led us through marble halls and gilded salons to the relatively small dining room where the pope normally takes his meals. Along three walls of the room were massive glassed-in cupboards holding crystal and porcelain dishes, all collected by earlier popes; on the shelf of one cupboard was a carved wooden replica of the Last Supper, the gift of a visitor from the Holy Land. A simple painting of a Polish mountain winter landscape, a gift from Polish President Henryk Jablonski in 1979, was the only addition to the room's furnishings that John Paul had brought from Poland.

A metal chandelier hung from the center of the ceiling above the oblong dining table, which took up most of the space in the room. The table could accommodate eight persons easily, but there were only four of us to dine that evening—the pope, Monsignor Dziwisz, Navarro, and I. We were served by an Italian waiter in a simple uniform. Our wineglasses were already filled with a local white Frascati, though the pope's glass was only half filled, a sign that he is not a wine enthusiast. When we sat down, the waiter filled our water glasses with cool San Pellegrino mineral water, and he quickly replenished our wineglasses as they were emptied (the pope scarcely touched his wine, though he drank copiously of water).

John Paul entered the room without ceremony, his amiable, informal manner putting us instantly at ease. An inner tranquillity was reflected in his ruddy face, unlined and far more youthful than you would expect in a sixty-six-year-old man—and this after bearing the burdens of the papacy for seven years.

As he took my hand he recalled with warmth the many times I had traveled with him on those long international voyages. With a chuckle he pointed to his attire and apologized "for not being dressed officially." The pope was wearing a full-length white cotton cassock, without even the usual sash, and his head was bare.

Despite this easy formality, I found the pope a far more intense person than he seems to be in public. Because of his good humor and contempt for protocol, John Paul appears publicly to have a great deal in common with the late Pope John, who projected the image of an indulgent grandfather. The similarity in fact is only on the surface. I couldn't help thinking that in a similar situation Pope John would have spent half the evening asking me about my family and my life. With this pope, time is too precious to waste in small talk. As the evening moved on and the conversation became more involved, Monsignor Dziwisz whispered to Navarro that he would appreciate our somehow suggesting it was time to go. It is the pope's prerogative to terminate such an encounter, but when he gets involved in intense discussion John Paul often is oblivious to the passing of time. He had other things to do after dinner, and his secretary could see that "he is ready to go on like this for hours." Navarro tactfully brought it to an end by asking papal permission for me to ask "just one more question." John Paul got the point and after he had answered one more question, he patted the table gently, smiled warmly, and with a "Well . . . ," signaled that dinner had ended.

During the dinner, Monsignor Dziwisz sat at the head of the table. The pope sat on one side alone, facing Navarro and me. His menu differed from ours. The three of us were served a first course of fresh melon with prosciutto, a main course of breast of chicken, peas cooked with ham, and roasted potatoes, and a basket of fresh fruit for dessert. The pope was served a mushy rice soup as a starter, followed by what looked like some kind of Polish crepe. His dessert was stewed fruit.

It very quickly became clear that food could not compete with ideas at the papal table. John Paul managed to get through his soup, afterwards picking up the empty bowl and setting it aside on the table without waiting for the waiter to take it away, an absentminded gesture that was a sure sign this man had not always dwelt in marble halls. After the soup, he scarcely touched his food. As we got into the conversation, he began leaning over the table, his blue eyes squeezed almost shut as he pulled his thoughts together, his hand sometimes covering his eyes in a characteristic gesture. While talking, he often toyed with his cutlery, picking up a knife or fork in one hand, squeezing it, twirling it around, and eventually tossing it aside, oblivious of what he was doing.

We wasted no time moving into the Curran case. To this pope, the issue was clear, simple, uncomplicated: "We could not permit a Catholic theologian teaching in a Catholic university to teach that which is contrary to what the Church teaches. There already was too much confusion, and that kind of teaching only added to the confusion. We have to present our teaching clearly."

I reminded him of Curran's arguments that he was dealing with moral issues on which no pope ever had made an infallible ruling, questions of birth control and homosexuality and extramarital sex. Doesn't a moral theologian have the right to dissent on these "non-infallible" teachings?

The pope covered his eyes with his hand and again leaned across the table, a pause obviously not to collect his thoughts but to make the right choice of words. He then answered: "Of course, the Church has made no solemn declaration of infallibility regarding moral issues, but infallible declarations on any subject have been extremely rare and exceptional in the history of the Church. If you believe only those declarations, you have very little left to

believe. But moral questions are covered by the 'ordinary' magisterium, and it is our duty to insist on their being obeyed. After
all, no solemn declaration of infallibility ever was made regarding
the Ten Commandments, or the commandment to love your
neighbor. Does that mean you have the right to dissent on those
teachings?"

During his interchanges with the doctrinal congregation,
Father Curran had listed a number of cases in which he said the
Church had changed its teaching on moral issues. To the pope,
I mentioned as an example the fact that Thomas Aquinas—a
doctor of the Church—had taught that "ensoulment" of the
human fetus takes place forty days after conception. This would
mean that abortion before the fortieth day would not mean taking
a human life. Yet the pope himself insists that the human person
exists from the moment of conception and thereby rules out abortion under any conditions. Isn't that a change in Church teaching?

In this case, the pope simply disagreed with Thomas Aquinas: "This was the theory of some theologians of the time, including Thomas, but it was never accepted by the magisterium of the
Church. It was a theory based on ideas of Aristotle. But modern
biology makes it absolutely clear that at the moment of conception
a human person exists. Abortion therefore violates the most fundamental of human rights, the right to life."

It was during this conversation that I fully understood what
a wide gap yawned between this Polish pope and those liberal
American Catholics who believe that Christian teachings should
be subjected to debate and discussion, with conclusions based on
consensus. Just as the Church of antiquity took on the external
trappings and some of the political structure of imperial Rome, so
many American Catholics today try to apply the democratic
structures of the United States to the Church. To Pope John Paul,
such an application is unthinkable. To him, Christian teaching is
a deposit of faith entrusted to the Church by Christ, something
to be accepted, not discussed.

When I mentioned that there was a strong negative reaction
in the United States to the handling of the Curran case, the pope

responded with tranquillity: "I believe the American people are divided on this issue. We have been flooded with letters from American Catholics supporting our action on Curran, American Catholics who are scandalized by what he was teaching."

But he went on to make clear that whether or not he had popular support on the issue was not the point: "It is a mistake to apply American democratic procedures to the faith and to the truth. You cannot take a vote on the truth. They must not confuse the 'sensus fidei' with 'consensus.' Truth is not determined by voting. It is something that must be accepted."

John Paul then sat back in his chair and tapped himself on the chest with both hands.

"This is not my teaching we are talking about. This is the teaching of the Church, and it is my responsibility to insist that it be obeyed. I cannot change that teaching. I have no *right* to change it!"

EPILOGUE:
THE CHARISM
OF PETER

As the reader by now is aware, I have written a book not about the papacy but about a trio of remarkable individuals who have occupied that office. In a sense their story is that of the predominance of the individual over the office, of human personality over structures. There is remarkable continuity from one of these popes to the next, and from St. Peter to each of them, and yet they emerge as very distinct and unforgettable personalities, men who rose to the occasion to meet the specific needs of specific moments in the history of the Church.

On ceremonial occasions honoring the pope at the Vatican the Sistine Chapel choir still intones the hymn "Tu es Petrus" ("Thou art Peter"), and indeed there is a close identification between a reigning pope and the Prince of the Apostles who received the keys of the kingdom from Christ. Pope Leo the Great in the fifth century enunciated the concept that each pope is direct successor to Peter—not to the pope immediately before him—and that Peter continues to carry out his responsibilities through whoever occupies the Holy See as his successor.

On one occasion I asked Pope John Paul II about Leo's concept and whether he felt imbued with the spirit of Saint Peter.

"No, not with the spirit of Peter," he explained to this ignorant layman. "We are imbued with the Holy Spirit. I prefer to call it a personal charism from Peter."

Receiving this charism, or gift, as John Paul pointed out, does not mean that each pope in some miraculous way is an incarnation of Peter. It means instead that the pope has received the gift of personality and individuality enabling him to bear the burdens of the office and to perform the very special tasks he faces.

The history of recent popes suggests that in some way not easily explainable in human terms the old cardinals locked up in each successive conclave chose as pope precisely the personality most needed at the moment. We have seen, for example, that Paul VI might have been elected in 1958 yet was not chosen because of a slight shift in circumstances. Had he been elected that year, there would not have been a Vatican Council, with all the sweeping and necessary reforms it brought to the Church.

Instead of Paul, the cardinals chose John XXIII, who possessed the confidence and decisiveness to summon the council and open it up to change. His reign was short, less than five years, yet he may have achieved as much as he would have if he had reigned twenty years. It was as though he had been chosen providentially to open things up, to summon the council, and then to pass away and leave to others the great task of putting the impact of his spirit into actions.

Paul's turn came in 1963, and he too appears to have been the right person for the time. Diplomat, bureaucrat, and legalist, the patient, long-suffering Paul was the ideal choice to steer the council to an orderly conclusion, to put the spirit of John into Church law and practice. It is my opinion that if Paul had not followed John, the latter's spirit of reform might well have died with the passing of years. But under Paul, it may be said, "John's word became flesh."

Paul's successor John Paul I, the lovable "smiling pope," reigned only thirty-three days, and yet you can see even in that short reign an important message that signaled a major change in the history of the papacy. His very frailty may have been a symbol of the weakness of the remaining group of Italian cardinals, a signal that the time had come to break the pattern of electing Italian popes. Responding to that signal, the cardinals looked beyond Italy and elected the Polish Karol Wojtyla.

After all the confusion, dissent, and experimentation that followed the council, the Church seemed to need a tough disciplinarian to define its course and restore clarity to Christian teaching without undoing the reforms of the council. If so, the cardinals could not have chosen a more suitable candidate. It could be said that the Polish pope reconciled Peter and John XXIII, that which is permanent with that which must change. And, consistent with his choice of a name, John Paul in many ways was a synthesis of John and Paul, a charismatic personality who exuded goodness and love, combined with a legalist who would not tolerate dissent from the traditional teachings of the Church.

They may say, as Paul did when he prayed with the World Council of Churches in Geneva, "Our Name is Peter." They may consider themselves immediate successors to the fisherman-disciple. But they will be remembered in history not as faceless successors to the Prince of the Apostles. Each will be remembered as an individual, by the name that each chose on that fateful day inside the conclave when he was asked: "Quo nomine vis vocari?"

SOURCES

Helpful sources that I tapped to supplement my reporting included Roland Flamini's *Pope, Premier, President* (New York, 1980), a most valuable account of Vatican diplomacy under Pope John XXIII; Hansjakob Stehle's *Eastern Politics of the Vatican, 1917–1918*, translated by Sandra Smith (Athens, Ohio, 1981), which offers an especially well-documented account of the Vatican's abortive attempts to set up a clandestine hierarchy in the Soviet Union in the twenties; Francis X. Murphy's *The Papacy Today* (London, 1981); Malachi Martin's *Three Popes and the Cardinal* (New York, 1972); Peter Hebblethwaite's *The Year of the Three Popes* (London, 1978); J. L. Gonzalez and T. Perez's *Paul VI*, translated by Edward Heston (Boston, 1964); Robert Kaiser's *Inside the Council* (New York, 1963), which contains good material on the first session of the Vatican Council under Pope John; Giulio Andreotti's *A Ogni Morte di Papa* (Milan, 1980), an excellent account of this politician's relations with Pope John; Paul Johnson's *Pope John XXIII* (London, 1975); Frank Korn's *From Peter to John Paul II* (Canfield, Ohio, 1980); Gianfranco Piazzesi and Sandra Bonsanti's *La Storia di Roberto Calvi* (Milan, 1984); and Pope John XXIII's own *Il Giornale del'Anima e Altri scritti de pietà* (Rome, 1964).

For history of the papacy and the Church I found most useful Patrick Granfield's *The Papacy in Transition* (Dublin, 1980); J. N. D. Kelly's *The Oxford Dictionary of Popes* (Oxford, 1986); Orville Prescott's *Princes of the Renaissance* (London, 1969); Sam Waagenaar's *Il Ghetto Sul Tevere* (Milan, 1972); Beny Lai's *Finanze e*

Finanzieri Vaticani fra L'800 e il 900" (Milan, 1979), a scholarly history of Vatican finances before World War I, including an account of the robbery of the Vatican Bank at the turn of the century.

Earlier historical works I consulted include Eusebius, *The History of the Church,* translated by G. A. Williamson (Middlesex, England, 1965); Francesco Guicciardini's *The History of Italy,* translated by Sidney Alexander (Princeton, 1969); Ferdinand Gregorovius's *Rome and Medieval Culture: Selections from History of the City of Rome in the Middle Ages,* translated by Mrs. Gustavus W. Hamilton (Chicago, 1971); and Gregorovius's *The Ghetto and Jews of Rome,* translated by Moses Hadas (New York, 1948).

For much of the diplomatic history of the Vatican I relied on my interviews, and those of other *Time* correspondents, with Jesuit father Robert Graham. For the background of early Vatican-American diplomatic relations, I found especially useful his article on the subject in the English-language edition of *L'Osservatore Romano* of June 25, 1970. For details of the abortive council prepared by Pope Pius XII I am indebted to Father Giovanni Caprile in his article "Pio XII e Un Nuovo Progetto di Concilio Ecumenico," in *La Civiltà Cattolica,* Rome, August 6/20, 1966.

In the Italian press, I found helpful for background on Pope Paul's attempts to mediate in Vietnam two articles in the weekly *Panorama*—"Il Messaggero Che Scotta," by Stefano Malatesta, March 8, 1973; and "Messaggero del Papa," by Gianluigi Melega, March 22, 1973. For a brief account of the Vatican press office under Pope Pius XII, I found useful a piece by Bruno Bartoloni in Milan's *Corriere della Sera,* February 9, 1986. A good short summary on the history of papal travel may be found in Curtis G. ("Bill") Pepper's article "Putting the Pope on the Road," in *Signature,* January 1985. Pepper also did a fine job of reporting for *Life* magazine on Pope Paul's decision on birth control. And to refresh my memory, I sifted carefully through all the *Time* cover stories on popes from John XXIII through John Paul II.

Reference materials I have consulted include *The Documents of Vatican II,* edited by Walter Abbott (New York, 1966); *Actes*

et Documents du Saint Siège Relatifs à la Seconde Guerre Mondiale,
edited by Robert Graham, Pierre Blet, and Angelo Martini (Libreria Editrice Vaticana, 1981), which contains documentation
regarding John XXIII's years as a diplomat in Istanbul and his
move to Paris as nuncio, and regarding Pope Pius XII's help to
European Jews during the war; *Annuario Pontificio* and *Encyclopedia Britannica.*

INDEX

INDEX · 273

About the Author

WILTON WYNN has lived abroad for forty years, of which thirty-five were spent as a correspondent for *Time* magazine. He has also been a broadcast correspondent for the Voice of America and CBS. In 1979 he became *Time*'s bureau chief in Rome. Since his retirement in 1985 he has continued to work as Vatican consultant for *Time* and to write on the papacy.